INTRODUCTION TO
MICROSOFT VISUAL BASIC 4

INTRODUCTION TO
MICROSOFT VISUAL BASIC 4

Gary B. Shelly
Thomas J. Cashman
John F. Repede

SHELLY
CASHMAN
SERIES

boyd & fraser

A DIVISION OF COURSE TECHNOLOGY
ONE MAIN STREET
CAMBRIDGE MA 02412

an International Thomson Publishing company I(T)P

CAMBRIDGE • ALBANY • BONN • CINCINNATI • LONDON • MADRID • MELBOURNE
MEXICO CITY • NEW YORK • PARIS • SAN FRANCISCO • TOKYO • TORONTO • WASHINGTON

© 1996 boyd & fraser publishing company
A Division of Course Technology
One Main Street
Cambridge, Massachusetts 02142

I(T)P® International Thomson Publishing
boyd & fraser publishing company is an ITP company.
The ITP logo is a registered trademark of International Thomson Publishing.

Printed in the United States of America

For more information, contact boyd & fraser publishing company:

boyd & fraser publishing company
A Division of Course Technology
One Main Street
Cambridge, Massachusetts 02142, USA

International Thomson Editores
Campos Eliseos 385, Piso 7
Colonia Polanco
11560 Mexico D.F. Mexico

International Thomson Publishing Europe
Berkshire House
168-173 High Holborn
London, WC1V 7AA, United Kingdom

International Thomson Publishing GmbH
Konigswinterer Strasse 418
53227 Bonn, Germany

Thomas Nelson Australia
102 Dodds Street
South Melbourne
Victoria 3205 Australia

International Thomson Publishing Asia
Block 211, Henderson Road #08-03
Henderson Industrial Park
Singapore 0315

Nelson Canada
1120 Birchmont Road
Scarborough, Ontario
Canada M1K 5G4

International Thomson Publishing Japan
Hirakawa-cho Kyowa Building, 3F
2-2-1 Hirakawa-cho, Chiyoda-ku
Tokyo 102, Japan

ISBN 0-7895-0728-5

2 3 4 5 6 7 8 9 10   BC   0 9 8 7

INTRODUCTION TO
MICROSOFT VISUAL BASIC 4

CONTENTS

Microsoft Visual Basic 4 — VB 1

 **Preface**

Shelly Cashman Series® Microsoft Windows 95 Books

Since the introduction of Microsoft Windows version 3.1, the personal computing industry has moved rapidly toward establishing Windows as the de facto user interface. The majority of software development funds in software vendor companies are devoted to Windows applications. Virtually all PCs purchased today, at any price, come preloaded with Windows and, often, with one or more Windows applications packages. With an enormous installed base, it is clear that Windows is the operating environment for both now and the future.

The Windows environment places the novice as well as the experienced user in the world of the mouse and a common graphical user. An up-to-date educational institution that teaches applications software to students for their immediate use and as a skill to be used within industry must teach Windows-based applications software.

Objectives of This Textbook

Introduction to Microsoft Visual Basic 4 was specifically developed for a course that covers the essentials of Microsoft Visual Basic 4. No mathematics beyond the high school freshman level is required. The objectives of this book are as follows:

▶ To teach the fundamentals of Windows and Microsoft Visual Basic 4

▶ To acquaint the student with the three-step approach to building Windows applications using Visual Basic 4

▶ To use practical problems to illustrate application-building techniques

▶ To take advantage of the many new capabilities of building applications in a graphical environment

The textbook covers all essential aspects of Visual Basic 4 for Windows. When students complete a course using this book, they will have a firm knowledge of Visual Basic 4 and will be able to develop a wide variety of Windows applications.

Student Version of Microsoft Visual Basic 4

A student version of Microsoft Visual Basic 4 for Windows 95, also called Working Model, is optionally available with this textbook (ISBN 0-7895-1317-X). The Working Model can be used by schools that do not have Microsoft Visual Basic 4 on their systems or by students who prefer to do their laboratory work at home on their own computers.

The Working Model is available on CD-ROM. Minimum system requirements are a personal computer with a 486 or higher processor, Microsoft Windows 95, 6 MB of memory, 20 MB of hard disk space, a VGA or higher resolution monitor, and a mouse unit.

The Working Model includes the same controls as the Standard Edition and has the Enterprise Edition Help file. The only limitations of the Working Model are that it does not provide the MAKE.OLE DLLs command, the MAKE.EXE command, Crystal Reports Controls, or the setup wizard, and the user is limited to two forms or modules.

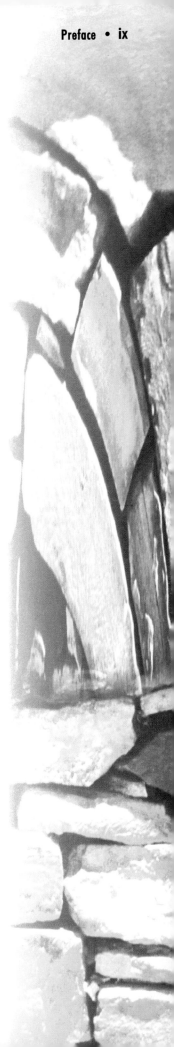

The Shelly Cashman Approach

The Shelly Cashman Series Windows Applications books present word processing, spreadsheet, database, programming, presentation graphics, and Windows itself by showing the actual screens displayed by Windows and the applications software. Because the student interacts with pictorial displays when using Windows, written words in a textbook do not suffice. For this reason, the Shelly Cashman Series emphasizes screen displays as the primary means of teaching Windows applications software. Every screen shown in the Shelly Cashman Series Windows Applications books appears in color, because the student views color on the screen. In addition, the screens display exactly as the student will see them. The screens in this book were captured while using the software. Nothing has been altered or changed except to highlight portions of the screen when appropriate.

The Shelly Cashman Series Windows Applications books present the material using a unique pedagogy designed specifically for the graphical environment of Windows. The textbooks are primarily designed for a lecture/lab method of presentation, although they are equally suited for a tutorial/hands-on approach wherein the student learns by actually completing each project following the step-by-step instructions. Features of this pedagogy include the following:

▶ Project Orientation: Each project in the book solves a complete problem, meaning that the student is introduced to a problem to be solved and is then given the step-by-step process to solve the problem.

▶ Step-by-Step Instructions: Each of the tasks required to complete a project is identified throughout the development of the project. For example, a task might be to add a control to a form or change a control's properties using Visual Basic. Then, each step to accomplish the task is specified. The steps are accompanied by screens. The student is not told to perform a step without seeing the result of the step on a color screen. Hence, students learn from this book the same as if they were using the computer. This attention to detail in accomplishing a task and showing the resulting screen makes the Shelly Cashman Series Windows Applications textbooks unique.

▶ Multiple Ways to Use the Book: Because each step to accomplish a task is illustrated with a screen, the book can be used in a number of ways, including: (a) Lecture and textbook approach — The instructor lectures on the material in the book. The student reads and studies the material and then applies the knowledge to an application on a computer; (b) Tutorial approach — The student performs each specified step on a computer. At the end of the project, the student has solved the problem and is ready to solve comparable student assignments; (c) Reference — Each task in a project is clearly identified. Therefore, the material serves as a complete reference because the student can refer to any task to determine how to accomplish it.

▶ Windows/Graphical User Interface Approach: Windows provides a graphical user interface. All of the examples in the book use this interface. Thus, the mouse is used for the majority of control functions and is the preferred user communication tool. When specifying a command to be executed, the sequence is as follows: (a) If a button invokes the command, use the button; (b) If a button is not available, use the command from a menu; (c) If a button or a menu cannot be used, only then is the keyboard used to implement a Windows command.

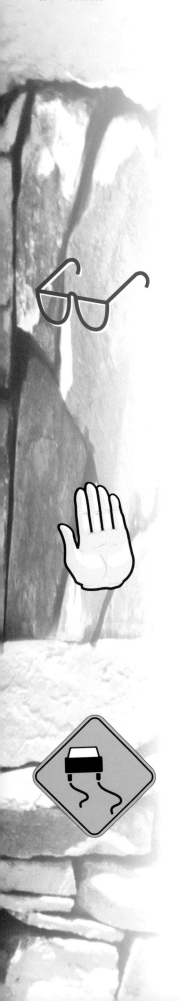

▶ **Emphasis on Windows Techniques:** The most general techniques to implement commands, enter information, and generally interface with Windows are presented. This approach allows the student to move from one application software package to another under Windows with a minimum amount of relearning with respect to interfacing with the software. An application-specific method is taught only when no other option is available.

▶ **Reference for All Techniques:** Even though general Windows techniques are used in all examples, a Quick Reference chart at the end of each project details not only the mouse and menu methods for implementing a command, but also contains the keyboard shortcuts for the commands presented in the project. Therefore, students are exposed to all means for implementing a command.

Organization of This Textbook

Introduction to Microsoft Visual Basic 4 provides detailed instruction on how to use Microsoft Visual Basic 4 for Windows. The material is divided into five projects as follows:

Project 1 – Building an Application   In Project 1, students are introduced to the major elements of Visual Basic by developing a currency conversion application. The process of building the application consists of three steps: Create the User Interface, Set Properties, and Write Code. Topics include starting Visual Basic; designing a form and adding labels, text boxes, and command buttons; changing the properties of controls; specifying an event procedure; running and saving applications; starting a new project or opening an existing project; and accessing information about Visual Basic using online Help and the online tutorial.

Project 2 – Working with Controls   Project 2 introduces students to building more complex applications than the one in Project 1. Additional properties of the controls used in Project 1, as well as several new controls, are used to create the movie box office application. Students learn more about writing code by writing six event subroutines and a declaration procedure. Topics include copying controls; copying code between subroutines; using variables in code statements; and using code statements to concatenate string data.

Project 3 – Applications with Multiple Forms and Working with the Debug Window
Project 3 extends the basics of building applications that were presented in Project 1 and Project 2. The loan payment calculator application in this project consists of multiple forms and dialog boxes. Topics include additional properties of the controls presented in Project 1 and Project 2; WindowState and modality; adding an icon to a form; using image, line, and scroll bar controls; and debugging applications using the features of Visual Basic's Debug window.

Project 4 – Using Color, Menus, the Data Control, and General Procedures   Project 4 further extends the basics of building applications presented in the first three projects. The geography database viewer interface is made more sophisticated through the use of menus and the Color dialog box. The Data control is introduced to link the application to a database file. Topics include using color within applications; creating menus; using a control array; writing code that uses the For...Next statement; and writing general procedures.

Project 5 – Building Applications with Drag-and-Drop Functionality In Project 5, students use the three-step approach to build the traffic sign tutorial application. The application introduces students to incorporating dragging and dropping of objects within applications. More complex code is written using nested structures, the Select Case structure, and the Do..Loop structure. Topics include Visual Basic data types; calls to subroutines; using the InputBox and UCase$ functions; adding remark statements to code; and printing a record of the application.

End-of-Project Student Activities

Each project ends with a wealth of student activities including these notable features:

▶ A list of key terms for review

▶ A Quick Reference that lists the ways to carry out a task using the mouse, menu, or keyboard shortcuts.

▶ Six Student Assignments for homework and classroom discussion.

▶ Three Computer Laboratory Exercises that usually require the student to load and manipulate a Visual Basic program from the Student Diskette that accompanies this book

▶ Four Computer Laboratory Assignments that require the student to develop a complete project assignment; the assignments increase in difficulty from a relatively easy assignment to a case study.

Course Tools

A comprehensive instructor's support package accompanies this textbook in the form of an electronic Instructor's Manual and teaching and testing aids on CD-ROM. The Instructor's Manual and most of the aids also are available to registered instructors on the Shelly Cashman Online home page (http://www.bf.com/scseries.html). The CD-ROM (ISBN 0-7895-0729-3) is available through your Course Technology representative or by calling 1-800-648-7450. The contents of the Instructor's Manual and additional ancillaries on the CD-ROM are listed below.

▶ **Instructor's Manual** The Instructor's Manual includes the following for each project: project objectives; project overview; detailed lesson plans with page number references; teacher notes and activities; answers to the end-of-project exercises; test bank of 110 questions for every project (50 true/false, 25 multiple-choice, and 35 fill-in-the blanks); and transparency references.

▶ **CD-ROM** The CD-ROM includes the following:

  ● **Figures on CD-ROM** Illustrations for every screen in the textbook are available. Use this ancillary to create a slide show from the illustrations for lecture or to print transparencies for use in lecture with an overhead.

  ● **ElecMan** ElecMan stands for *Elec*tronic *Man*ual. ElecMan is a Microsoft Word version of the Instructor's Manual, including all lecture notes and the test bank. The files allow you to modify the lecture notes or generate quizzes and exams from the test bank using your word processor.

- **Course Test Manager**   Designed by Course Technology, this cutting edge Windows-based testing software helps instructors design and administer tests and pre-tests. The full-featured online program permits students to take tests at the computer where their grades are computed immediately following completion of the exam. Automatic statistics collection, student guides customized to the student's performance, and printed tests are only a few of the features.

- **Lecture Success System**   Lecture Success System files are for use with the application software, a personal computer, and projection device to explain and illustrate the step-by-step, screen-by-screen development of a project in the textbook without entering large amounts of data.

- **Instructor's Lab Solutions**   Solutions and required files for all the Computer Laboratory Assignments at the end of each project are available.

- **Student Files**   All the files that are required by the student to complete the Computer Laboratory Exercises or advanced projects are included.

Shelly Cashman Online

Shelly Cashman Online is a World Wide Web service available to instructors and students of computer education. Visit Shelly Cashman Online at http://www.bf.com/scseries.html. Shelly Cashman Online is divided into four areas:

- **Series Information**   Information on the Shelly Cashman Series products.

- **The Community**   Opportunities to discuss your course and your ideas with instructors in your field and with the Shelly Cashman Series team.

- **Teaching Resources**   This area includes password-protected data from Instructor's Floppy Disks that can be downloaded, course outlines, teaching tips, and ancillaries such as ElecMan.

- **Student Center**   Dedicated to students learning about computers with Shelly Cashman Series textbooks and software. This area includes cool links, data from Student Floppy Disks that can be downloaded, and much more.

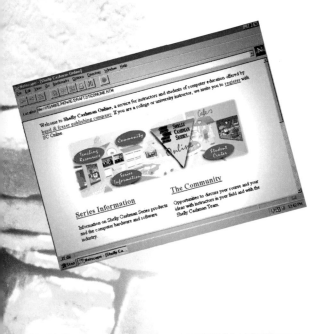

Acknowledgments

The Shelly Cashman Series would not be the leading computer education series without the contributions of outstanding publishing professionals. First, and foremost, among them is Becky Herrington, director of production and designer. She is the heart and soul of the Shelly Cashman Series, and it is only through her leadership, dedication, and tireless efforts that superior products are made possible. Becky created and produced the award-winning Windows 95 series of books.

Under Becky's direction, the following individuals made significant contributions to these books: Peter Schiller, production manager; Ginny Harvey, series administrator and manuscript editor; Ken Russo, senior illustrator and cover artist; Mike Bodnar, Stephanie Nance, Greg Herrington, and Dave Bonnewitz, Quark artists and illustrators; Patti Garbarino and Lora Wade, editorial assistants; Jeanne Black, Quark expert; Cristina Haley, indexer; Nancy Lamm, proofreader; Henry Blackham, cover photographer; and Kent Lauer, cover glass work. Special mention must go to Ken Russo for the cover design. Special recognition also must go to Bill Lisowski, director of marketing. The efforts of Jim Quasney, series editor, are unmatched in publishing. Without Jim, none of this happens.

Gary B. Shelly
Thomas J. Cashman
John F. Repede

Visit Shelly Cashman Online at
http://www.bf.com/scseries.html

Shelly Cashman Series - Traditionally Bound Textbooks

The Shelly Cashman Series presents computer textbooks across the entire spectrum including both Windows- and DOS-based personal computer applications in a variety of traditionally bound textbooks, as shown in the table below. For more information, see your Course Technology representative or call 1-800-648-7450.

COMPUTERS	
Computers	Using Computers: A Gateway to Information, World Wide Web Edition
	Using Computers: A Gateway to Information, World Wide Web Brief Edition
	Using Computers: A Gateway to Information, World Wide Web Edition and Exploring Computers: A Record of Discovery with CD-ROM
	Using Computers: A Gateway to Information
	Using Computers: A Gateway to Information, Brief Edition
	Exploring Computers: A Record of Discovery with CD-ROM
	A Record of Discovery for Exploring Computers
	Study Guide for Using Computers: A Gateway to Information, World Wide Web Edition
	Study Guide for Using Computers: A Gateway to Information
and Windows Apps	Using Computers: A Gateway to Information and Microsoft Office (also in spiral bound)
	Using Computers: A Gateway to Information and Microsoft Works 3.0 (also in spiral bound)
and Programming	Using Computers: A Gateway to Information and Programming in QBasic

WINDOWS APPLICATIONS	
Integrated Packages	Microsoft Office 95: Introductory Concepts and Techniques (also in spiral bound)
	Microsoft Office 95: Advanced Concepts and Techniques (also in spiral bound)
	Microsoft Office 4.3 running under Windows 95: Introductory Concepts and Techniques (also in spiral bound)
	Microsoft Office: Introductory Concepts and Techniques (also in spiral bound)
	Microsoft Office: Advanced Concepts and Techniques (also in spiral bound)
	Microsoft Works 4.0 for Windows 95*
	Microsoft Works 3.0 (also in spiral bound)* • Microsoft Works 2.0 (also in spiral bound)
	Microsoft Works 3.0—Short Course
Windows	Microsoft Windows 95: Introductory Concepts and Techniques (96-page)
	Introduction to Microsoft Windows 95 (224-page)
	Microsoft Windows 95: Complete Concepts and Techniques
	Microsoft Windows 3.1 Introductory Concepts and Techniques
	Microsoft Windows 3.1 Complete Concepts and Techniques
Windows Applications	Microsoft Word 2.0, Microsoft Excel 4, and Paradox 1.0 (also in spiral bound)
Word Processing	Microsoft Word 7* • Microsoft Word 6* • Microsoft Word 2.0
	WordPerfect 6.1* • WordPerfect 6* • WordPerfect 5.2
Spreadsheets	Microsoft Excel 7* • Microsoft Excel 5* • Microsoft Excel 4
	Lotus 1-2-3 Release 5* • Lotus 1-2-3 Release 4* • Quattro Pro 6 • Quattro Pro 5
Database Management	Microsoft Access 7* • Microsoft Access 2
	Paradox 5 • Paradox 4.5 • Paradox 1.0 • Visual dBASE 5/5.5
Presentation Graphics	Microsoft PowerPoint 7* • Microsoft PowerPoint 4*

DOS APPLICATIONS	
Operating Systems	DOS 6 Introductory Concepts and Techniques
	DOS 6 and Microsoft Windows 3.1 Introductory Concepts and Techniques
Integrated Package	Microsoft Works 3.0 (also in spiral bound)
Word Processing	WordPerfect 6.1 • WordPerfect 6.0
	WordPerfect 5.1 Step-by-Step Function Key Edition • WordPerfect 5.1 Function Key Edition
Spreadsheets	Lotus 1-2-3 Release 4 • Lotus 1-2-3 Release 2.4 • Lotus 1-2-3 Release 2.3
	Lotus 1-2-3 Release 2.2 • Lotus 1-2-3 Release 2.01
	Quattro Pro 3.0 • Quattro with 1-2-3 Menus (with Educational Software)
Database Management	dBASE 5 • dBASE IV Version 1.1 • dBASE III PLUS (with Educational Software)
	Paradox 4.5 • Paradox 3.5 (with Educational Software)

PROGRAMMING AND NETWORKING	
Programming	Introduction to Microsoft Visual Basic 4* (available with Student version of Visual Basic 4)
	Microsoft Visual Basic 3.0 for Windows*
	QBasic • QBasic: An Introduction to Programming • Microsoft BASIC
	Structured COBOL Programming
Networking	Novell NetWare for Users
	Business Data Communications: Introductory Concepts and Techniques
Internet	The Internet: Introductory Concepts and Techniques (UNIX)
	Netscape Navigator 3: An Introduction • Netscape Navigator 2 running under Windows 3.1
	Netscape Navigator: An Introduction (Version 1.1)
	Netscape Navigator Gold: Creating Web Pages

SYSTEMS ANALYSIS	
Systems Analysis	Systems Analysis and Design, Second Edition

*Also available as a Double Diamond Edition, which is a shortened version of the complete book

Shelly Cashman Series - Custom Edition® Program

If you do not find a Shelly Cashman Series traditionally bound textbook to fit your needs, the Shelly Cashman Series' unique **Custom Edition** program allows you to choose from a number of options and create a textbook perfectly suited to your course. Features of the **Custom Edition** program are:

▶ Textbooks that match the content of your course

▶ Windows- and DOS-based materials for the latest versions of personal computer applications software

▶ Shelly Cashman Series quality, with the same full-color materials and Shelly Cashman Series pedagogy found in the traditionally bound books

▶ Affordable pricing so your students receive the **Custom Edition** at a cost similar to that of traditionally bound books

The table on the right summarizes the available materials.

For more information, see your Course Technology representative or call 1-800-648-7450.

For Shelly Cashman Series information, visit Shelly Cashman Online at http://www.bf.com/scseries.html

COMPUTERS	
Computers	Using Computers: A Gateway to Information, World Wide Web Edition
	Using Computers: A Gateway to Information, World Wide Web Brief Edition
	Using Computers: A Gateway to Information
	Using Computers: A Gateway to Information, Brief Edition
	A Record of Discovery for Exploring Computers (available with CD-ROM)
	Study Guide for Using Computers: A Gateway to Information, World Wide Web Edition
	Study Guide for Using Computers: A Gateway to Information
	Introduction to Computers (32-page)
OPERATING SYSTEMS	
Windows	Microsoft Windows 95: Introductory Concepts and Techniques (96-page)
	Introduction to Microsoft Windows 95 (224-page)
	Microsoft Windows 95: Complete Concepts and Techniques
	Microsoft Windows 3.1 Introductory Concepts and Techniques
	Microsoft Windows 3.1 Complete Concepts and Techniques
DOS	Introduction to DOS 6 (using DOS prompt)
	Introduction to DOS 5.0 or earlier (using DOS prompt)
WINDOWS APPLICATIONS	
Integrated Packages	Microsoft Works 4.0 for Windows 95*
	Microsoft Works 3.0*
	Microsoft Works 3.0—Short Course
	Microsoft Works 2.0
Microsoft Office	Using Microsoft Office (16-page)
	Object Linking and Embedding (OLE) (32-page)
	Schedule+ 7
Word Processing	Microsoft Word 7* • Microsoft Word 6* • Microsoft Word 2.0
	WordPerfect 6.1* • WordPerfect 6* • WordPerfect 5.2
Spreadsheets	Microsoft Excel 7* • Microsoft Excel 5* • Microsoft Excel 4
	Lotus 1-2-3 Release 5* • Lotus 1-2-3 Release 4*
	Quattro Pro 6 • Quattro Pro 5
Database Management	Microsoft Access 7* • Microsoft Access 2*
	Paradox 5 • Paradox 4.5 • Paradox 1.0 • Visual dBASE 5/5.5
Presentation Graphics	Microsoft PowerPoint 7* • Microsoft PowerPoint 4*
DOS APPLICATIONS	
Integrated Package	Microsoft Works 3.0
Word Processing	WordPerfect 6.1 • WordPerfect 6.0
	WordPerfect 5.1 Step-by-Step Function Key Edition
	WordPerfect 5.1 Function Key Edition
	Microsoft Word 5.0
Spreadsheets	Lotus 1-2-3 Release 4 • Lotus 1-2-3 Release 2.4 • Lotus 1-2-3 Release 2.3
	Lotus 1-2-3 Release 2.2 • Lotus 1-2-3 Release 2.01
	Quattro Pro 3.0 • Quattro with 1-2-3 Menus
Database Management	dBASE 5 • dBASE IV Version 1.1 • dBASE III PLUS
	Paradox 4.5 • Paradox 3.5
PROGRAMMING AND NETWORKING	
Programming	Introduction to Microsoft Visual Basic 4* (available with Student version of Visual Basic 4) • Microsoft Visual Basic 3.0 for Windows*
	Microsoft BASIC
	QBasic
Networking	Novell NetWare for Users
Internet	The Internet: Introductory Concepts and Techniques (UNIX)
	Netscape Navigator 3: An Introduction
	Netscape Navigator 2 running under Windows 3.1
	Netscape Navigator: An Introduction (Version 1.1)
	Netscape Navigator Gold: Creating Web Pages

*Also available as a mini-module

PROGRAMMING

USING MICROSOFT VISUAL BASIC 4 FOR WINDOWS

MICROSOFT VISUAL BASIC 4 FOR WINDOWS

▼

BUILDING AN APPLICATION

OBJECTIVES You will have mastered the material in this project when you can:

▸ Start Visual Basic
▸ Describe the Visual Basic design environment
▸ Change the size and location of a form
▸ Add controls to a form
▸ Describe the function of labels, text boxes and command buttons
▸ Move and resize controls on a form

▸ Set properties of controls
▸ Name a form
▸ Write an event procedure
▸ Save a Visual Basic project
▸ Start a new Visual Basic project
▸ Open an existing Visual Basic project
▸ Use Visual Basic online Help

▸ WHAT IS VISUAL BASIC?

 A user interface allows you to communicate with a computer. Microsoft Windows is called a **graphical user interface (GUI)** because it lets you use both text and graphical images to communicate with the computer. **Applications software**, or **applications**, are computer programs that perform a specific function such as a calendar, word processor, or spreadsheet.

Numerous application software packages are available from computer stores, and several applications are included when you purchase Microsoft Windows. Although many of these Windows applications are created by different companies or individuals, they have a similar *look and feel* to the computer user. They *look* similar because they contain many of the same graphical images, or **objects**. A typical Windows application with common Windows objects is shown in Figure 1-1. Different Windows applications *feel* similar because they respond to the same kinds of user actions, such as clicking or dragging with a mouse.

Visual Basic is itself a Windows application. Its function, however, is to help you build your own special-purpose Windows applications. With Visual Basic, professional-looking applications using the graphical user interface of Windows can be created by persons who have no previous training or experience in computer programming.

VB2

Visual Basic Editions

Visual Basic 4 is available in four editions: Working Model, Standard, Professional, and Enterprise. These editions vary in the programming features they provide. The Visual Basic 4 Working Model is included with this book. Refer to Appendix A for minimum system requirements and installation instructions. The major difference between the Working Model and other editions is that it has fewer controls in the toolbox and cannot make .exe files. All of the projects presented in this book can be built with any one of these editions.

Mouse Usage

In this book, the mouse is used as the primary way to communicate with Visual Basic. You can perform six operations with a mouse: point, click, right-click, double-click, drag, and right-drag.

Point means you move the mouse across a flat surface until the mouse pointer rests on the item of choice on the screen. As you move the mouse, the mouse pointer moves across the screen in the same direction. **Click** means you press and release the left mouse button. The terminology used in this book to direct you to point to a particular item and then click is, Click [item]. For example, Click the Bold button assumes you will point to the Bold button before clicking.

Right-click means you press and release the right mouse button. As with the left mouse button, you normally will point to an item on the screen prior to right-clicking.

Double-click means you quickly press and release the left mouse button twice without moving the mouse. In most cases, you must point to an item before double-clicking. **Drag** means you point to an item, hold down the left mouse button, move the item to the desired location on the screen, and then release the left mouse button. **Right-drag** means you point to an item, hold down the right mouse button, move the item to the desired location, and then release the right mouse button.

The use of the mouse is an important skill when working with Visual Basic.

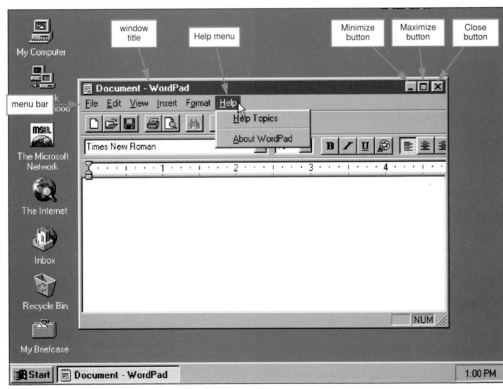

FIGURE 1-1

▶ PROJECT ONE – CONVERTING DOLLARS TO FRANCS

To illustrate the major features of Microsoft Visual Basic, this book presents a series of projects using Visual Basic to build Windows applications. Project 1 uses Visual Basic to build the currency conversion application shown in Figure 1-2. In this application, the user enters a number in the box labeled DOLLARS. When the user clicks the CONVERT button, the amount is converted to French francs and appears in the box labeled FRANCS. The Dollars To Francs Converter has some of the common features of Windows applications. It occupies a window that the user can move on the desktop, it can be maximized or minimized, and it has a Close button.

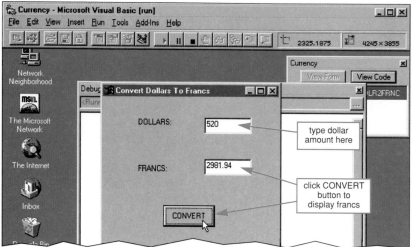

FIGURE 1-2

▶ STARTING VISUAL BASIC

When you start Visual Basic, several windows are added to the desktop. Generally, you should minimize or close all other windows on the desktop before starting Visual Basic. This will make it easier for you to work with the Visual Basic windows. Perform the following steps to start Visual Basic.

TO START VISUAL BASIC ▼

STEP 1 ▶

Point to the Start button on the taskbar (Figure 1-3).

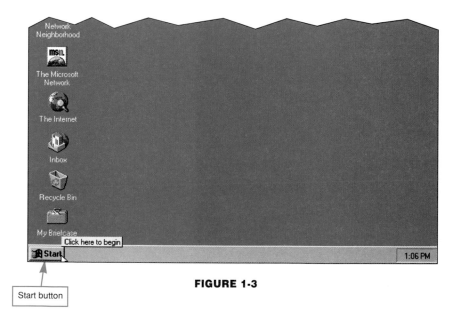

FIGURE 1-3

Start button

STEP 2 ▶

Click the Start button.

The Start menu displays on the desktop (Figure 1-4).

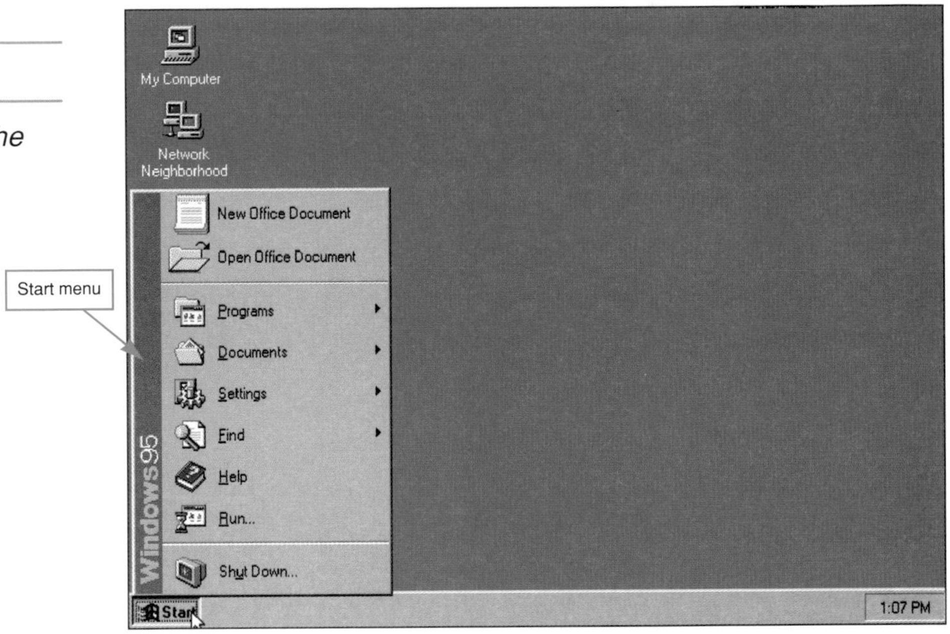

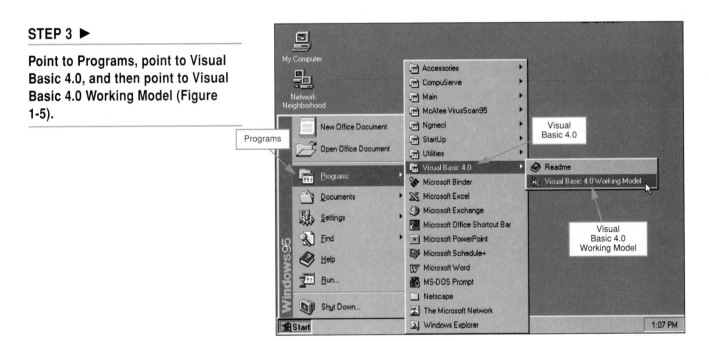

FIGURE 1-4

STEP 3 ▶

Point to Programs, point to Visual Basic 4.0, and then point to Visual Basic 4.0 Working Model (Figure 1-5).

FIGURE 1-5

STEP 4 ▶

**Click Visual Basic 4.0
Working Model.**

*The desktop now
displays five windows
that make up the **Visual Basic
programming environment** (Figure 1-6).*

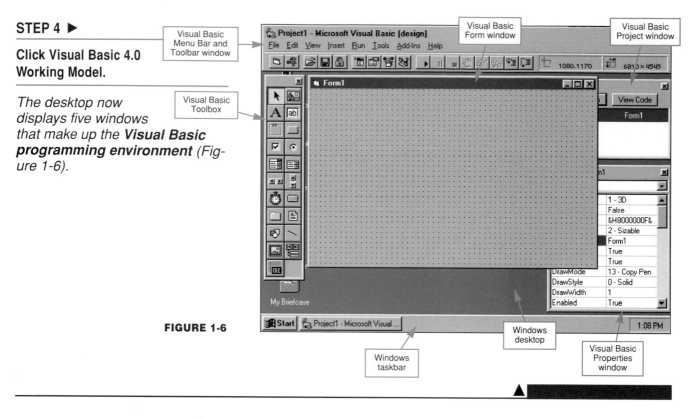

FIGURE 1-6

When you start Visual Basic, several windows are added to the desktop. It is
possible to work with Visual Basic without clearing the desktop. However, if other
windows are already open, the desktop becomes cluttered.

The Active Window

To work in any one of the Visual Basic windows, it must be the active window. Perform the following steps to make the Project window active and then
make the Properties window active.

TO MAKE A WINDOW ACTIVE ▼

STEP 1 ▶

**Point to any part of the Project
window (Figure 1-7).**

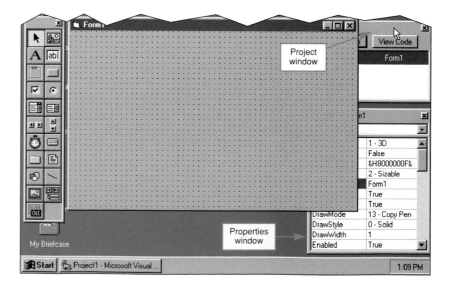

FIGURE 1-7

STEP 2 ▶

Click the Project window.

The Project window appears on top of the other windows, and its title bar changes to the active title bar color (Figure 1-8).

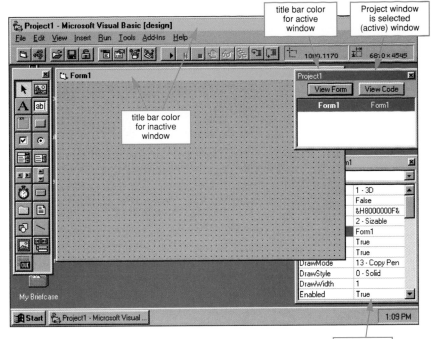

FIGURE 1-8

STEP 3 ▶

Repeat Steps 1 and 2 for the Properties window.

The Properties window appears on top of the other windows (Figure 1-9). Its title bar changes to the active title bar color. The Project window's title bar changes back to the inactive title bar color.

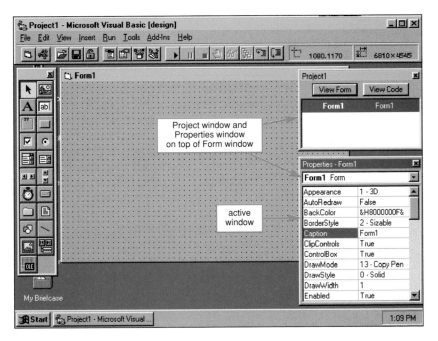

FIGURE 1-9

You can arrange the Visual Basic windows on the desktop in many different ways without affecting Visual Basic's functions. As you become more experienced, you may find a different arrangement that you prefer to work with. For now, use the default sizes and arrangement of the windows as shown in Figure 1-9 on the previous page.

Design Time and Run Time

The time when you build an application in Visual Basic is called **design time**. In contrast, the time when you use an application for its intended purpose is called **run time**. In Visual Basic, the applications you build are called **projects**. A project always begins with a **form**. At run time, a form becomes the window the application occupies on the desktop. Begin building the Dollars To Francs application shown in Figure 1-2 on page VB4 by specifying the size and location where you want the application's window to appear on the desktop during run time.

▶ SETTING THE SIZE AND LOCATION OF FORMS

T
he size and location that the application's window will occupy on the desktop during run time is specified by adjusting the size and location of the form during design time. Adjustments to the form's size and location can be made at any time during design time.

Setting the Size of a Form

Perform the following steps to set the size of the Dollars To Francs form.

TO SET THE SIZE OF A FORM ▼

STEP 1 ▶

Point to the Form window's title bar (Figure 1-10).

The color of the title bar indicates it is an inactive window.

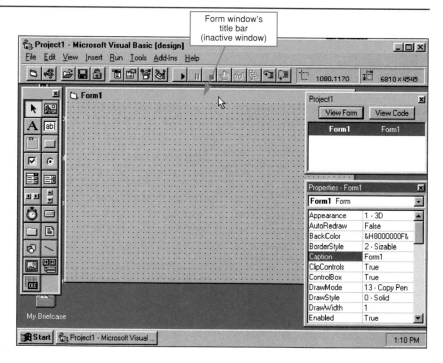

FIGURE 1-10

STEP 2 ▶

Click the title bar.

The Form window becomes the active window (Figure 1-11). This can be seen by the color of the title bar and the Form window moving on top of the Project and Properties windows.

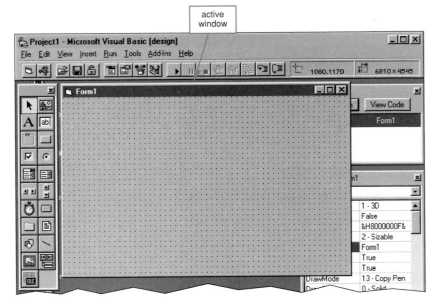

FIGURE 1-11

STEP 3 ▶

Point to the form's right border.

The pointer changes to a double arrow (⇔) (Figure 1-12).

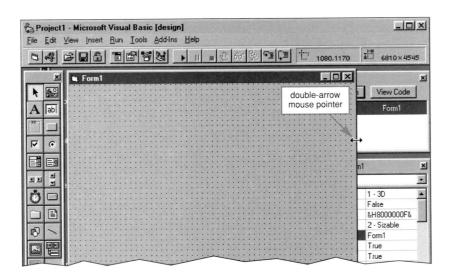

FIGURE 1-12

STEP 4 ▶

Drag the form's right border approximately three inches toward the left side of the screen.

The border's new location appears as a shaded line (Figure 1-13).

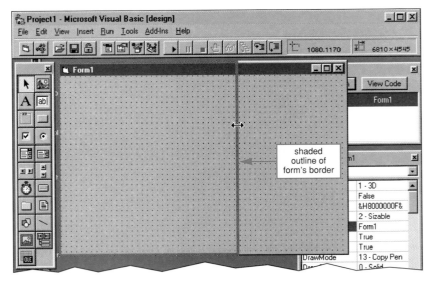

FIGURE 1-13

STEP 5 ►

Release the left mouse button.

The form's right border moves to the location of the shaded line (Figure 1-14). The Project and Properties windows again become visible.

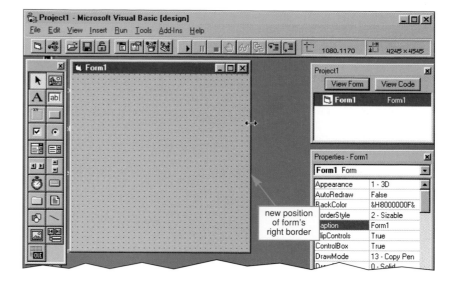

FIGURE 1-14

STEP 6 ►

Drag the form's bottom border toward the top of the screen approximately one inch.

The border's new location appears as a shaded line (Figure 1-15).

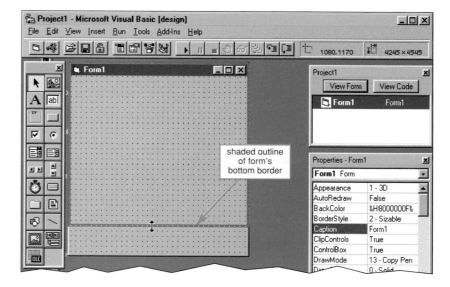

FIGURE 1-15

STEP 7 ►

Release the left mouse button.

The form's bottom border moves to the location of the shaded line (Figure 1-16). The width and height of the form are shown as two numbers (4245 × 3855) located in the lower right corner of the Menu Bar and Toolbar window.

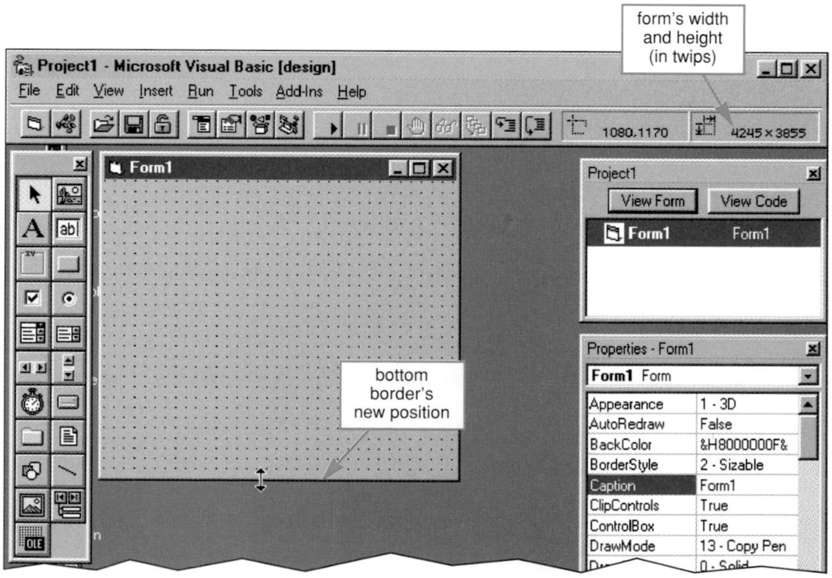

FIGURE 1-16

In the preceding example, the form's width and height were set by dragging the form's right and bottom borders. You can drag any of the form's four borders in either an inward or outward direction to change its size. The form's width and height are measured in units called **twips**. The dimensions of Form1 appear as 4245 × 3855 twips in the lower right corner of the Menu Bar and Toolbar window (Figure 1-16). A twip is a printer's measurement equal to 1/1440 inch. However, the width of a twip can vary slightly from one computer monitor to another.

Positioning a Form

Use the following steps to set the location on the desktop for the Dollars To Francs window.

TO POSITION A FORM ▼

STEP 1 ▶

Point to the title bar of the Form window (Figure 1-17).

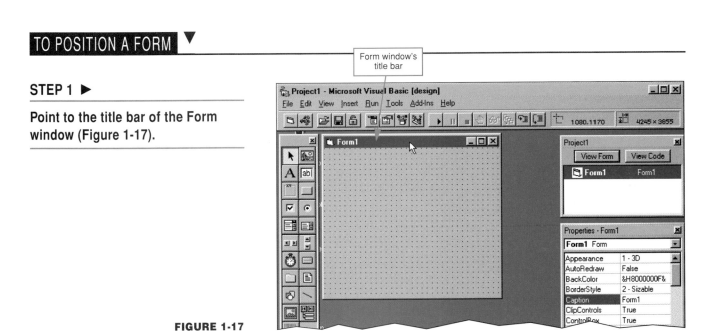

FIGURE 1-17

STEP 2 ▶

Drag the Form window down and to the right.

The Form window's new location appears as a shaded gray outline on the desktop (Figure 1-18).

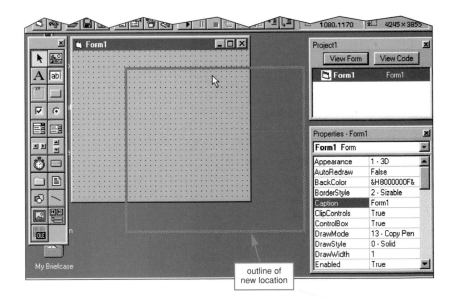

FIGURE 1-18

STEP 3 ▶

When the form is approximately centered on the desktop, release the left mouse button.

The form moves to the location outlined by the shaded lines (Figure 1-19). The location of the form's upper left corner is shown as two numbers (2325, 1875) in the lower right corner of the Menu Bar and Toolbar window.

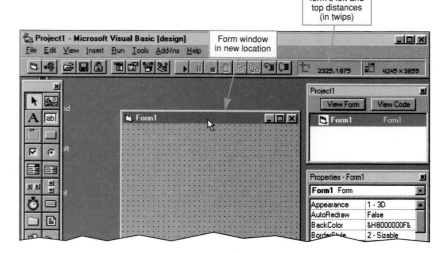

FIGURE 1-19

In the preceding steps, you set the form's location by dragging the form to the desired position. The form's location is given as two numbers. The first number (2325) is the distance in twips between the left side of the desktop and the left border of the form. The second number (1875) is the distance in twips between the top of the desktop and the top border of the form.

The form's location can be changed as often as desired during design time. Sometimes it is useful to temporarily move the form to work more easily in the other Visual Basic windows.

▶ ADDING AND REMOVING CONTROLS

F igure 1-1 on page VB3 shows some of the graphical images, or objects, common to many Windows applications. In Visual Basic, these objects also are called **controls**. The Dollars To Francs application contains three different types of controls (Figure 1-20). These controls and their functions are:

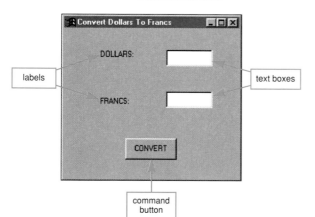

FIGURE 1-20

▶ **Label** A **label** is used to display text on a form. At run time the person using the application cannot change the text on a label, such as DOLLARS.

▶ **Text box** A **text box** also is used to display text on a form, but their contents can be changed at run time by the person using the application. It frequently is used as a way for the user to supply information to the application.

▶ **Command button** A **command button** is used during run time to initiate actions called **events.**

Adding Controls to a Form

Controls are added to a form by using tools from the group of tools found in the Visual Basic window called the **Toolbox**. Twenty-one tools are in the Toolbox of Visual Basic's Working Model. Additional controls are available in the other editions of Visual Basic and from third-party vendors. Specific controls and their functions will be discussed as they are used throughout the projects in this book. Figure 1-21 shows the Toolbox containing the three tools that are used to draw controls in Project 1 (Label, TextBox, and Command-Button). The following steps use these tools to add controls to the form.

The names of all tools in the Toolbox are summarized in Figure 1-87 at the bottom of page VB44.

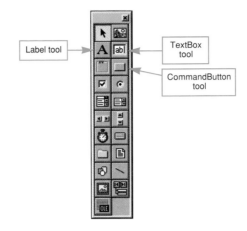

FIGURE 1-21

TO DRAW LABELS ON A FORM ▼

STEP 1 ▶

Point to the Label tool in the Toolbox (Figure 1-22).

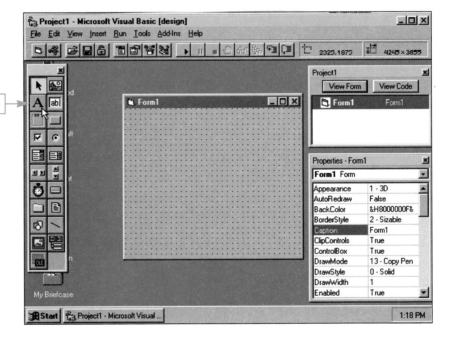

FIGURE 1-22

STEP 2 ▶

Click the Label tool. Place the cross hair near the upper left corner of the form by moving the mouse pointer.

The Label tool in the Toolbox is highlighted, and the mouse pointer changes to a cross hair (+) when it is over the form (Figure 1-23). The upper left corner of the label control will be positioned here.

FIGURE 1-23

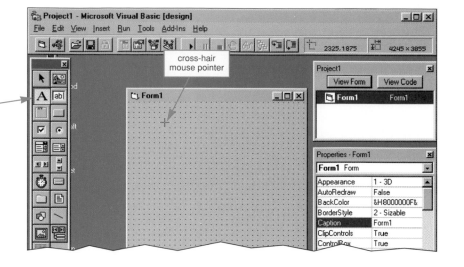

STEP 3 ▶

Drag the cross hair down and to the right.

A gray outline of the label control appears (Figure 1-24).

FIGURE 1-24

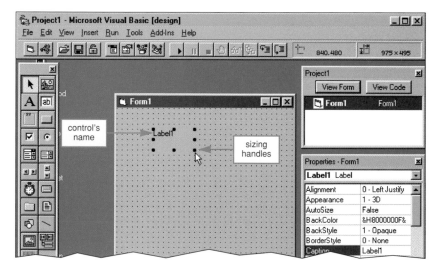

STEP 4 ▶

When the label control outline is the desired size, release the left mouse button.

*The gray outline changes to a solid background. The name of the label control (Label1) appears on the control. Small solid boxes called **sizing handles** appear at each corner and in the middle of each side of the label control (Figure 1-25).*

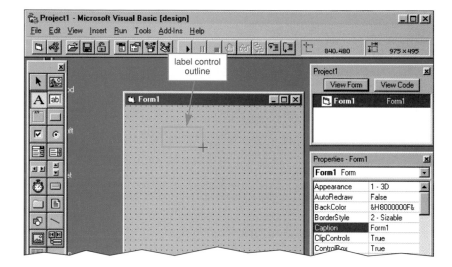

FIGURE 1-25

STEP 5 ▶

Repeat Steps 1 through 4 to draw a
second label control on the form as
shown in Figure 1-26.

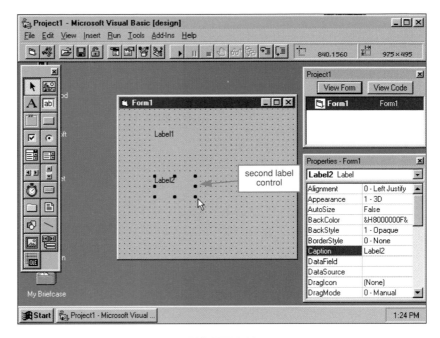

FIGURE 1-26

Two Label controls now have been added to the form by drawing them with
the Label tool selected from the Toolbox. Complete the following steps to add two
text box controls to the form.

TO DRAW TEXT BOXES ON A FORM ▼

STEP 1 ▶

Point to the TextBox tool in the
Toolbox (Figure 1-27).

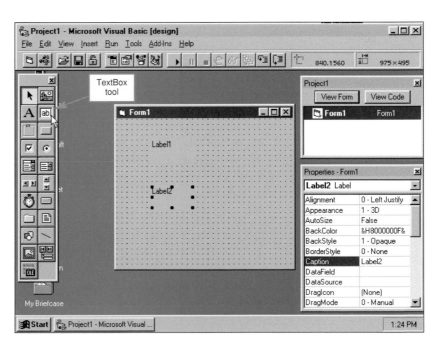

FIGURE 1-27

STEP 2 ▶

Click the TextBox tool. Place the cross hair toward the middle right side of the form.

The TextBox tool is highlighted in the Toolbox and the mouse pointer changes to a cross hair (Figure 1-28). The upper left corner of the label control will be positioned here.

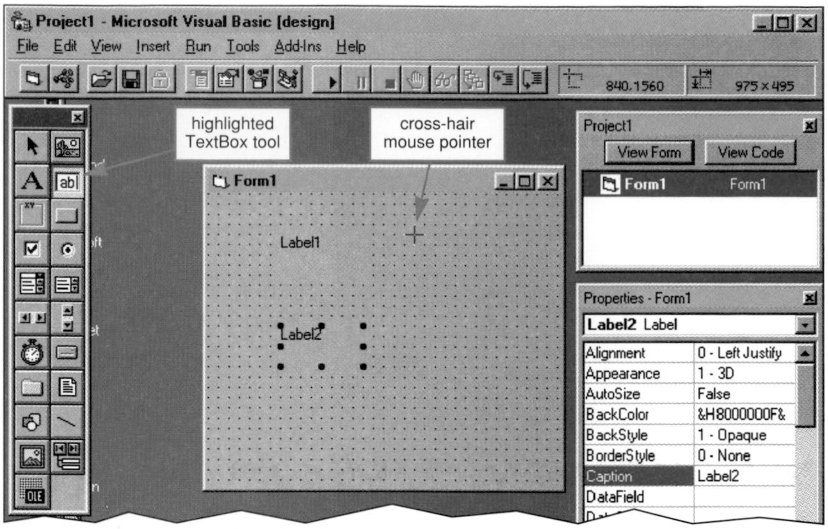

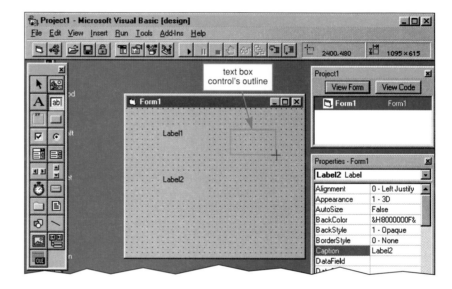

FIGURE 1-28

STEP 3 ▶

Drag the pointer down and to the right.

A gray outline of the text box control appears (Figure 1-29).

FIGURE 1-29

STEP 4 ▶

When the text box control outline is the size you want, release the left mouse button.

The gray outline changes to a solid background. The name of the text box control (Text1) appears on the control. Sizing handles appear at each corner and in the middle of each side of the text box control (Figure 1-30).

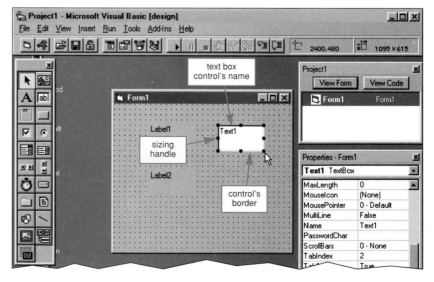

FIGURE 1-30

STEP 5 ▶

Repeat Steps 1 through 4 to place a second text box control on the form as shown in Figure 1-31.

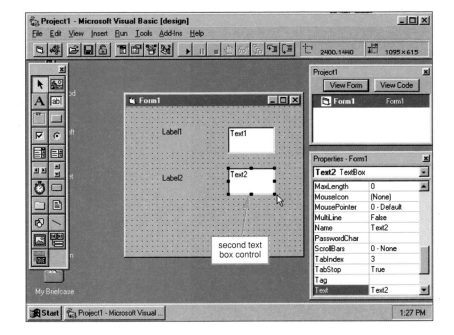

FIGURE 1-31

Two text boxes were added to the form in the same way as the two labels by selecting the tool in the Toolbox and then drawing the control's outline on the form. This method can be used for adding any of the controls in the Toolbox to a form. However, this method is not the only way to add controls to a form.

The following steps use an alternative method to add a command button to the Dollars To Francs form.

TO ADD CONTROLS BY DOUBLE-CLICKING ▼

STEP 1 ▶

Point to the CommandButton tool in the Toolbox (Figure 1-32).

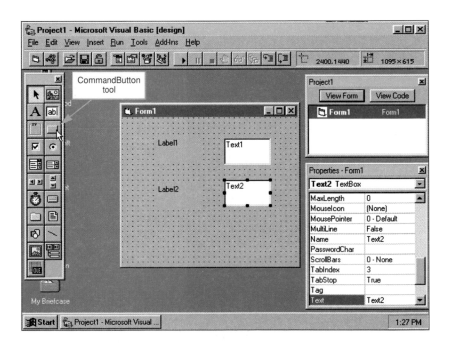

FIGURE 1-32

STEP 2 ▶

Double-click the CommandButton tool.

The command button control appears in the center of the form. The control's name, Command1, appears on the control. Sizing handles appear around the command button control (Figure 1-33).

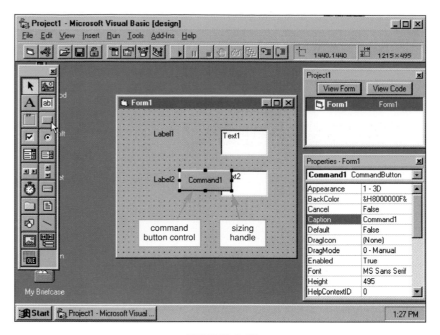

FIGURE 1-33

As you have just seen, double-clicking a tool in the Toolbox adds a default-sized control to the center of the form. If another control already is located in the center of the form, this method will add the new control on top of the previous control.

Removing Controls

If you choose the wrong control in the Toolbox or want to modify the project, controls can be removed from the form at any time during design time. Use the following steps to remove a control.

TO REMOVE A CONTROL

Step 1: Point to the control you want to remove.
Step 2: Click the control to select it.
Step 3: Press the DELETE key.

▶ CHANGING THE LOCATION AND SIZE OF CONTROLS

I f you add a control to a form by double-clicking a tool in the Toolbox, you will need to move the control from the center of the form, and you frequently will want to change its size from the default. The location and size of any of the controls on a form can be changed at any time during design time.

Moving a Control on a Form

A control can be moved by dragging it to a new location. Perform the following steps to move the command button control from the center of the Dollars To Francs form.

TO MOVE A CONTROL ON A FORM ▼

STEP 1 ▶

Point to a location in the interior (not on any of the handles) of the Command1 command button control (Figure 1-34).

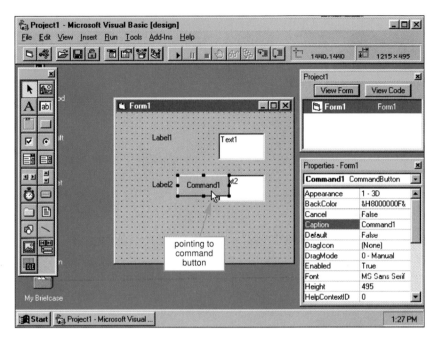

FIGURE 1-34

STEP 2 ▶

Drag the Command1 control toward the bottom of the form.

A gray outline of the command button control appears (Figure 1-35).

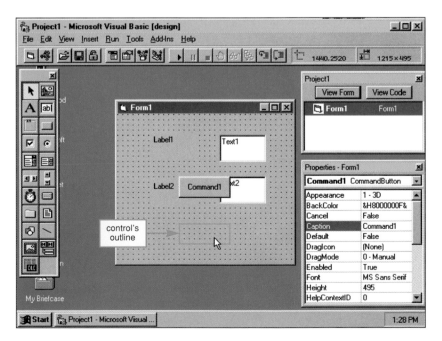

FIGURE 1-35

STEP 3 ▶

Move the pointer until the gray outline is at the desired location on the form, and then release the left mouse button.

The control moves to the location of the outline (Figure 1-36).

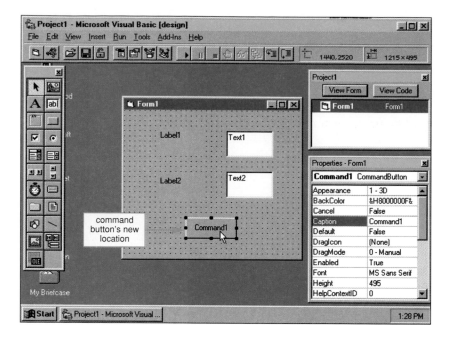

FIGURE 1-36

The location given to a control by dragging it across a form during design time is where the control will appear at the beginning of run time. However, a control doesn't have to remain in that location during run time. Changing a control's location during run time will be covered in a later project.

Changing the Size of a Control

Controls can be made larger or smaller by dragging the sizing handles located around the control. Perform the following steps to make the Text1 control smaller.

TO CHANGE A CONTROL'S SIZE ▼

STEP 1 ▶

Select the Text1 text box control by clicking it.

Handles appear around the control (Figure 1-37).

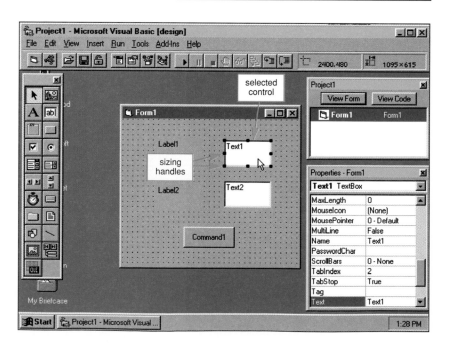

FIGURE 1-37

STEP 2 ▶

Point to the handle located at the center of the bottom border of the control.

The mouse pointer changes to a double arrow (Figure 1-38).

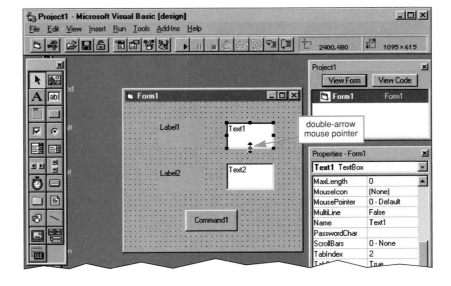

FIGURE 1-38

STEP 3 ▶

Drag the border toward the top of the screen approximately one-quarter inch.

The new position of the bottom border appears as a shaded gray line (Figure 1-39). Dragging a handle located in the center of one of the borders of a control moves that one border. Dragging one of the handles located at the corner of a control simultaneously moves the two borders that form the corner.

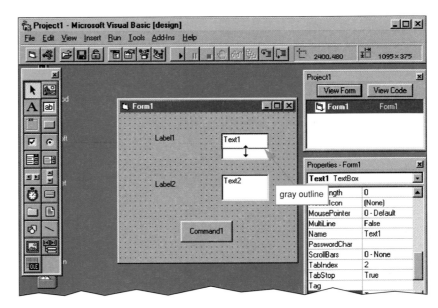

FIGURE 1-39

STEP 4 ▶

Release the left mouse button.

The bottom line of the Text1 text box control moves to the location of the outline (Figure 1-40).

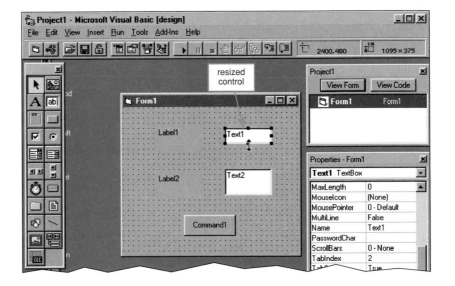

FIGURE 1-40

STEP 5 ▶

Repeat Steps 1 through 4 to resize
the Text2 text box control to the size
shown in Figure 1-41.

*The Form window now resembles
the one shown in Figure 1-41.*

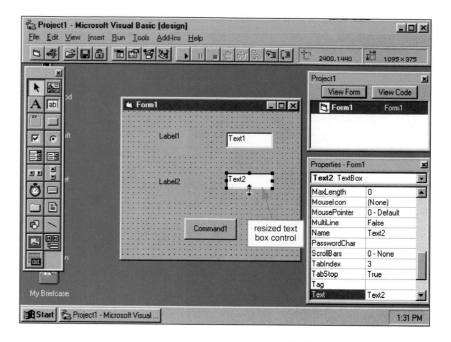

FIGURE 1-41

Notice how similar the procedures are for setting the location and size of the
form and for setting the locations and sizes of the labels, text boxes, and command
button on the form. This similarity should not be surprising, though, because a
Visual Basic form is a type of control. You will work more with form controls in
Project 3.

▶ SETTING PROPERTIES

Now that controls have been added to the form, the next step in Visual
Basic application development is to set the controls' **properties**.
Properties are characteristics or attributes of a control, such as its color
or the text that appears on top of it.

Properties are set at design time by using the
Properties window (Figure 1-42). The Properties
window consists of two sections:

▶ **Object box** The **Object box** displays the
name of the control whose properties are
being set.

▶ **Properties list** The Properties list displays
the set of properties belonging to the control
named in the Object box and the current value
of the properties.

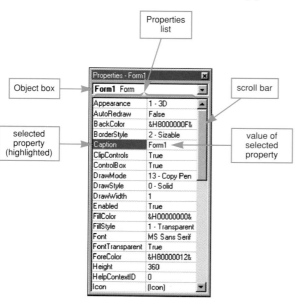

FIGURE 1-42

Different controls have different sets of properties. Because some controls' Properties lists are very long, the Properties window has a scroll bar to move through the list. It is not necessary to set every property of each control because Visual Basic assigns initial values for each of the properties. Change only the properties that you want to differ from their initial values, called **default values**. The major properties of controls will be discussed as they are used throughout the projects in this book.

The following example sets the **Caption property** of the *Label1* label control. The Caption property of a control contains text that you want to appear on the control.

TO SET THE CAPTION PROPERTY ▼

STEP 1 ▶

Select the Label1 label control by clicking the control on the form.

Handles appear around the selected control. The control's name (Label1) appears in the Object box of the Properties window. The currently selected property (Font) is highlighted in the Properties list, with its current value (MS Sans Serif) (Figure 1-43). Another property may be highlighted on your screen.

FIGURE 1-43

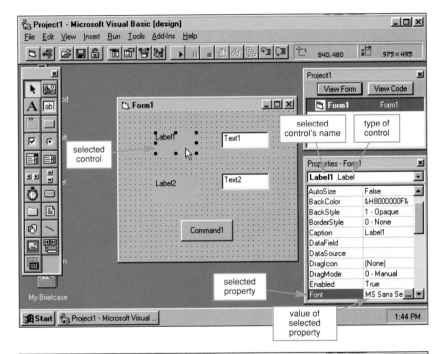

STEP 2 ▶

Point to the Caption property in the Properties list.

If the property you want to change is not visible in the Properties list (Figure 1-44), use the scroll bar on the Properties window to move the Properties list within the Properties window.

FIGURE 1-44

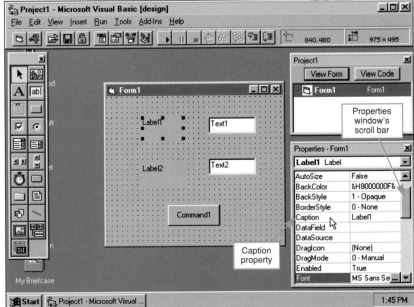

STEP 3 ▶

Double-click the Caption property.

The Caption property is highlighted in the Properties list. The current value of the property, Label1, is highlighted (Figure 1-45).

FIGURE 1-45

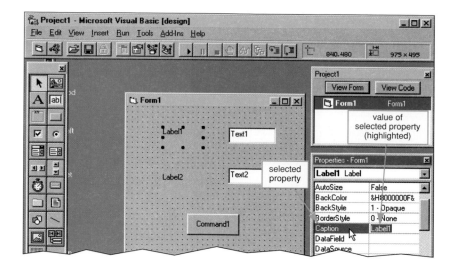

STEP 4 ▶

Type DOLLARS: **as the entry.**

When you type the first character, the old value of the caption is replaced by that character. As you continue typing characters, they appear in the Properties list and on the label control on the form (Figure 1-46). If you make a mistake while typing, you can correct it by using the BACKSPACE *key or the* LEFT ARROW *and* DELETE *keys.*

FIGURE 1-46

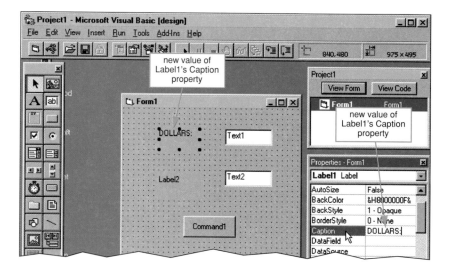

STEP 5 ▶

Repeat Steps 1 through 4 to change the caption of the second label control from Label2 to FRANCS:.

STEP 6 ▶

Repeat Steps 1 through 4 to change the caption of the command button control to CONVERT.

STEP 7 ▶

Select the form control by pointing to an empty area of the form that does not contain any other controls and clicking form (Figure 1-47).

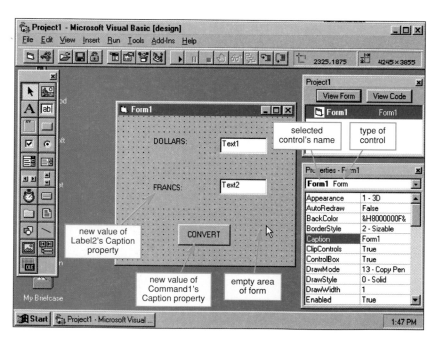

FIGURE 1-47

STEP 8 ▶

Repeat the procedures shown in Steps 2 through 4 to change the form control's caption from Form1 to Convert Dollars To Francs.

The form resembles the one shown in Figure 1-48.

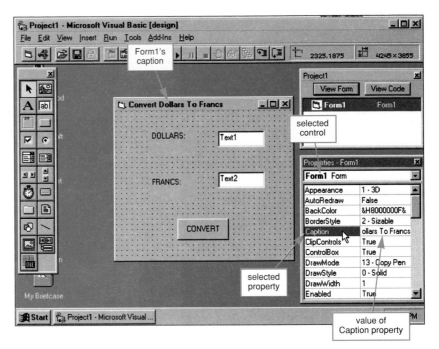

FIGURE 1-48

In the preceding steps, you changed the Caption property of four different types of controls. The caption of a label appears as text in the label control's location. This method is frequently used to place text in different locations on a form. The Caption property of a form appears as text on the title bar of the form.

An alternative method of selecting the control whose properties you want to change is to click the arrow to the right of the Object box (Figure 1-49), and then click the control's name from the drop-down list box that appears. This list expands as you add more controls to a form.

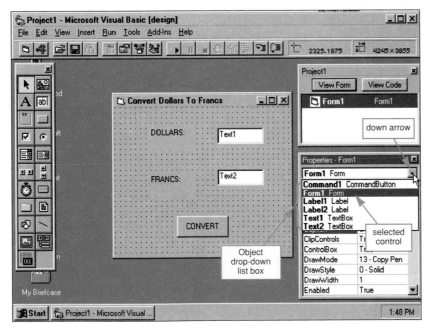

FIGURE 1-49

▶ THE TEXT PROPERTY

he **Text property** of a text box is similar to the Caption property of a label. That is, whatever value you give to the Text property of a text box control appears in the text box at the beginning of run time. Later in this project you will see how to change the Text property during run time.

The default value of a text box's Text property (the text that appears within its borders) is the name of the control. In the Dollars To Francs application, the two text boxes should be empty when the application begins, so you will set their Text property to be blank, as described in the following steps.

TO SET THE TEXT PROPERTY ▼

STEP 1 ▶

Select the Text1 text box control by clicking the control on the form.

The selected control's name appears in the Object box of the Properties window (Figure 1-50).

FIGURE 1-50

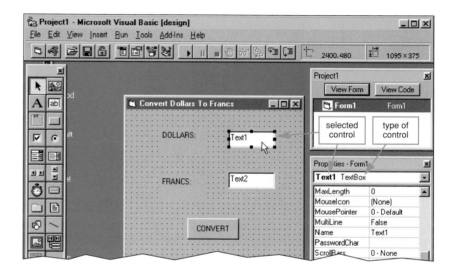

STEP 2 ▶

Point to the Text property in the Properties list.

If the property you want to change is not visible in the Properties list (Figure 1-51), use the scroll bar of the Properties window to move the Properties list within the Properties window.

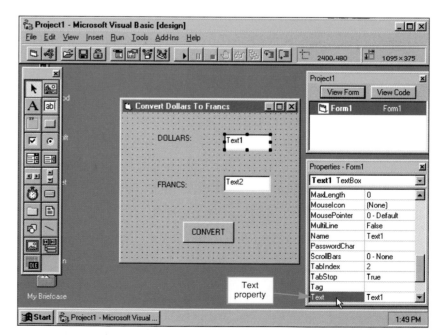

FIGURE 1-51

STEP 3 ▶

Double-click the Text property.

The Text property is highlighted in the Properties list, and the current value of the property, Text1, is highlighted (Figure 1-52).

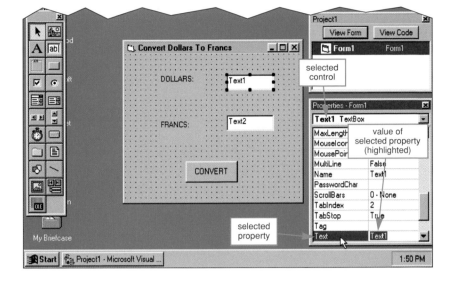

FIGURE 1-52

STEP 4 ▶

Change the contents of the Settings box to be blank by pressing the DELETE key.

The selected text box no longer has any text appearing within its borders (Figure 1-53).

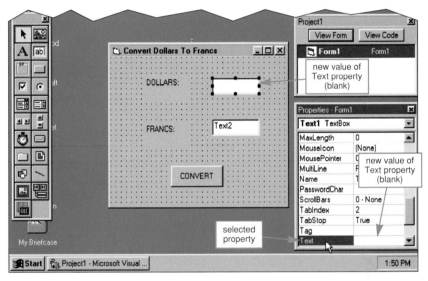

FIGURE 1-53

STEP 5 ▶

Repeat Steps 1 through 4 for the Text2 text box control.

The form appears as shown in Figure 1-54.

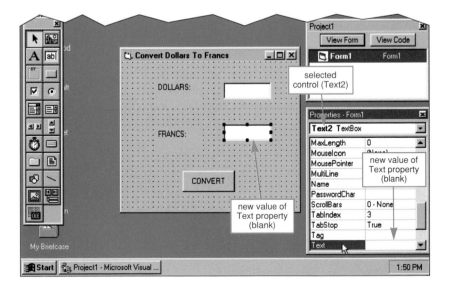

FIGURE 1-54

Notice how similar the procedures are for setting the Text property of the text boxes and for setting the Caption property of the labels. This same basic procedure is used for setting most of the properties of any type of control.

▶ NAMING CONTROLS

Visual Basic assigns unique **default names** to controls, such as Form1, Label1, Label2, Text1, and Command1. Although Visual Basic initially sets the caption of some controls to be equal to the name of the control, the name of a control and the caption of a control are two different properties. For example, the caption of the command button in your application is CONVERT; its name is Command1.

Each control has its own unique name to distinguish it from a class of similar objects. For example, the Dollars To Francs application has more than one text box. It is very important in the application to distinguish which text box gets what text printed in it. Many times it is useful to give a different name to a control. This renaming often is useful with forms, which are themselves a type of control.

You will see in Project 3 that a single Visual Basic project can have more than one form and that forms created in one project can be used in other projects. For these reasons, it is useful to give each form you create a unique name. Forms are named by setting the **Name property** of the *form* control.

Perform the following steps to change the Name property of the Form1 control.

TO CHANGE A CONTROL'S NAME ▼

STEP 1 ▶

Point to an empty area of the form that does not contain any other control.

Pointing to an empty area allows you to select the form instead of one of the controls on the form (Figure 1-55).

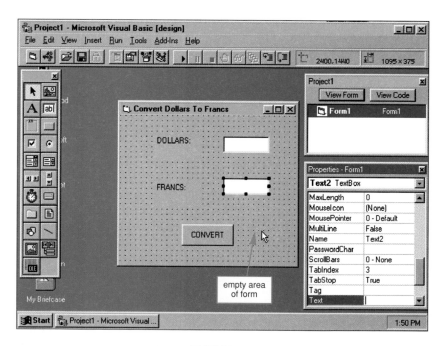

FIGURE 1-55

STEP 2 ▶

Select the Form1 control by clicking it.

The form becomes the active window as indicated by the high-lighted title bar. The form's name appears in the Object box of the Properties window (Figure 1-56).

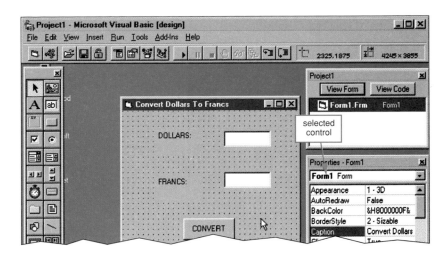

FIGURE 1-56

STEP 3 ▶

Point to the down scroll arrow of the Properties box and click the left mouse button several times to bring the Name property into view.

As you click the left mouse button, the Properties list advances within the Properties window (Figure 1-57). An alternative to clicking the down scroll arrow is to drag the scroll box downward.

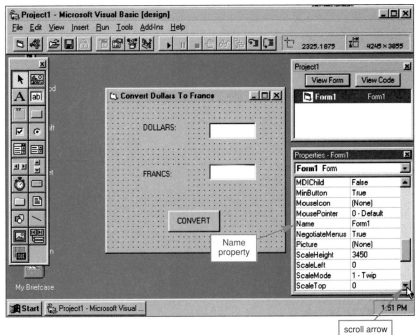

FIGURE 1-57

STEP 4 ▶

Select the Name property by double-clicking the Name property in the Properties list.

The Name property is highlighted in the Properties list, and the value of the property, Form1, is highlighted (Figure 1-58).

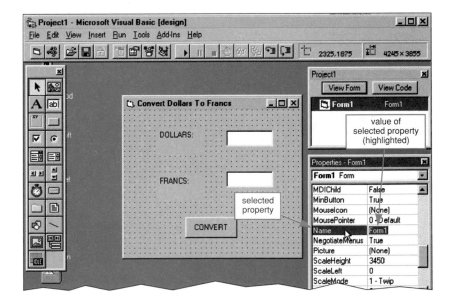

FIGURE 1-58

STEP 5 ▶

Type DLR2FRNC **and press the**
ENTER key.

The value of the form's name in
the Settings box is changed to
DLR2FRNC (Figure 1-59). Note
that the form's caption in the title
bar is unchanged because this
property is different from the
Name property.

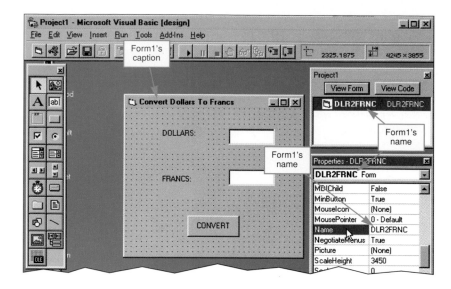

FIGURE 1-59

When you save a Visual Basic project, forms are saved as separate files with a
file extension **.frm**. The default filename for the form is the current value of the
form's Name property. However, you can assign a filename different from the
form's Name property.

▶ EVENT PROCEDURES

Development of the Dollars To Francs application began by building the
user interface, which consisted of a form and controls. The properties of
the controls were then set. The remaining step in developing the application is to write the **event procedures** or **events** that will occur within the
application. Events are the actions that occur when the application runs.

Events can be actions by the user, such as clicking or dragging a control.
Events also can be **code statements**, sometimes just called **code**. Code statements
are instructions to the computer written at design time for the computer to execute at run time. Visual Basic has its own **language**, the words and symbols used
to write these instructions. This language is very similar to Beginner's All-Purpose
Symbolic Instruction Code (**BASIC**).

Students who have had previous experience with BASIC language programming will be able to move to much more complex event procedures quite easily.
However, all of the BASIC or BASIC-like code needed for the projects in this book
will be explained at the time it is presented.

In Visual Basic, many predefined events are common to many of the different
types of controls. A control's name is used to associate common events with a specific control on a form. For example, clicking the left mouse button, the **Click**
event, is common to most types of Visual Basic controls. Text boxes are one type,
or *class*, of objects that can be associated with the Click event. Each individual
text box on a form is called an *instance* of the class and can be uniquely identified
by its name. When the mouse is clicked with its pointer positioned on a specific
instance of a class, such as the Text1 instance of the text box class, these elements
combine to form a unique event, Text1_Click.

Many times, the things you want to occur in response to events can be expressed as changes in the values of the properties of objects on the form. Although Visual Basic is not truly an Object-Oriented Programming language, this type of application development is often referred to as being **event-driven**, and **object-oriented**.

The following steps add the event procedure that converts dollars to francs and displays the result in the Text2 text box when the CONVERT button is clicked during run time.

TO WRITE AN EVENT ▼

STEP 1 ►

Point to the Command1 command button control with a caption of CONVERT.

Although you changed the command button's caption to CONVERT (Figure 1-60), its name is still Command1, the name supplied by Visual Basic when you added the control to the form. If you had more than one command button on the form, you might want to change the control's name to cmdConvert or something that more clearly identifies its function.

FIGURE 1-60

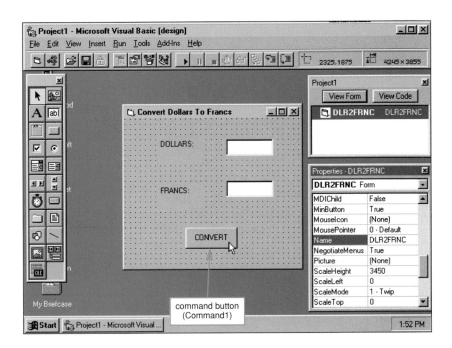

STEP 2 ►

Double-click the command button control on the form.

*The **Code window** opens on the desktop (Figure 1-61). The name of the control you selected appears in the Object box of the Code window. Two lines of code for the Click event procedure display in the Code window.*

FIGURE 1-61

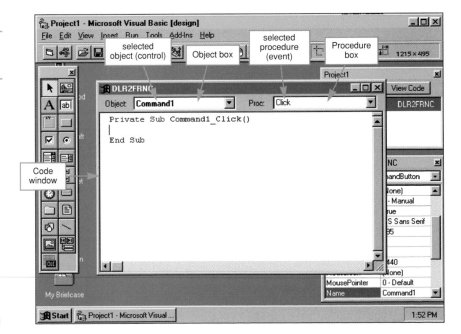

STEP 3 ▶

Click the arrow to the right of the Procedure box.

A Procedure list box containing all the event procedures that can be associated with the Command1 control displays (Figure 1-62).

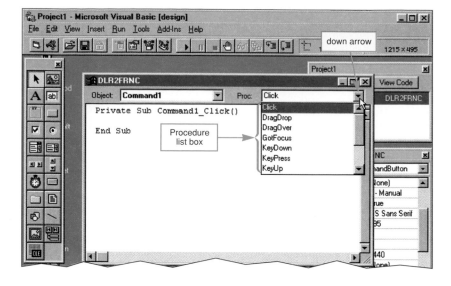

FIGURE 1-62

STEP 4 ▶

Point to the Click event procedure in the Procedure list box (Figure 1-63).

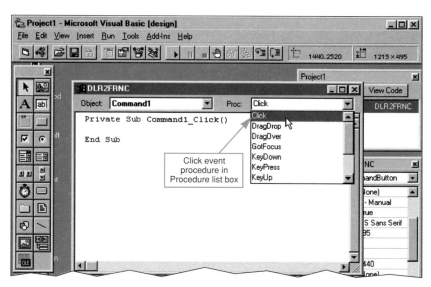

FIGURE 1-63

STEP 5 ▶

Click the Click event procedure in the list.

The insertion point (|) appears at the beginning of a blank line in between the two code statements (Figure 1-64).

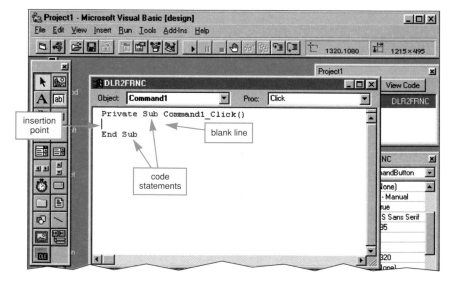

FIGURE 1-64

STEP 6 ▶

Type `text2.text = text1.text * 5.7345` **on one line as shown in Figure 1-65.**

The code appears in the second line of the Code window. This code statement changes the value of the text property of the Text2 control to equal the value of the text property of the Text1 control times 5.7345, the exchange rate between dollars and francs. This statement will execute whenever the CONVERT button is clicked during run time.

FIGURE 1-65

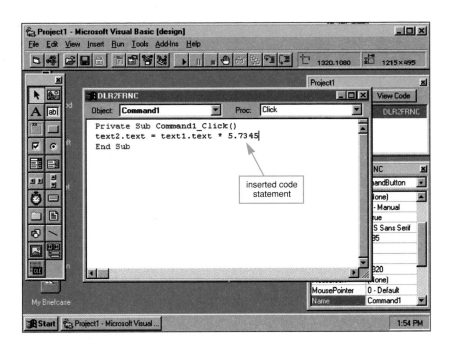

STEP 7 ▶

Close the Code window by clicking the Code window's Close button (Figure 1-66).

FIGURE 1-66

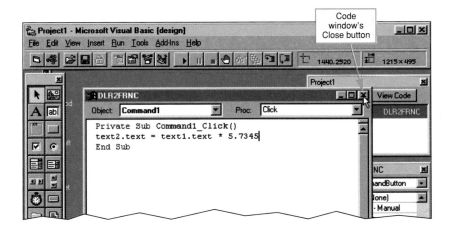

The event procedures in Visual Basic are written in blocks of code called **subroutines**. Each block begins with a statement that includes the subroutine's name and ends with a statement that indicates no further instructions are within that subroutine. These first and last statements are supplied by Visual Basic when you begin a new event subroutine.

The Code window functions as a text editor for writing your code statements. You can add and change text within the window in the same manner as you would with a text editor such as WordPad.

▶ SAVING A PROJECT

The Dollars To Francs application is now complete. Before starting a new Visual Basic project or exiting Visual Basic, you should save your work. You also should save your project periodically while you are working on it and before you run it for the first time.

Visual Basic projects are saved as a set of files. Forms are saved as files with a filename and a .frm extension. Visual Basic creates an additional file to save the project. This file has a filename and a **.vbp** extension. You specify the path and filename for these files using the Save File As dialog box and the Save Project As dialog box. The Save File As and Save Project As boxes are the same in many different Windows applications. They are called common dialog boxes.

The following example illustrates how to save a project to drive A. It is assumed you have a formatted diskette in drive A.

TO SAVE A PROJECT ▼

STEP 1 ►

Click the Save Project button on the toolbar.

The Save File As dialog box opens (Figure 1-67). The default filename in the dialog box is the name you gave to the form previously.

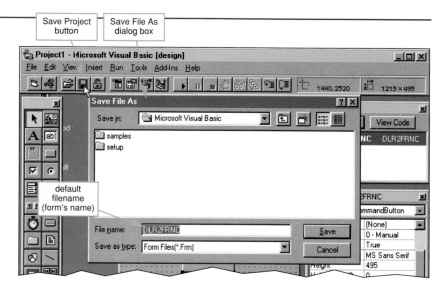

FIGURE 1-67

STEP 2 ►

Click the Save in box arrow.

The Save in drop-down list appears (Figure 1-68).

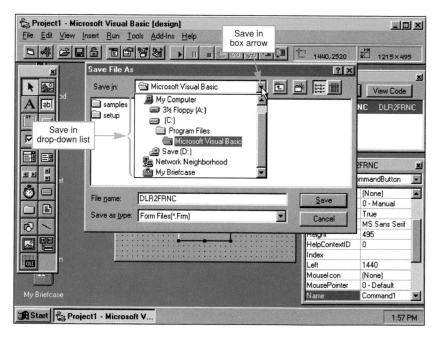

FIGURE 1-68

STEP 3 ▶

Click 3½ Floppy [A:].

The drop-down list closes and drive A becomes the selected drive (Figure 1-69).

FIGURE 1-69

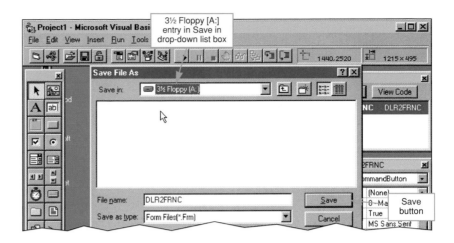

STEP 4 ▶

Click the Save button in the Save File As dialog box.

The form is saved as the file dlr2frnc.frm, and the Save Project As dialog box appears (Figure 1-70). The default project name, Project1, appears in the File Name box.

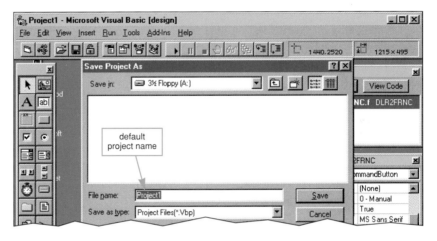

FIGURE 1-70

STEP 5 ▶

Type Currency **as the entry.**

The default name for the project is replaced in the File name box with the characters you typed (Figure 1-71). If you make an error while typing, you can use the BACK-SPACE key or the LEFT ARROW and DELETE keys to erase the mistake and then continue typing.

STEP 6 ▶

Click the Save button in the Save Project As dialog box.

The project is saved as Currency.vbp and the dialog box closes.

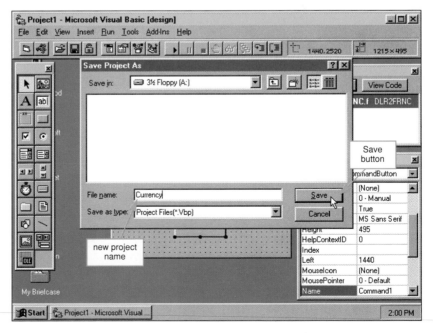

FIGURE 1-71

In the Save File As dialog box you specified the drive used to save the form file, but you did not need to change the drive in the Save Project As dialog box. After you change a drive or directory in any of the common dialog boxes, it remains current in all the dialog boxes until you change it again.

You can resave your work without opening the common dialog box by clicking the Save Project button on the toolbar. If you want to save your work with a different filename, directory, or drive, you must choose the Save File As command after selecting the File menu on the menu bar.

▶ STARTING, OPENING, AND RUNNING PROJECTS

his section shows how to start a new project, open an existing project, and run a project within the Visual Basic environment.

Starting a New Project

When you started Visual Basic, a new project opened automatically. The form had no controls or event procedures, and all properties had their default values. It is not necessary to restart Visual Basic each time you want to build a new application. Before beginning a new application, you should be certain that you have saved any work you don't want to lose. Because you already have saved the Dollars To Francs application, perform the follow steps to begin another project.

TO START A NEW PROJECT ▼

STEP 1 ▶

Click File on the menu bar.

The File menu displays (Figure 1-72).

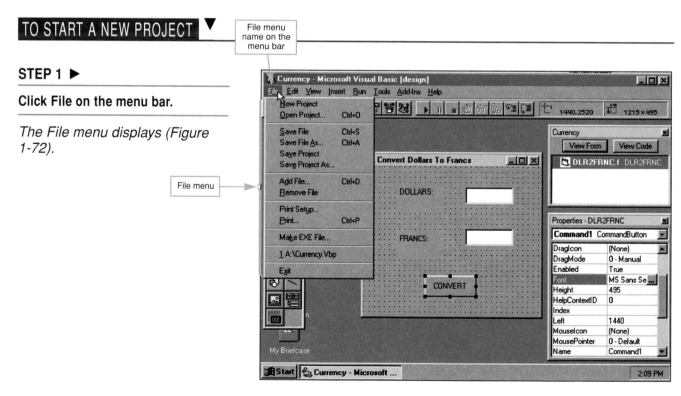

FIGURE 1-72

STEP 2 ▶

Point to the New Project command from the File menu (Figure 1-73).

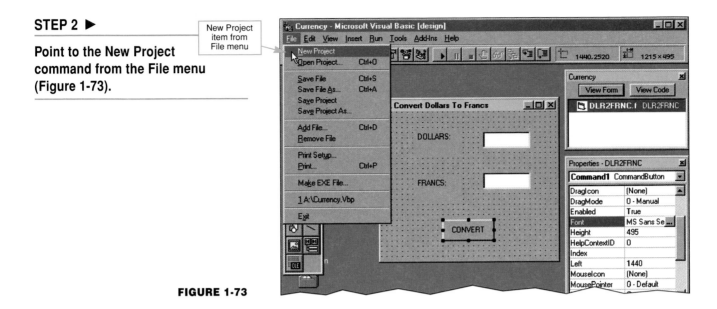

FIGURE 1-73

STEP 3 ▶

Click New Project.

Five Visual Basic windows appear on the desktop with an empty form (Figure 1-74). The new form has the default form name, Form1, and the project has the default project name, Project1.

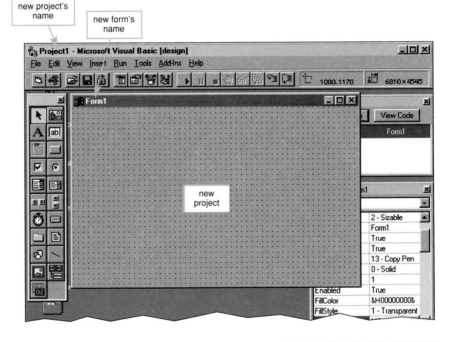

FIGURE 1-74

Each time you start Visual Basic, a new project is opened. In the preceding steps you learned it is not necessary to restart Visual Basic to begin a new project. If you attempt to open a new project before saving the current project, Visual Basic will display a message box asking if you want to save the previous work.

Opening a Project

Once a project has been saved, you can return to that project and make changes. You tell Visual Basic which project you want to use through an Open Project dialog box that is similar to the Save File As dialog box. The example on the following page opens the project previously completed.

TO OPEN A PROJECT ▼

STEP 1 ▶

Click the Open Project button on the Toolbar.

The Open Project dialog box appears (Figure 1-75). If drive A is not the selected drive, you can change it in the same way you changed the selected drive when you saved the form file.

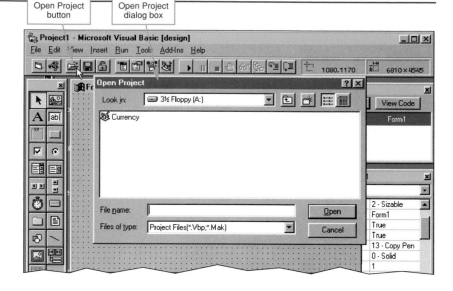

FIGURE 1-75

STEP 2 ▶

Point to the project's name, Currency, in the File list box.

If the project's name is not visible in the File list box, use the scroll bar to move the list until its name is visible (Figure 1-76).

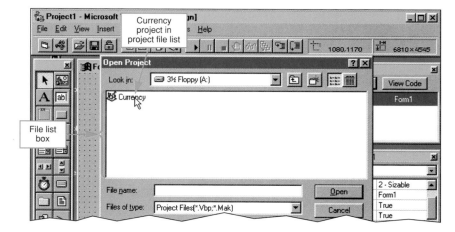

FIGURE 1-76

STEP 3 ▶

Double-click Currency.

The files are read into memory, and the Project window listing all of the files associated with the project opens on the desktop (Figure 1-77). The Form window is reopened by clicking the View Form button. The Properties window is empty until a form is selected.

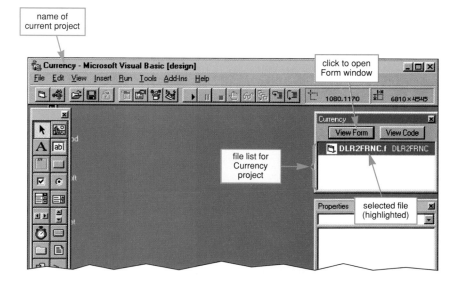

FIGURE 1-77

When you save a project, save the form file first and then save the project file. When you open a project, open only the project file. Any other files associated with that project are automatically opened. All of these files are listed in the Project window.

Running an Application

In the following example, the Dollars To Francs application is run from within the Visual Basic environment and the application is started by using the toolbar.

TO RUN AN APPLICATION ▼

STEP 1 ▶

Click the Start button on the toolbar.

The word design *in the Visual Basic title bar changes to* run. *The application's window appears on the desktop, and the cursor moves to the first text box (Figure 1-78).*

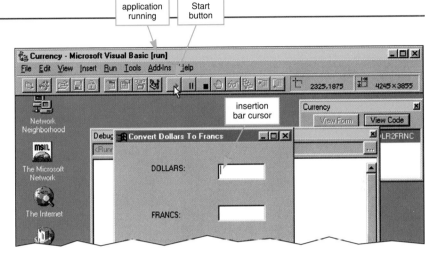

FIGURE 1-78

STEP 2 ▶

Type 520 **as the entry.**

The number appears in the first text box (Figure 1-79). You can change or edit your entry using the BACKSPACE *key or the* LEFT ARROW *and* DELETE *keys.*

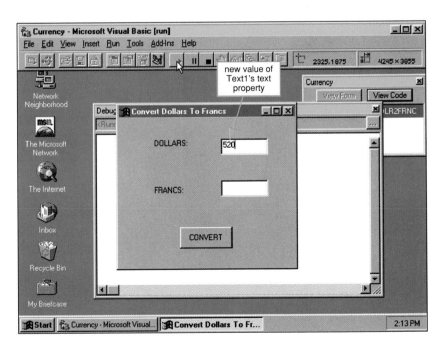

FIGURE 1-79

STEP 3 ▶

Click the command button with the CONVERT caption.

The number 2981.94 appears in the second text box (Figure 1-80). Thus, $520 = 2981.94 Francs.

STEP 4 ▶

Click the End button on the toolbar.

The application closes, and the design environment returns to the desktop.

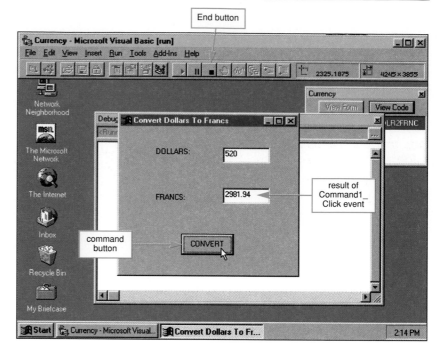

FIGURE 1-80

Run your application again, trying different numbers for the dollars amount. You do not need to restart the application each time you want to do another conversion. Use the mouse to click the first text box, press the DELETE key several times to erase your entry, and type a new number. Click the CONVERT button.

You also can close (end) the application by clicking the Close button on the application's window, like other Windows applications.

▶ EXITING VISUAL BASIC

J ust like other Windows applications, Visual Basic can be minimized to allow you to temporarily work with another application such as a spreadsheet or word processing document. You then can return by clicking the Visual Basic button on the taskbar.

When you have completed working with Visual Basic, you should exit the Visual Basic program to conserve memory space for other Windows applications. The following step shows how to exit Visual Basic.

TO EXIT VISUAL BASIC ▼

STEP 1 ▶

Click the Visual Basic Close button.

If you made changes to the project since the last time it was saved, Visual Basic displays a dialog box (Figure 1-81). Click the Yes button to resave your project and exit. Click the No button to exit without saving the changes. Click the Cancel button to remove the dialog box.

FIGURE 1-81

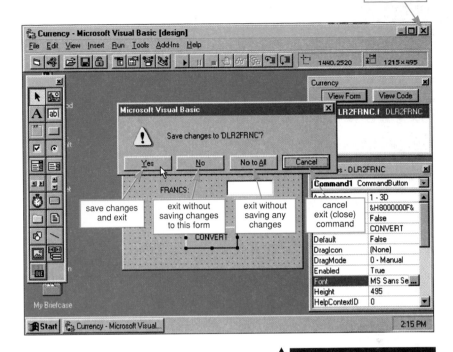

An alternative method of exiting Visual Basic is to choose the Exit command from the File menu.

▶ VISUAL BASIC ONLINE HELP

he Visual Basic programming system includes an extensive online Help. You can access online Help any time you are working with Visual Basic by selecting the Help menu on the menu bar (Figure 1-82).

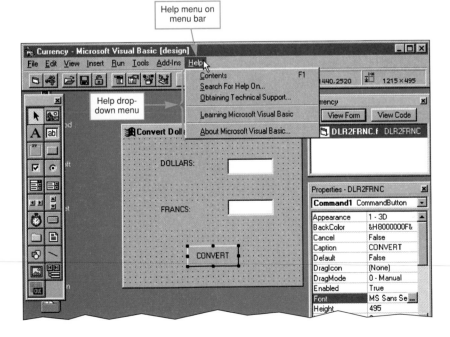

FIGURE 1-82

Help Menu

The Visual Basic Help menu includes a table of contents (Figure 1-83) and a Find tab for navigating around online Help (Figure 1-84). Once you have opened online Help, you can get information about how to use it by pressing function key F1.

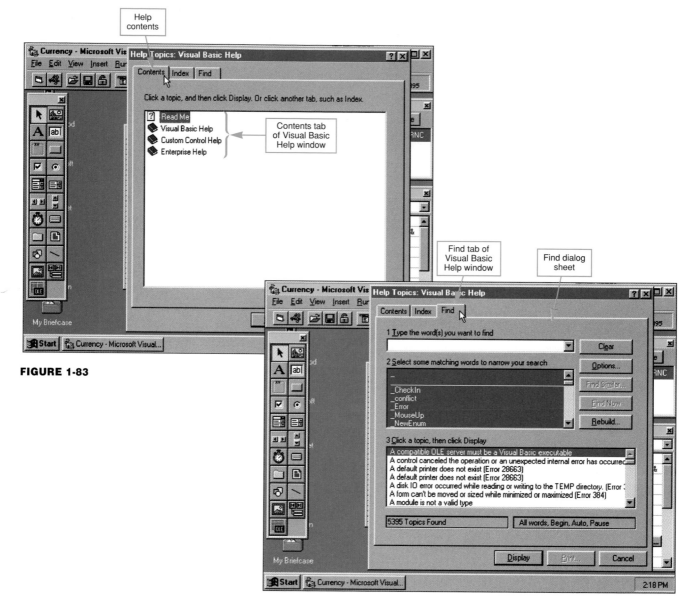

FIGURE 1-83

FIGURE 1-84

Context-Sensitive Help

You can get help on many parts of Visual Basic without using the Help menu. This feature is called **context-sensitive help**. You can get help on any context-sensitive part of Visual Basic by pressing function key F1. For example, to get help about the toolbar, click the title bar of the Visual Basic Menu Bar and Toolbar window, and then press F1. Visual Basic opens online Help and displays the section on the toolbar (Figure 1-85).

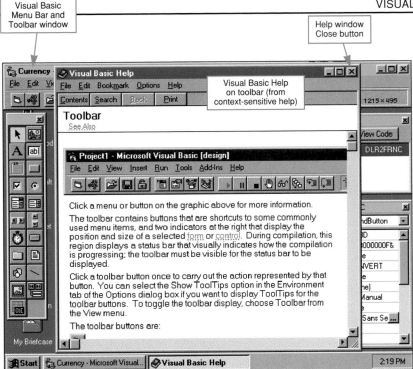

FIGURE 1-85

Click the Help window's Close button to exit online Help and return to the design environment.

Visual Basic Tutorial

You can improve your Visual Basic skills by working through the online **tutorial**. The tutorial is accessed by choosing the Learning Microsoft Visual Basic command on the Help menu. The tutorial contains nine Visual Basic lessons (Figure 1-86). Before starting any of these lessons, you first should complete the lesson on how to use the tutorial by clicking the Instructions button.

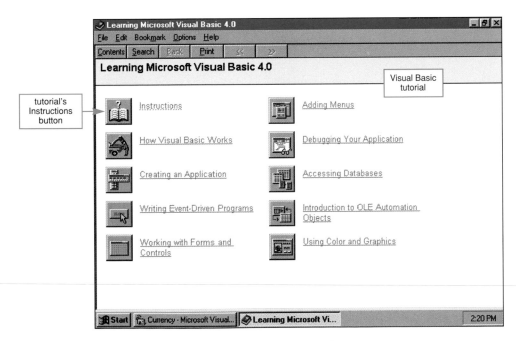

FIGURE 1-86

▶ PROJECT SUMMARY

Project 1 introduced the major elements of Visual Basic by developing a Windows application. The process to build the application consisted of three steps:

- ▶ **Create the interface**   Draw the form and controls (objects)
- ▶ **Set properties**   Set values of properties for the objects added to the form
- ▶ **Write code**   Create the events and actions that will occur when the application runs

You learned how to start Visual Basic, design a form, and add labels, text boxes, and command buttons to a form. You learned the process for changing the properties of controls by setting Caption, Text, and Name properties. After the graphical user interface of your application was built, you learned how to specify an event procedure. You then learned how to run and save your application and how to start a new project or open an existing project. At the end of Project 1 you learned how to access information about Visual Basic through online Help and online tutorial.

▶ KEY TERMS AND INDEX

applications (*VB2*)
application software (*VB2*)
BASIC (*VB30*)
Caption property (*VB23*)
click (*VB3*)
Click event (*VB30*)
code (*VB30*)
code statements (*VB30*)
Code window (*VB31*)
command button (*VB13*)
context-sensitive help (*VB42*)
controls (*VB12*)
default names (*VB28*)
default values (*VB23*)
design time (*VB8*)
double-click (*VB3*)
drag (*VB3*)
event (*VB13, VB30*)

event-driven (*VB31*)
event procedures (*VB30*)
form (*VB8*)
.frm (*VB30*)
graphical user interface (GUI)
  (*VB2*)
online Help (*VB41*)
label (*VB12*)
language (*VB30*)
menu bar (*VB3*)
Name property (*VB28*)
Object box (*VB22*)
object-oriented (*VB31*)
objects (*VB2*)
point (*VB3*)
Procedure list box (*VB32*)
project (*VB8*)
properties (*VB22*)

Properties list (*VB22*)
right-click (*VB3*)
right-drag (*VB3*)
run time (*VB8*)
sizing handles (*VB14*)
subroutines (*VB33*)
text box (*VB12*)
Text property (*VB26*)
toolbar (*VB6*)
Toolbox (*VB13*)
tutorial (*VB43*)
twips (*VB11*)
Visual Basic programming
  environment (*VB6*)
.vbp (*VB34*)

▶ TOOLBAR AND TOOLBOX REFERENCE

The Toolbar and Toolbox Reference shown in Figure 1-87 identifies the buttons on the toolbar and the tools in the Toolbox.

Toolbar

Toolbox

FIGURE 1-87

In Visual Basic you can accomplish a task in a number of ways. The following table provides a quick reference to each of the major tasks presented for the first time in the project with some of the available options. The commands listed in the Menu column can be executed using either the keyboard or mouse.

Task	Mouse	Menu	Keyboard Shortcuts
Activate a Window	Click the window to be activated	From Window menu, choose window title	Press ALT+F6 to toggle between last two active windows
Add a Control to a Form	Double-click control's tool in Toolbox		Press ENTER to add the selected tool in the Toolbox
End (Close) an Application	Click End button on toolbar	From Run menu, choose End	Press CTRL+BREAK
Open a Code Window	Click View Code button in Project window	From View menu, choose Code	Press F7
Open the Help Facility		From Help menu, choose appropriate command	Press F1 for context-sensitive help
Remove a Selected Control from a Form			Press DELETE
Resave a Modified Form with the Same Filename	Click Save Form button on toolbar	From File menu, choose Save File	
Resave a Modified Project with the Same Filename	Click Save Project button on toolbar	From File menu, choose Save Project	
Save a Form File with a New Filename		From File menu, choose Save File As	Press CTRL+A (when Form window is active)
Save a Project File with a New Filename		From File menu, choose Save Project As	
Select a Control on a Form	Click on control to be selected		Press TAB to cycle through control on form (Form window must be active window)
Select a Tool in the Toolbox	Click on tool in Toolbox		Use arrow keys to move through tools (Toolbox must be active window)
Select a Control in the Active Properties Window	Click Object box arrow to open Object drop-down list. Click control's name in objects list		Press SHIFT+TAB to give Object box focus. Press F4 to open list. Use UP and DOWN ARROWS to move through list and press ENTER.
Select a Property in the Active Properties Window	Use scroll bar to move through list and click property's name		Use UP and DOWN ARROWS to move through list and press ENTER
Start (Run) an Application	Click Start button on toolbar	From Run menu, choose Start	Press F5

STUDENT ASSIGNMENT 1
True/False

Instructions: Circle T if the statement is true or F if the statement is false.

T F 1. Visual Basic is a Windows application.
T F 2. Visual Basic is used to build Windows applications.
T F 3. A form can be resized by dragging its borders.
T F 4. The text in a label control can be changed by the user at run time.
T F 5. Controls are added to the form by selecting them from the control list in the Code window.
T F 6. The location of a control on a form is changed by dragging the control to the new location.
T F 7. The Object box of the Properties window is where you enter a value for a specific property.
T F 8. All controls have the same set of properties.
T F 9. At design time, you must set the values of all properties of the controls on a form.
T F 10. A form is a control.
T F 11. A project cannot have the same name as a form used within that project.
T F 12. Forms are saved as a file with a filename and .vbp extension.
T F 13. Double-clicking a control will open the Code window and show the event code for that control.
T F 14. You must exit Visual Basic before you can switch to another Windows application.
T F 15. A new project is opened each time you start Visual Basic.
T F 16. You can open previously saved projects by using the Save File As dialog box.
T F 17. Projects must be saved in the Microsoft Visual Basic folder.
T F 18. To activate the online Help, press function key F3.
T F 19. To get help about using online Help, press function key F1 twice.
T F 20. To get help about any topic, you always must use the Help menu.

STUDENT ASSIGNMENT 2
Multiple Choice

Instructions: Circle the correct response.

1. You specify the text you want to appear in a form's title bar by setting the _____ property of the form.
   a. Text   c. Caption
   b. Title   d. Name
2. The purpose of handles is to _____.
   a. move a form   c. grab a drop-down menu list box
   b. select controls from the toolbox   d. resize controls
3. The Code window contains a drop-down list of _____.
   a. properties   c. code statements
   b. controls   d. .frm files
4. The _____ property of a command button contains text that will appear on the control.
   a. Name   c. Text
   b. Caption   d. Label
5. You select a property from the Properties list by _____ the name of the property.
   a. clicking   c. double-clicking
   b. pointing to   d. dragging
6. Forms are saved as files that have a filename and _____ extension.
   a. .vbp   c. .bas
   b. .frm   d. .vbx

7. The Visual Basic window that contains buttons representing frequently used menu commands is the
   _____.
   a. Toolbox   c. Menu Bar and Toolbar window
   b. Project window   d. menu box
8. The last code statement in an event procedure is _____.
   a. run   c. return
   b. end sub   d. run
9. The Visual Basic tutorial is accessed by choosing _____ on the Help menu.
   a. About Microsoft Visual Basic...
   b. Introducing Microsoft Visual Basic
   c. Learning Microsoft Visual Basic
   d. Microsoft Visual Basic Tutorial
10. Context-sensitive help _____.
   a. is not available in Visual Basic
   b. accesses Help without going through the Help menu
   c. can be accessed from the Help menu
   d. provides help on using online Help

STUDENT ASSIGNMENT 3
Understanding the Visual Basic Environment

Instructions: In Figure SA1-3, arrows point to the windows that make up the Visual Basic programming environment. Identify these windows in the spaces provided.

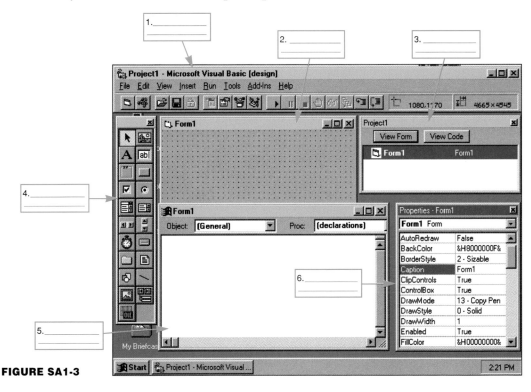

FIGURE SA1-3

1. _____
2. _____
3. _____
4. _____
5. _____
6. _____

STUDENT ASSIGNMENT 4
Understanding the Toolbox and Properties Window

Instructions: In Figure SA1-4, arrows point to some of the tool buttons in the Toolbox and to the major components of the Properties window. Identify these in the spaces provided.

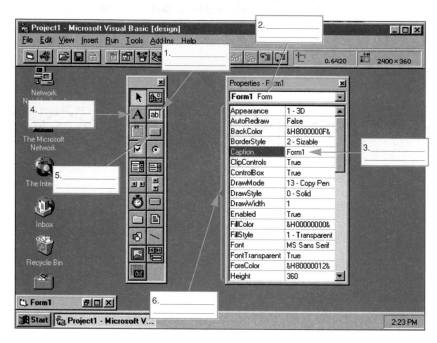

FIGURE SA1-4

1. _____

2. _____

3. _____

4. _____

5. _____

6. _____

STUDENT ASSIGNMENT 5
Understanding the Menu Bar, Toolbar, and Code Window

Instructions: In Figure SA1-5, arrows point to some of the important components of the menu bar, toolbar, and Code window. Identify these components in the spaces provided.

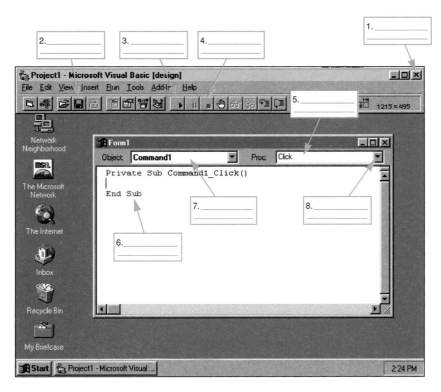

FIGURE SA1-5

1. _____
2. _____
3. _____
4. _____
5. _____
6. _____
7. _____
8. _____

STUDENT ASSIGNMENT 6
Understanding Control Names, Properties, and Property Values

Instructions: Three different examples of the Properties window are shown in Figure SA1-6 on the next page. For each of these examples, identify the following:

    a. the name of the selected control
    b. the type of control
    c. the selected property
    d. the value of the selected property

(continued)

STUDENT ASSIGNMENT 6 (continued)

FIGURE SA1-6a   **FIGURE SA1-6b**   **FIGURE SA1-6c**

a. _____   a. _____   a. _____

b. _____   b. _____   b. _____

c. _____   c. _____   c. _____

d. _____   d. _____   d. _____

C O M P U T E R   L A B O R A T O R Y   E X E R C I S E S

COMPUTER LABORATORY EXERCISE 1
Using the Help Menu, Context-Sensitive Help, and Visual Basic Tutorial

Instructions: Perform the following tasks using a computer:

1. Start Visual Basic.
2. Choose Contents on the Help menu on the Menu bar.
3. Click the Contents tab.
4. Double-click Visual Basic Help.
5. Double-click Using Visual Basic.
6. Double-click Creating The Interface.
7. Click the word Toolbox in the Creating The Interface Help window.
8. Use the scroll bar to read about Visual Basic's controls.
9. Click the Help window's Close button.
10. Click the Caption property in the Properties list of the Properties window.
11. Press function key F1 for context-sensitive help.
12. Read about the Caption property in the Help window.
13. Click the Close button on the Help window.
14. Choose Learning Microsoft Visual Basic from the Help menu on the menu bar.
15. Click How Visual Basic Works and read through the tutorial.
16. Exit the tutorial.

STEP 5 ▶

Point to the form's right border and drag the border toward the left side of the screen to the position shown in Figure 2-8.

The mouse pointer's shape again changes to a horizontal double arrow, and the shaded outline of the right border is moved toward the left side of the screen.

FIGURE 2-8

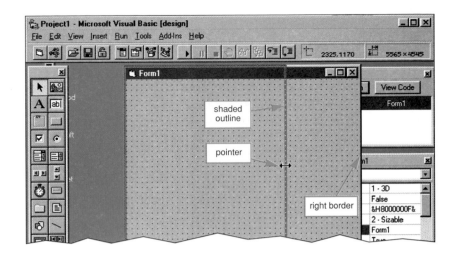

STEP 6 ▶

Release the left mouse button.

The form's right border moves to the position of the shaded line, and the new width appears on the right side of the toolbar (Figure 2-9).

FIGURE 2-9

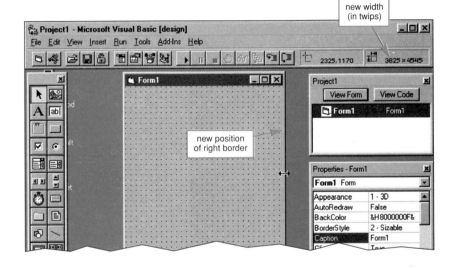

STEP 7 ▶

Point to the form's bottom border and drag the border downward to the position shown in Figure 2-10.

The pointer changes to a vertical double arrow. As you drag the border, the form's new shape appears as shaded lines.

FIGURE 2-10

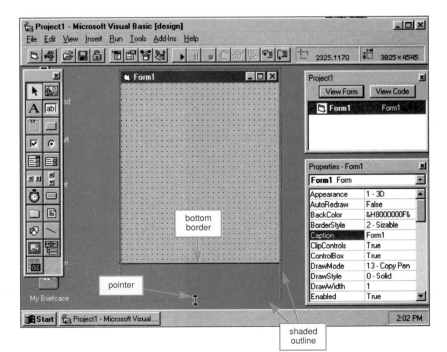

STEP 8 ▶

Release the left mouse button.

The bottom border moves to the position of the shaded line, and the form's new height appears on the right side of the toolbar (Figure 2-11).

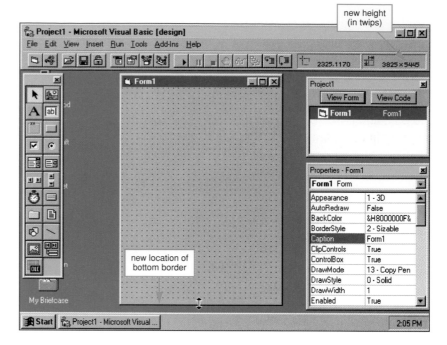

FIGURE 2-11

With the form's size set, the entire form now can be dragged to a position on the desktop where it will appear at run time, as was done in Project 1. However, its current position (Figure 2-11) is satisfactory for the Movie Box Office application.

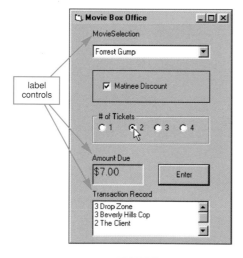

FIGURE 2-12

Adding Labels and Setting the AutoSize Property

The next step is to add the three label controls in the Movie Box Office project shown in Figure 2-12. Recall that unlike a text box, the contents of a label control cannot be directly changed by the user of the application at run time. For example, the word *MovieSelection* can only be changed with code statements at run time because that word is the caption of one of the label controls.

When the **AutoSize property** of a label is set to True, the label's size automatically is adjusted to the size of the label's caption. Although setting properties normally is performed after building the interface, the AutoSize property of three of the labels will be set to make room for the other controls that will be added to the form. The following steps add one label control to the form and set its AutoSize property.

TO ADD AN AUTOSIZE LABEL CONTROL ▼

STEP 1 ►

Double-click the Label tool in the Toolbox, and point to the AutoSize property in the Properties list.

A default-size label is added to the center of the form. The Label1 control is the selected control. Its properties appear in the Properties window (Figure 2-13).

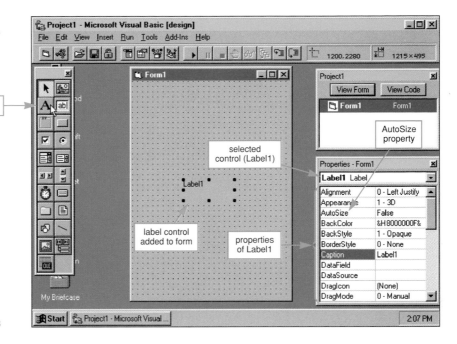

FIGURE 2-13

STEP 2 ►

Double-click the AutoSize property in the Properties list.

The value of the label's AutoSize property size is changed from False to True in the Properties window, and its size is adjusted on the form (Figure 2-14).

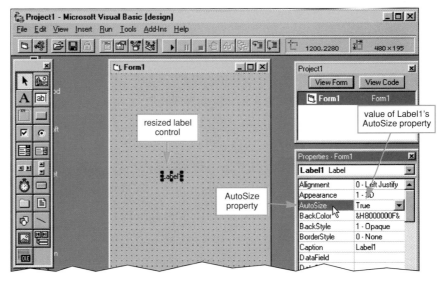

FIGURE 2-14

STEP 3 ►

Drag the Label1 control to the position shown in Figure 2-15.

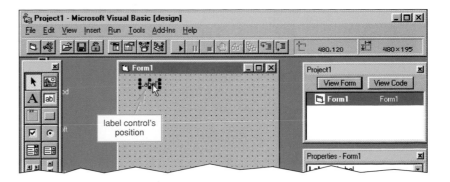

FIGURE 2-15

In Project 1, properties were set by typing their values in the Properties window. When a property has fixed values, such as the False/True values of the AutoSize property, you can switch between those values by double-clicking the name of the property in the Properties list.

Copying Controls

The two additional label controls identified in Figure 2-12 on page VB62 are similar to the one that was just added. When you want to add multiple similar controls to a form, it often is easier to copy the control to the Clipboard and then paste copies of it from the Clipboard to the form. The following steps add two copies of the Label1 control to the form.

TO COPY CONTROLS ▼

STEP 1 ▶

Click Edit on the menu bar.

The Edit menu displays (Figure 2-16).

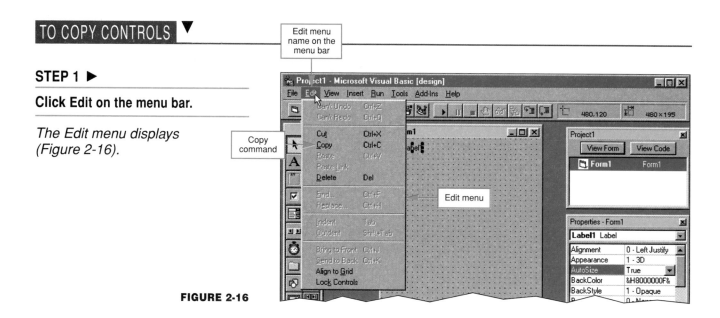

FIGURE 2-16

STEP 2 ▶

Click the Copy command on the Edit menu.

The selected control (Label1) is copied to the Clipboard, and the Edit menu closes (Figure 2-17). The selected control changes to Form1 in the Properties window.

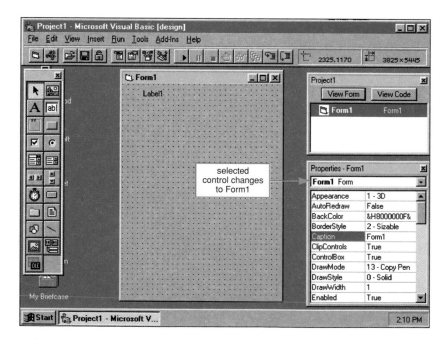

FIGURE 2-17

STEP 3 ▶

Click Edit on the menu bar and click the Paste command. Point to No in the dialog box.

The dialog box shown in Figure 2-18 displays. The pointer points to No in the dialog box.

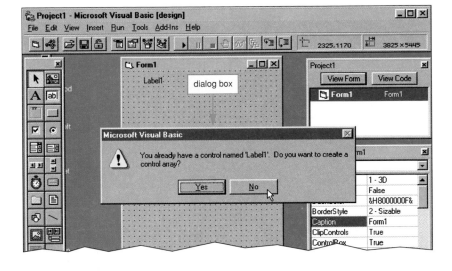

FIGURE 2-18

STEP 4 ▶

Click No in the dialog box.

The dialog box closes, and a copy of the control is added to the form (Figure 2-19). The control is automatically named Label2 and is the selected control.

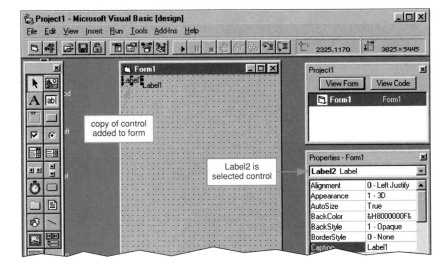

FIGURE 2-19

STEP 5 ▶

Drag the new label control to the position shown in Figure 2-20.

The label's name shown in the Properties window is Label2, but its caption is Label1.

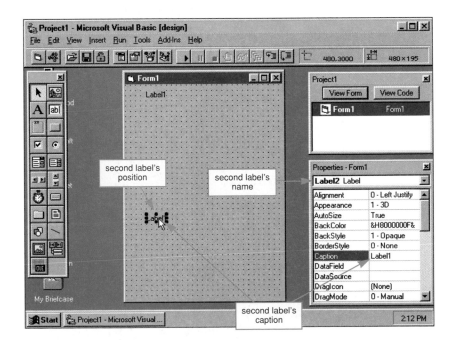

FIGURE 2-20

STEP 6 ▶

Repeat the procedures shown in
Steps 3 and 4 to add the third label,
and drag it to the position shown in
Figure 2-21.

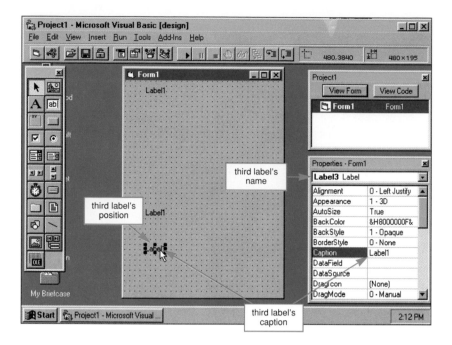

FIGURE 2-21

When you copy a control, the pasted control has a new name but has all of
the other properties of the control you copied. Thus, both additional controls are
AutoSized and have the same caption, Label1. The captions will be changed later
in this project. Once a control is copied to the Clipboard, multiple copies can be
pasted without having to copy the control to the Clipboard each time.

The List Box and Combo Box Controls

List box and **combo box** controls are used in applications to present lists of
choices. In a list box, part or all of the list of choices displays. When the list of
choices is longer than can appear in the list box, a scroll bar automatically is added
to move the list up or down. When an item is selected from the list by clicking it,
the item appears in a highlighted color.

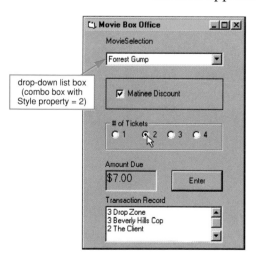

FIGURE 2-22

The Movie Box Office application contains a combo box
control with properties set so that the movies appear in a drop-
down list of choices (Figure 2-22). With a **drop-down list,** the
list of choices appears only when you click the down arrow
located next to the list box. When you select an item from the
list by clicking it, the drop-down list closes, and only the
selected item appears in the list box.

At run time, list box controls always have one way to
select an item from the list. Combo box controls can have
different selection methods and can appear differently, depending on how the properties are set. The appearance of list box
controls and combo box controls and the method of selecting
an item from these controls at run time are summarized in
Table 2-1.

▸ **TABLE 2-1 LIST BOX AND COMBO BOX CONTROLS**

CONTROL	APPEARANCE OF LIST	SELECTION FROM LIST
List box	List always shows; scroll bar added if list is longer than control's size	Click item from list
Combo box (style 0)	Drop-down list	Click item in list or type item directly in combo box
Combo box (style 1)	List always shows; scroll bar added if list is longer than control's size	Click item in list or type item directly in combo box
Combo box (style 2)	Drop-down list	Click item in list

The following steps add a combo box to the Movie Box Office form. Later, its style is set to 2 (see Table 2-1) to make it a drop-down list box.

TO ADD A COMBO BOX CONTROL ▾

STEP 1 ▶

Double-click the ComboBox tool in the Toolbox.

A default-sized combo box is added to the form (Figure 2-23).

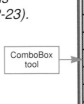

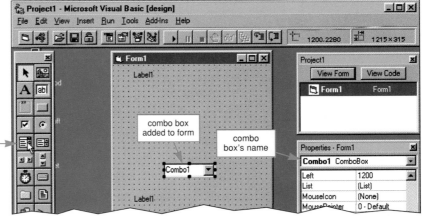

FIGURE 2-23

STEP 2 ▶

Drag the combo box to the position shown in Figure 2-24. Point to the right center sizing handle.

The combo box is moved, and the pointer points to the right center sizing handle.

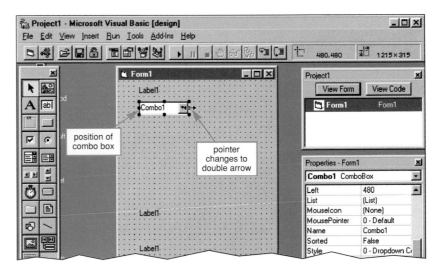

FIGURE 2-24

STEP 3 ▶

Drag the sizing handle on the center right side of the combo box to the position shown in Figure 2-25.

The shaded outline of the control appears on the form.

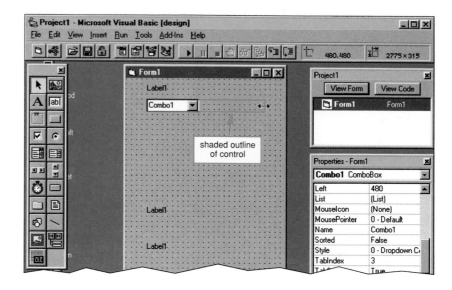

FIGURE 2-25

STEP 4 ▶

Release the left mouse button.

The combo box is resized on the form (Figure 2-26).

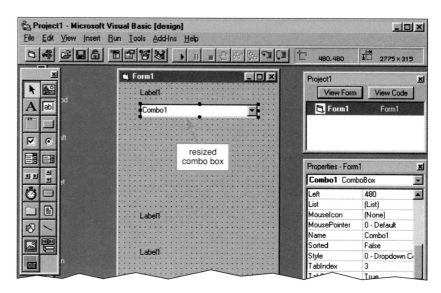

FIGURE 2-26

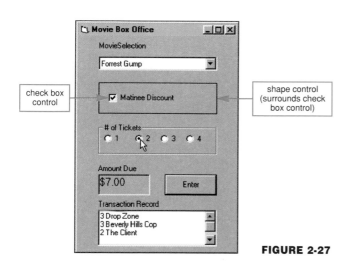

FIGURE 2-27

The names of the movies will be added to the drop-down list box by using code statements later in this project.

The Shape Control

The **shape control** is used to add a rectangle, square, oval, or circle to a form. The Movie Box Office application uses a rectangular shape as a border surrounding the Matinee Discount check box (Figure 2-27). Its only purpose in this application is to enhance the visual balance of the controls on the form.

Perform the following steps to add the shape control to the form.

TO ADD THE SHAPE CONTROL ▼

STEP 1 ▶

Click the Shape tool in the Toolbox, and move the mouse under the lower left corner of the combo box, which is where the top left corner of the shape will appear (Figure 2-28).

The Shape tool is highlighted in the Toolbox, and the mouse pointer changes to a cross hair.

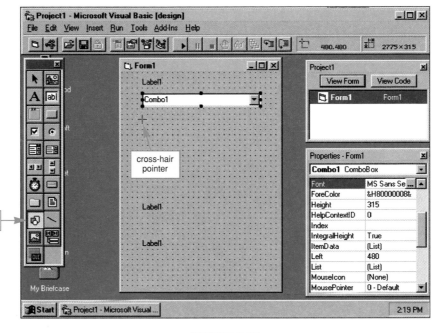

FIGURE 2-28

STEP 2 ▶

Drag the mouse pointer down and to the right as shown in Figure 2-29.

A shaded outline of the control appears on the form.

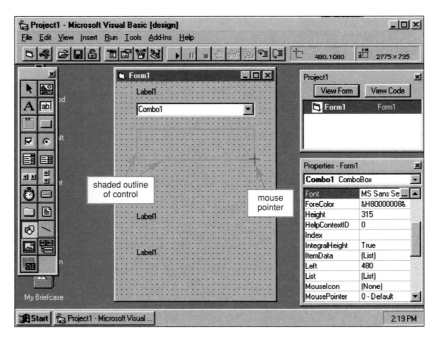

FIGURE 2-29

STEP 3 ▶

Release the left mouse button.

The control is sized to fit the area of the shaded outline (Figure 2-30).

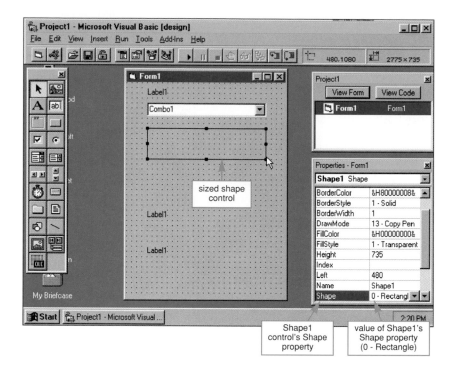

FIGURE 2-30

The different properties of the shape control, such as the Shape property, appear in the Properties list (Figure 2-30). The default shape of a shape control is a rectangle.

The Check Box Control

A **check box** control is used in applications to turn options on or off, such as the matinee discount (Figure 2-27 on page VB68). Clicking an empty check box places a ✓ in the box to indicate the option is selected. Clicking on a selected check box removes the ✓ to indicate the option is not selected.

TO ADD A CHECK BOX CONTROL ▼

STEP 1 ▶

Double-click the CheckBox tool in the Toolbox.

A default-sized check box is added to the form (Figure 2-31).

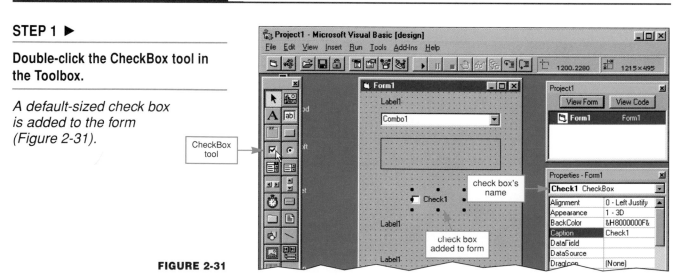

FIGURE 2-31

STEP 2 ►

Drag the check box to a position inside the shape control. Drag the sizing handle on the right of the control to extend its width, as shown in Figure 2-32.

The check box is positioned inside the shape control, and its width is extended.

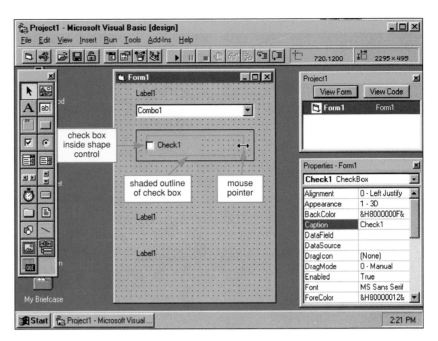

FIGURE 2-32

Check boxes are used to indicate the selection or deselection of individual options. For this reason, any number or combination of check boxes on a form can be checked at the same time. In the Movie Box Office application, the check box is used to switch between the two different prices of the tickets purchased. The two prices will be established later in the code for the application.

The Frame Control

The **frame control** is used as a container for other controls, as shown in Figure 2-33. It has several properties similar to the shape control, but it has some important differences:

- ▶ A frame can have only a rectangular shape.
- ▶ A frame can have a caption.
- ▶ When option buttons are added inside a frame, only one can be selected at a time during run time.

To add the frame control as illustrated in Figure 2-33, perform the steps on the next page.

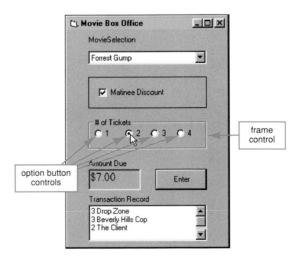

FIGURE 2-33

TO ADD THE FRAME CONTROL ▼

STEP 1 ▶

Click the Frame tool in the Toolbox, and move the mouse to the position where the top left corner of the frame will appear (Figure 2-34).

The Frame tool is high- lighted in the Toolbox, and the mouse pointer changes to a cross hair.

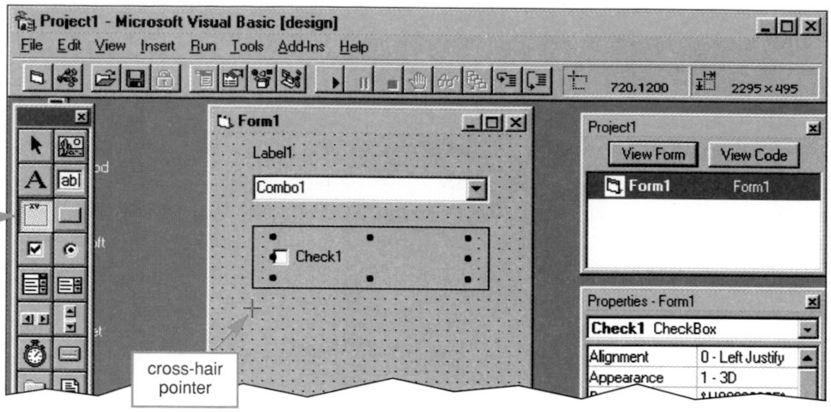

FIGURE 2-34

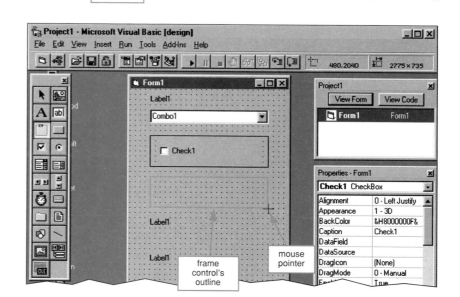

STEP 2 ▶

Drag the mouse pointer down and to the right as shown in Figure 2-35.

A gray outline of the control appears on the form.

FIGURE 2-35

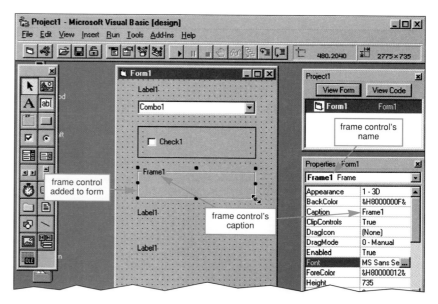

STEP 3 ▶

Release the left mouse button.

The control is sized to fit the area of the gray outline (Figure 2-36).

FIGURE 2-36

When controls have been added by drawing them inside a frame control, dragging the frame to a new position causes the controls inside to be moved as well.

The Option Button Control

Option buttons present a set of choices, such as the number of tickets bought in a single box office transaction (Figure 2-33 on page VB71). Option buttons are placed in groups that allow you to select only one choice from a group, such as the number of tickets sold. All of the option buttons on a form function as one group unless they are placed inside a frame. Multiple groups of option buttons can be created by adding another frame to the form for each option group.

For an option button to be part of a group, it must be added directly inside the frame. You cannot add an option button to the form and then drag it inside a frame if you want it to be part of the group formed by that frame.

The application in this project offers four choices for the number of tickets sold (1, 2, 3, or 4). Perform the following steps to create a group of five option buttons within the frame control already added. The reason for the fifth button will be explained later in this project.

TO BUILD AN OPTION BUTTON GROUP ▼

STEP 1 ▶

Click the OptionButton tool in the Toolbox, and move the mouse to the position where the top left corner of the button will appear (Figure 2-37).

The OptionButton tool is highlighted in the Toolbox, and the mouse pointer changes to a cross hair.

FIGURE 2-37

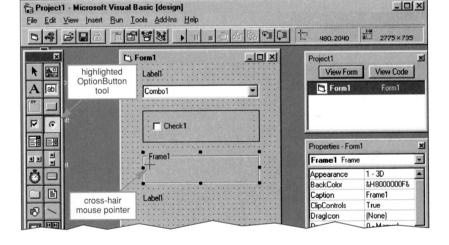

STEP 2 ▶

Drag the mouse pointer down and to the right as shown in Figure 2-38.

A shaded outline of the control appears on the form.

FIGURE 2-38

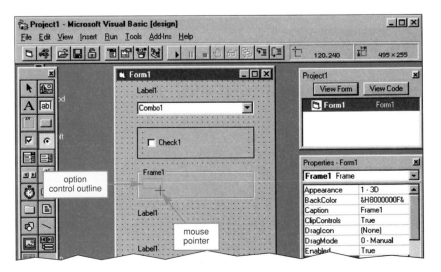

STEP 3 ▶

Release the left mouse button.

The control is sized to fit the area of the gray outline (Figure 2-39). Only part of the option button's caption, Option1, is visible on the form because of the size of the control.

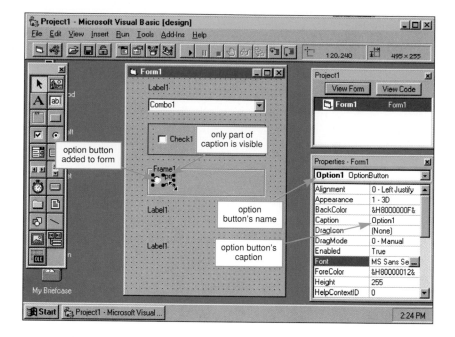

FIGURE 2-39

STEP 4 ▶

Repeat Steps 1 through 3 four times to add four more option buttons in the positions shown in Figure 2-40.

As the option button controls are added, Visual Basic assigns to them the default names Option2 through Option5.

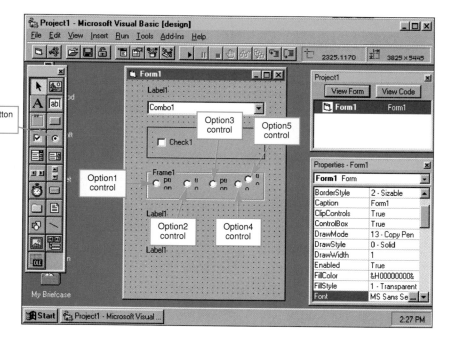

FIGURE 2-40

You may have wondered why Step 4 did not use the cut and paste method or the double-click method to add the last four option buttons. The reason is that both of these methods would have added the option buttons to the form, not to the frame control. To add the option buttons to a frame control, the preceding procedure should be used. The option buttons were added to the form inside the frame control in order to form an option group.

Adding the Remaining Controls

Three controls remain to be added to the form: one additional label, a command button, and a text box as shown in Figure 2-41. You should be familiar with working with these controls from Project 1.

In the Movie Box Office application, a label control with borders around it is used to contain the total cost of the transaction (number of tickets times the ticket price). The command button is used to clear the amount displayed in the label and to add the number of tickets purchased and the name of the movie to a list contained in the Transaction Record text box. Later, some additional properties of these controls will be presented. The following steps add these controls to the Movie Box Office form.

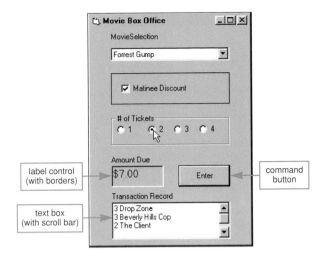

FIGURE 2-41

TO ADD A LABEL, COMMAND BUTTON, AND TEXT BOX ▼

STEP 1 ▶

Click the Label tool in the Toolbox, and position the cursor under the second label control as shown in Figure 2-42.

The Label tool is highlighted in the Toolbox, and the cursor changes to a cross hair.

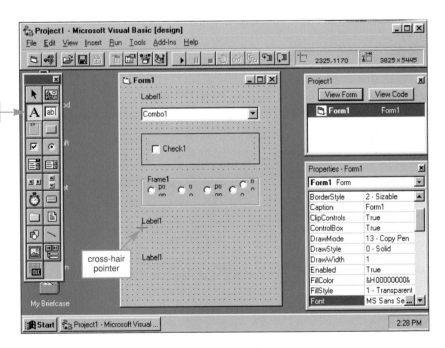

FIGURE 2-42

STEP 2 ▶

Drag the cursor down and to the right as shown in Figure 2-43.

As you drag the cursor, a gray out-line of the control is drawn.

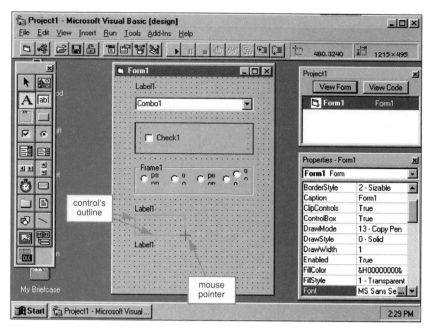

FIGURE 2-43

STEP 3 ▶

Release the left mouse button. Double-click the CommandButton tool in the Toolbox.

When the left mouse button is released, the Label4 control is sized to fit the outline. A default-sized command button is added to the form (Figure 2-44).

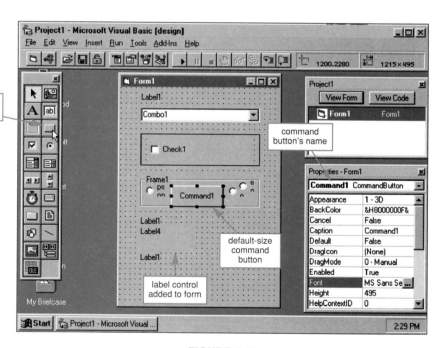

FIGURE 2-44

STEP 4 ▶

Drag the command button control's outline down and to the right to the position shown in Figure 2-45.

Dragging the command button control causes an outline of it to move.

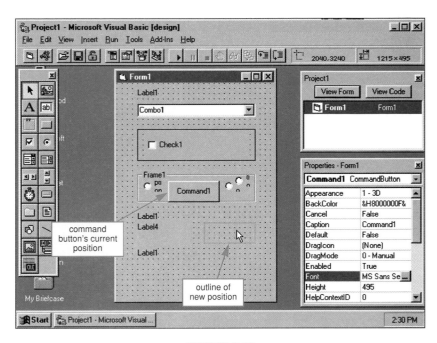

FIGURE 2-45

STEP 5 ▶

Release the left mouse button. Double-click the TextBox tool in the Toolbox.

When the mouse button is released, the Command1 control moves to the position of the outline. A default-sized text box named Text1 is added to the form (Figure 2-46).

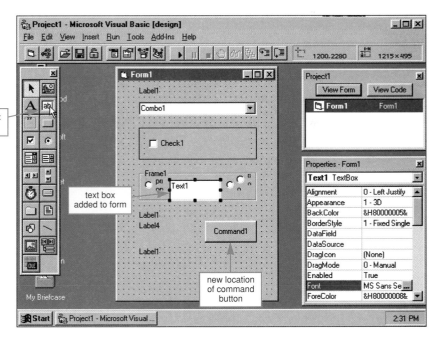

FIGURE 2-46

STEP 6 ▶

Drag the Text1 text box control's outline under the third label control to the position shown in Figure 2-47.

Dragging the text box control causes an outline of it to move.

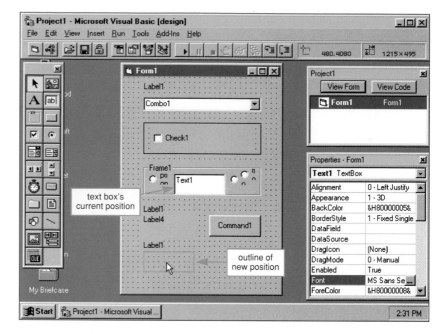

FIGURE 2-47

STEP 7 ▶

Release the left mouse button. Drag the lower right sizing handle of the text box down and to the right, as shown in Figure 2-48 and release the left mouse button.

When the mouse button is released, the Text1 control moves to the position of the outline. When you drag the text box control's handle, a gray outline of the control is drawn.

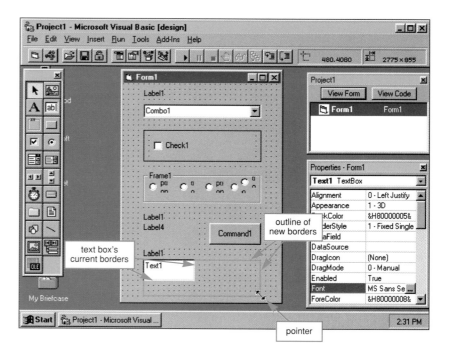

FIGURE 2-48

The text box's borders are moved to the position of the outline when the left mouse button is released. The interface for the Movie Box Office application is now finished. The form should appear as shown in Figure 2-49a. Figure 2-49b shows how the form will appear at run time after the properties of the controls have been set.

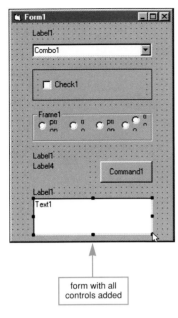

form with all
controls added

FIGURE 2-49a

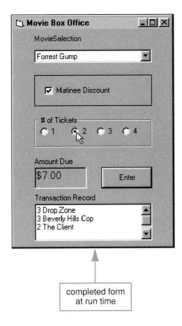

completed form
at run time

FIGURE 2-49b

▶ SETTING PROPERTIES

T he following section completes the second phase of application development, setting the properties of the controls.

Naming Controls

When you add controls to a form, Visual Basic assigns a name to the control,
which consists of the type of control and a number, such as Label1. It often is
easier to read and edit your
code if controls have names
that more closely represent
the purpose or function of
the control within the
application. The **name** of a
control is a property of a
control and can be changed
to whatever seems appropriate. Visual Basic has a
suggested standard for
naming controls. A control's
name should consist of a
three-letter prefix that
designates the type of
control followed by a
unique text description.
Control types and name
prefixes are listed in
Table 2-2.

▶ **TABLE 2-2 CONTROL TYPES AND NAME PREFIXES**

CONTROL	PREFIX	CONTROL	PREFIX
form	frm	label	lbl
check box	chk	line	lin
combo box	cbo	list box	lst
command button	cmd	menu	mnu
data	dat	OLE	ole
directory list box	dir	option button	opt
drive list box	drv	picture box	pic
file list box	fil	shape	shp
frame	fra	text box	txt
grid	grd	timer	tmr
horizontal scroll bar	hsb	vertical scroll bar	vsb
image	img		

The following steps assign new values of the **Name property** to several of the controls on the Movie Box Office form, following the Visual Basic conventions for naming controls. Table 2-3 lists the current (default) name of each control (shown in Figure 2-49a on the previous page), its function in the Movie Box Office application, and the new name that will be assigned.

▸ **TABLE 2-3 NAMES AND FUNCTIONS OF MOVIE BOX OFFICE CONTROLS**

CURRENT NAME	CONTROL'S FUNCTION	NEW NAME
Combo1	selects name of the movie	cboMovie
Check1	selects matinee discount price	chkMatinee
Label4	displays purchase amount	lblAmtdue
Command1	enters transaction in list	cmdEnter
Text1	contains a record of purchased tickets	txtRecord
Form1	the Movie Box Office form	frmMovies

TO NAME CONTROLS ▼

STEP 1 ▶

Select the control you want to change (Combo1) by clicking it on the form or by selecting its name from the Object drop-down list in the Properties window.

The name of the selected control and its properties appear in the Properties window (Figure 2-50).

FIGURE 2-50

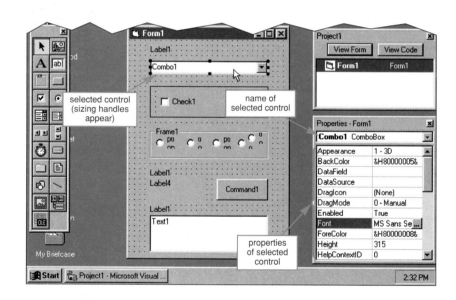

STEP 2 ▶

Click the Properties window scroll arrow several times until the Name property is shown. Double-click the Name property in the Properties window.

The current name of the control (Combo1) appears highlighted (Figure 2-51).

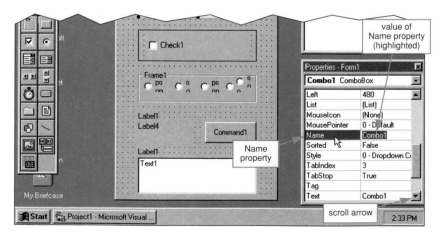

FIGURE 2-51

STEP 3 ▶

Type `cboMovie` as the new name, and press the ENTER key.

As you type, the name is replaced next to the Name property in the Properties list (Figure 2-52).

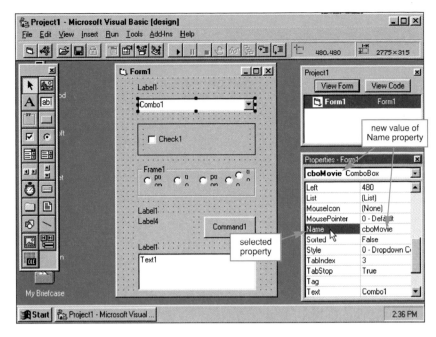

FIGURE 2-52

STEP 4 ▶

Repeat Steps 1 through 3 to name the Check1 control chkMatinee. Repeat Steps 1 through 3 to name the Label4 control lblAmtdue. Repeat Steps 1 through 3 to name the Command1 control cmdEnter. Repeat Steps 1 through 3 to name the Text1 control txtRecord. Repeat Steps 1 through 3 to name the Form1 control frmMovies.

STEP 5 ▶

Click the down arrow next to the Object box in the Properties window.

The Object drop-down list showing their new names appears (Figure 2-53).

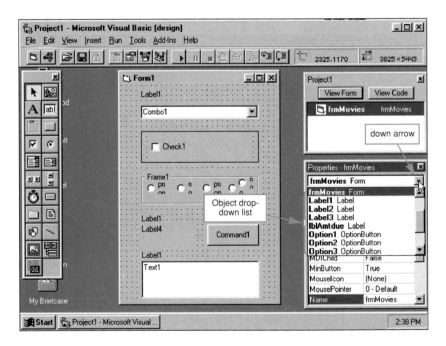

FIGURE 2-53

Changing the control names did not change their appearance on the form because the text that appears on the control is the control's caption, which is separate from the control's name.

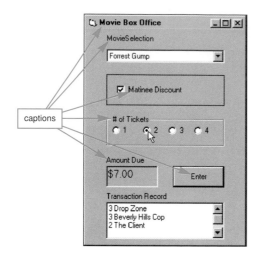

FIGURE 2-54

Setting the Caption Property

The following steps add meaningful captions to the controls on the form, as shown in Figure 2-54.

![TO SET THE CAPTION PROPERTY ▼]

STEP 1 ▶

Select the Label1 control by clicking its name in the Object drop-down list in the Properties window.

The name of the control and its properties appear in the Properties window (Figure 2-55).

FIGURE 2-55

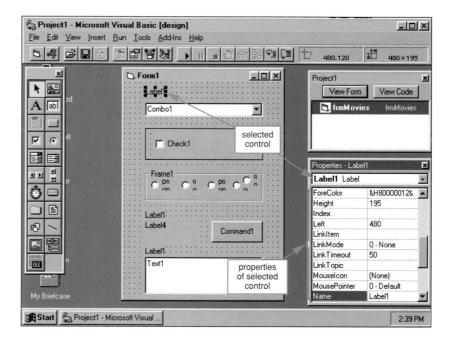

STEP 2 ▶

Scroll up through the Properties list until the Caption property is visible. Double-click the Caption property in the Properties list.

The current value of the control's Caption property appears highlighted (Figure 2-56).

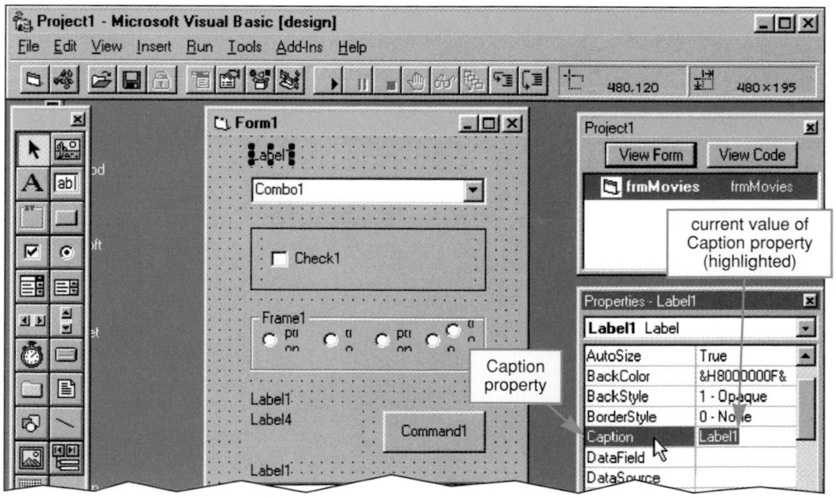

FIGURE 2-56

STEP 3 ▶

Type `MovieSelection` as the new caption and press the ENTER key.

As you type, the caption is replaced and appears next to the Caption property in the Properties list (Figure 2-57).

FIGURE 2-57

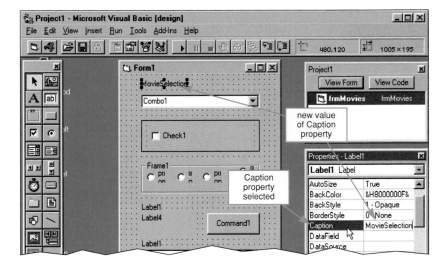

STEP 4 ▶

Repeat Steps 1 through 3 to change the captions of the controls as listed in the New Caption column in Table 2-4 below.

STEP 5 ▶

Follow the procedure in Steps 1 through 3 to change the txtRecord control's Text property to be blank and Combo1's Text property to be cboMovie.

The Movie Box Office form (frmMovies) appears as shown in Figure 2-58.

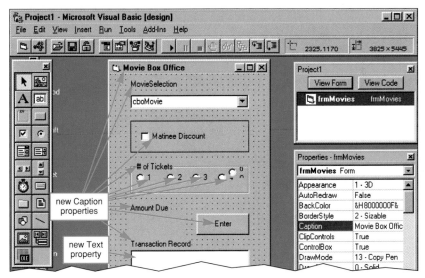

FIGURE 2-58

▶ **TABLE 2-4 MOVIE BOX OFFICE CONTROL CAPTIONS**

CONTROL	CURRENT CAPTION	NEW CAPTION
chkMatinee	Check1	Matinee Discount
Frame1	Frame1	# of Tickets
Option1	Option1	1
Option2	Option1	2
Option3	Option1	3
Option4	Option1	4
Label2	Label1	Amount Due
lblAmtdue	Label4	[blank]
cmdEnter	Command1	Enter
Label3	Label1	Transaction Record
frmMovies	Form1	Movie Box Office

Setting Combo Box Properties

The Movie Box Office application contains a drop-down list box for selecting the name of the movie. A combo box control indicated in Figure 2-59 was added to the form when the other controls were added. Recall from Table 2-1 on page VB67 that a drop-down list is one type of a combo box control. The type of combo box control is set by using the combo box's **Style property**. Perform the following steps to make the combo box (cboMovie) a drop-down list box.

TO MAKE A COMBO BOX A DROP-DOWN LIST BOX ▼

STEP 1 ▶

Select the combo box control by clicking it on the form or by selecting its name, cboMovie, from the Object drop-down list in the Properties window.

Sizing handles appear around the control and the control's properties appear in the Properties window (Figure 2-59).

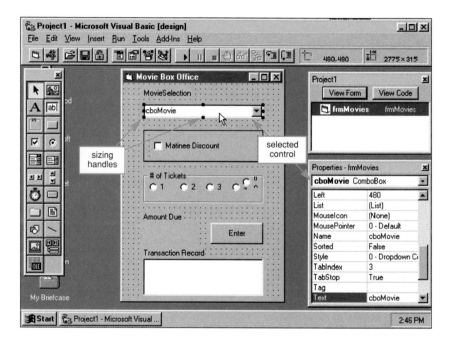

FIGURE 2-59

STEP 2 ▶

Click the Style property in the Properties list.

The default value of the Style property, 0 - Dropdown Combo, appears in the Properties list (Figure 2-60).

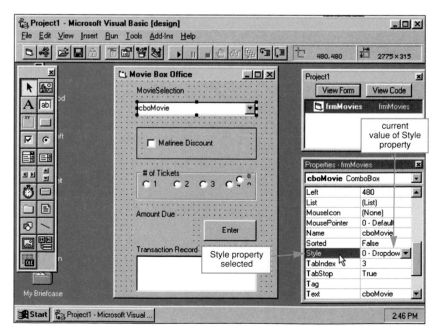

FIGURE 2-60

STEP 3 ▶

Click the down arrow located on the right of the property value.

A drop-down list of property values appears (Figure 2-61).

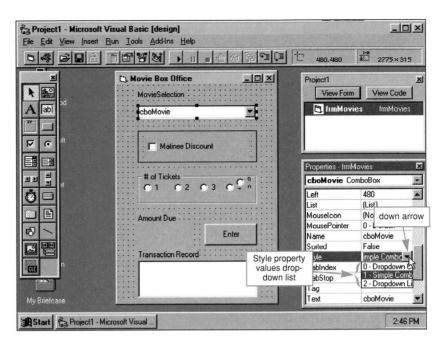

FIGURE 2-61

STEP 4 ▶

Click 2 - Dropdown List in the Property values list.

The selected value of the Style property appears. The drop-down list closes. (Figure 2-62).

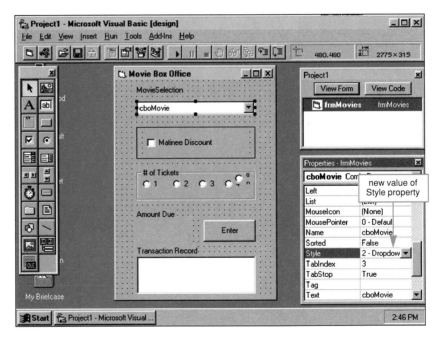

FIGURE 2-62

Although a separate Visual Basic control exists for a simple list box, the drop-down list box is one of three types of combo boxes specified by setting the Style property of the combo box control.

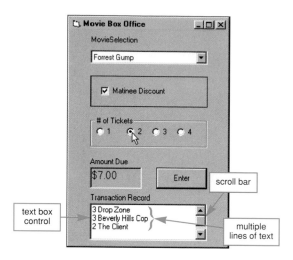

FIGURE 2-63

Setting Text Box Properties

The Movie Box Office application contains one text box control. Its appearance in Figure 2-63 is different from the text box controls that were used in Project 1. It contains multiple lines of text (three are visible at a time), and it has a vertical scroll bar to move up and down through the text that extends beyond the borders of the control. The following steps add these features by setting the **MultiLine property** and **ScrollBars property** of the text box control.

TO SET THE MULTILINE AND SCROLLBARS PROPERTIES OF TEXT BOXES ▼

STEP 1 ▶

Select the text box control by clicking it on the form or by selecting its name, txtRecord, from the Object drop-down list in the Properties window.

Sizing handles appear around the control, and the control's properties appear in the Properties window (Figure 2-64).

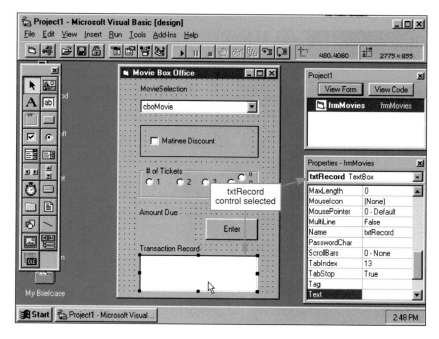

FIGURE 2-64

STEP 2 ▶

Double-click the MultiLine property in the Properties list.

The value of the MultiLine property changes from the default value of False to the new value, True (Figure 2-65).

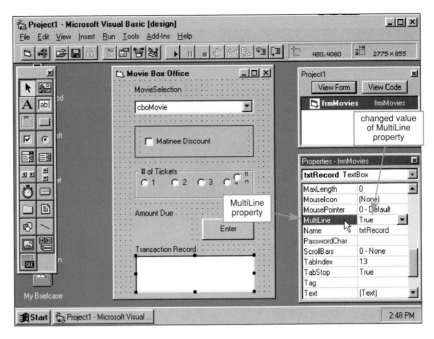

FIGURE 2-65

STEP 3 ▶

Select the ScrollBars property by clicking it in the Properties list. Click the down arrow located on the right of the ScrollBar property.

A drop-down list of ScrollBars property values appears (Figure 2-66).

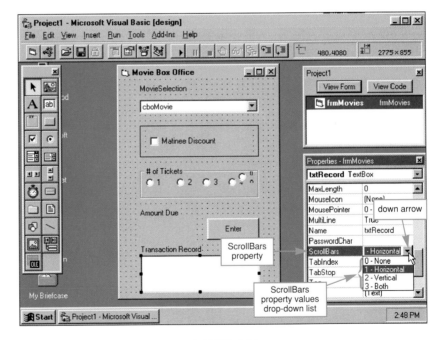

FIGURE 2-66

STEP 4 ▶

Click 2 - Vertical in the Property values list.

A vertical scroll bar is added to the control. The selected value of the property appears and the drop-down list closes (Figure 2-67).

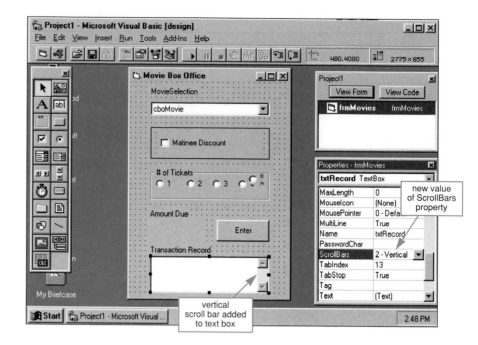

FIGURE 2-67

The drop-down list of property values for the ScrollBars property also has choices for a horizontal scroll bar or both horizontal and vertical scroll bars to be added to text box controls. If the ScrollBars property is not set and the size of the text box control is smaller than the text you want to appear, you are unable to view the text that extends beyond the borders of the text box.

Setting Label Properties

In the Movie Box Office application, a label control (lblAmtdue) is used to display the total purchase price (Figure 2-68). A label control is used instead of a text box so the user of the application cannot change the value displayed during run time. Two features of the label control (lblAmtdue) shown in Figure 2-68 make it different from the other label controls in the Movie Box Office application.

First, you may have thought it was a text box control because it has a border around it. Borders are added to a label control by setting the **BorderStyle property**. Second, the size of the characters inside the lblAmtdue control is larger than the size of the characters in the other labels on the Movie Box Office form (Figure 2-68). The size of the characters is set by using the **FontSize property** of the control.

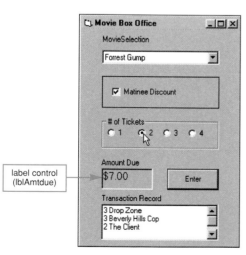

FIGURE 2-68

To set the BorderStyle property and FontSize property of labels, perform the following steps.

TO SET THE BORDERSTYLE PROPERTY AND FONTSIZE PROPERTY OF LABELS ▼

STEP 1 ▶

Select the label control (it appears only as a solid gray rectangle on the form) by clicking it or by selecting its name, lblAmtdue, from the Object drop-down list in the Properties window.

Sizing handles appear around the control, and the control's properties appear in the Properties window (Figure 2-69).

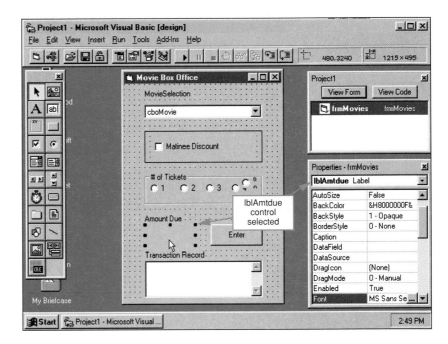

FIGURE 2-69

STEP 2 ▶

Double-click the BorderStyle property in the Properties list.

The value of the BorderStyle property changes from the default value of 0 - None to the new value, 1 - Fixed Single and a border appears around the control (Figure 2-70).

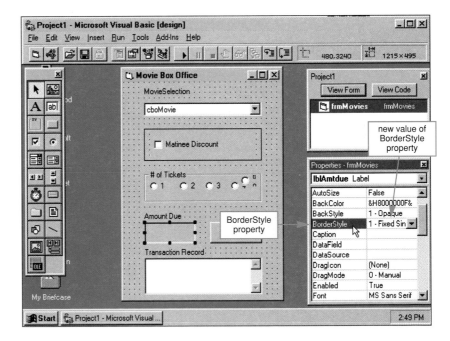

FIGURE 2-70

STEP 3 ▶

Scroll down through the Properties list until the Font property is visible. Select the Font property by clicking it in the Properties list. Click the Properties button located on the right of the Font property.

A dialog box of Font property values appears (Figure 2-71).

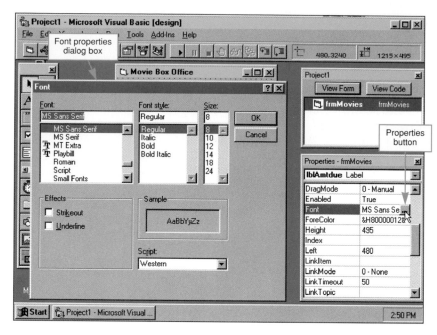

FIGURE 2-71

STEP 4 ▶

Click 12 in the Size Property list. Click OK.

The Font size is changed and the Font properties dialog box closes (Figure 2-72).

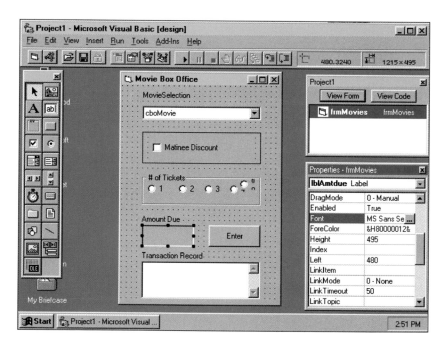

FIGURE 2-72

All controls that contain text or have Caption properties have the FontSize property. In addition, these controls have additional Font properties that you may have noticed in the Properties list. You will work with these other Font properties in later projects.

The Visible Property

The five option buttons that form the option group within the frame control are shown in Figure 2-73. In the earlier discussion of option buttons, you learned that only one option button in a group can be selected at one time. Selecting a second option button automatically deselects the first option button.

In the Movie Box Office application, you do not want any of the four option buttons representing the number of tickets purchased to be selected when the application starts. When you choose the Enter button on the form, you also want all four of these option buttons to be deselected. The way to accomplish this involves using the fifth option button added earlier.

Later, code will be written so the fifth option button is selected when the Enter button is chosen. Selecting the fifth option button automatically will deselect whichever of the other four had been selected. However, you will make it seem that no button is selected by making the fifth button invisible. The **Visible property** of a control determines whether the control can be seen at run time. Perform the following steps to make the Option5 control invisible.

TO SET THE VISIBLE PROPERTY ▼

STEP 1 ▶

Select the option button named Option5 by clicking it or by selecting its name from the Object drop-down list in the Properties window.

Sizing handles appear around the control, and the control's properties appear in the Properties window (Figure 2-73).

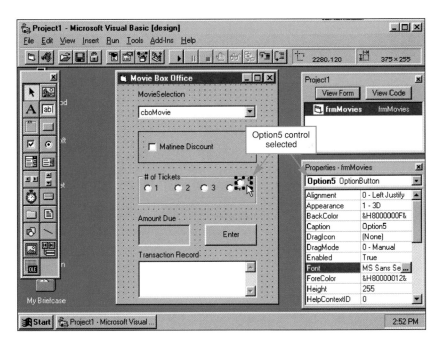

FIGURE 2-73

STEP 2 ▶

Scroll through the Properties list, and double-click the Visible property.

The value of the Visible property changes from the default value of True to the new value, False (Figure 2-74).

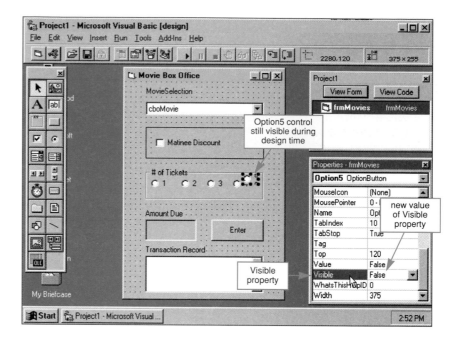

FIGURE 2-74

The Option5 control still is visible on the form during design time. At run time, however, the control will not appear on the form.

The Default Property of Command Buttons

The **Default property** of a command button allows you to press the ENTER key on the keyboard as a substitute for clicking a command button with the mouse during run time. Either action during run time will cause the code statements in the command button's Click event to be executed. Perform the following steps to set this property for the Enter button (cmdEnter) control.

TO SET THE DEFAULT PROPERTY ▼

STEP 1 ▶

Select the Enter button by clicking it or by selecting its name, cmdEnter, from the Object drop-down list in the Properties window.

Sizing handles appear around the control, and the control's proper-ties appear in the Properties window (Figure 2-75).

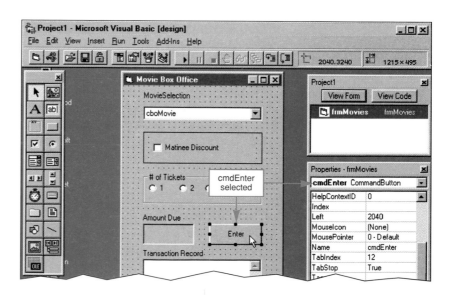

FIGURE 2-75

STEP 2 ►

Scroll up through the Properties list, and double-click the Default property.

The value of the Default property changes from the value of False to the new value, True (Figure 2-76).

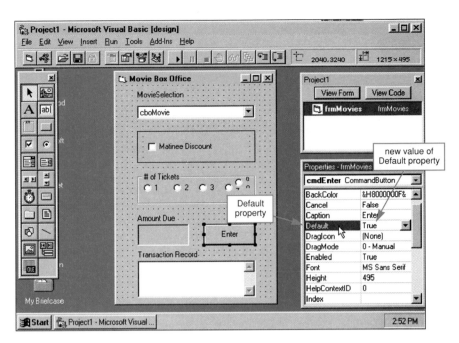

FIGURE 2-76

Only one command button on a form can have its Default property set to true, as has been done with the cmdEnter control in the Movie Box Office application. However, if there were more than one and you changed a second command button's Default property to true, Visual Basic would automatically change the first command button's Default property back to false.

► WRITING CODE

The interface now has been built, and the properties of the controls in the Movie Box Office application have been set. The remaining step is to write the code for the application. Project 1 introduced writing Visual Basic code through the use of statements that change the properties of controls during run time. These statements take the following general form:

```
controlname.property = value
```

The name of the control and the name of the property to be changed are separated with a period, and the value of the property to be set follows an equal sign.

This project requires more complex code statements that incorporate variables and the If...Then...Else statement. This project also shows how to cut and paste (copy) code from one subroutine to another.

Seven events in the Movie Box Office application require event procedures (subroutines). These events and their actions are listed in Table 2-5 on the next page.

▶ **TABLE 2-5 MOVIE BOX OFFICE EVENT SUMMARY**

CONTROL	EVENT	ACTIONS
General	Declarations	Creates a variable that will be used in several of the subroutines
Form	Load	Adds the movie names to the drop-down list
Option1	Click	Calculates the price of one ticket and displays the amount in the Amount Due box
Option2	Click	Calculates the price of two tickets and displays the amount in the Amount Due box
Option3	Click	Calculates the price of three tickets and displays the amount in the Amount Due box
Option4	Click	Calculates the price of four tickets and displays the amount in the Amount Due box
cmdEnter	Click	Adds the number of tickets and name of the movie to the transaction list; clears the option buttons, MovieSelection box, and Amount Due box

The code for the Movie Box Office application will be written one event at a time using the Code window. Before proceeding with the code writing, the form should be saved. In the following steps, the form is saved to a formatted diskette in the 3½ Floppy [A:] drive.

TO SAVE THE FORM

Step 1: Choose the Save File As command from the File menu.
Step 2: Type `Movies` in the File name box in the Save File As dialog box.
Step 3: Select 3½ Floppy [A:] from the Save in drop-down list box.
Step 4: Click the Save button.

The form is saved as movies.frm on the diskette in the 3½ Floppy [A:] drive and the Save File As dialog box closes.

The General Declarations Subroutine

Variables are sometimes used in code statements to store the temporary values used by other code statements. Visual Basic variables have a name you create and a data type. The **data type** determines what kind of data the variable can store (numeric or character). You must follow a few rules when choosing names for variables:

▶ The name must begin with a character.
▶ The name cannot be more than 40 characters.
▶ The name cannot contain punctuation or blank spaces.

The easiest way to create a variable is to assign a value to the variable's name in a code statement, such as `rate = 3.5` or `name = "John"`. Variables created in this way can hold either numbers (numeric data) or characters (string data). Character data, called a **string**, is placed within quotation marks. In addition, variables can be assigned the value of another variable or the value of a mathematical expression. Table 2-6 lists several examples of code statements that create a variable and assign a value to it.

▶ **TABLE 2-6 CODE STATEMENTS THAT CREATE VARIABLES**

EXAMPLE TYPE	STATEMENT
numeric data	price = 5
numeric data	discount = 1.15
string data	movie = "Sneakers"
value of another variable	cost = price
value of an expression	cost = price - discount
value of an expression	amountdue = price * 1.05

When variables are created simply by using them, they can be used only within the subroutine in which they were created. For code statements in different subroutines to use the value stored in a variable, the variable must be declared. Variables are **declared** in code statements in a special procedure, where both the variable name and data type must be specified. Data types will be discussed in greater detail in Project 5.

The Movie Box Office application uses a variable named *num* that stores the number of tickets to be purchased. The variable is used in more than one event subroutine, and therefore it must be declared. The following steps write a declaration for this variable.

TO DECLARE A VARIABLE ▼

STEP 1 ▶

Click the View Code button in the Project window.

The Code window opens (Figure 2-77). The cursor is located at the top left of the Code window.

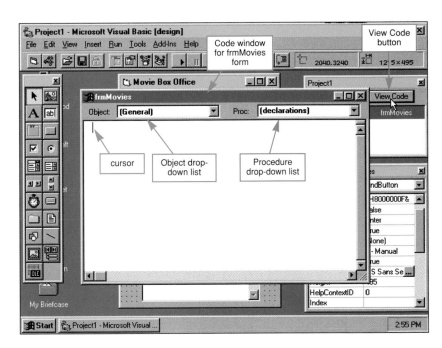

FIGURE 2-77

STEP 2 ▶

Enter the following statement in the Code window: `Dim num As Integer`

When you press the ENTER *key, the cursor moves to the beginning of the next line, and some of the typed characters change to uppercase or change color (Figure 2-78).*

FIGURE 2-78

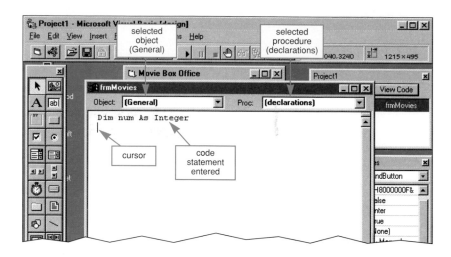

The declaration statement always has the following form:

```
Dim variablename As datatype
```

When you press the ENTER key at the end of a code statement, Visual Basic inspects the code for many common errors. If it finds an error, a dialog box opens. Some of the characters' case and color are automatically changed for ease in reading the code.

In Project 1, you learned how to open the Code window and select a control from the object list by double-clicking the control in the Form window. If you are going to write procedures for several controls, it can be awkward to move between the Form window and the Code window just to select different controls in the Code window. A more general way to enter, edit, or view a subroutine in the Code window involves these steps (refer to Figure 2-78):

▶ Select the control that you wish to assign code to from the Object drop-down list.
▶ Select the desired event from the Procedure drop-down list.
▶ Enter the code statements.

When the declaration statement was written, it was not necessary to select an object and a procedure from the drop-down lists in the Code window because the declarations procedure already is selected when the Code window is opened the first time.

The Form_Load Event

The **Form_Load** event causes a subroutine of code statements to be carried out when the form is loaded into the computer's memory at run time. For applications with a single form, such as the Movie Box Office application, this execution occurs when the application starts.

Recall from Table 2-5 on page VB94 that the Form_Load event adds items to the drop-down list of movie names (cboMovie).

Items such as the list of movie names are added to a list box or combo box by using the **AddItem** method in code statements. These statements take the following form:

```
controlname.AddItem "item to be added"
```

Each item (movie name) added to the list is given a consecutive number (**index**) by Visual Basic that can be used to reference that item in the list. The first item is given an index of 0. When an item is selected during run time, the **ListIndex property** of the control is given the value of that item's index. You can select an item from the list in a code statement by changing the control's ListIndex property.

The following steps write the code statements that will occur each time the application starts.

TO WRITE THE FORM_LOAD SUBROUTINE ▼

STEP 1 ▶

Display the drop-down list of controls by clicking the down arrow located next to the Object box in the Code window.

A list of the controls on the Movies form displays (Figure 2-79).

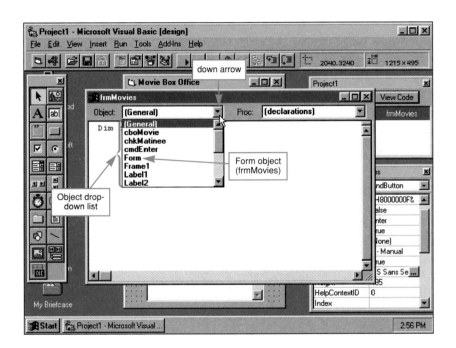

FIGURE 2-79

STEP 2 ▶

Select the form control by clicking the word Form in the Object drop-down list.

The Form_Load procedure appears in the Code window. The cursor appears at the beginning of a blank line located between the first and last statements of the subroutine (Figure 2-80).

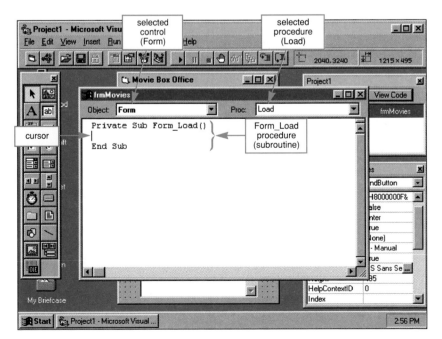

FIGURE 2-80

STEP 3 ▶

**Enter the following five statements
in the Code window:**

```
cboMovie.AddItem "The
Abyss"
cboMovie.AddItem "Beverly
Hills Cop"
cboMovie.AddItem "The
Client"
cboMovie.AddItem "Drop
Zone"
cboMovie.AddItem "Forrest
Gump"
```

*The Code window appears as
shown in Figure 2-81.*

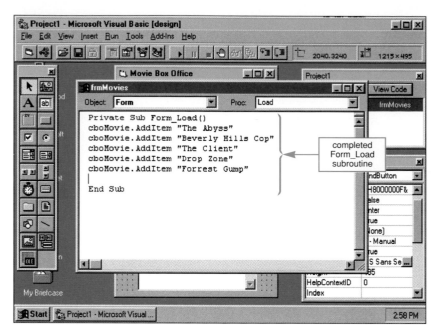

FIGURE 2-81

In the preceding steps you did not have to select the load procedure from the
Procedure drop-down list in the Code window because the load procedure is the
first one displayed when the form object is chosen from the Object drop-down list.

The Option1_Click Subroutine

The next step is to write the code for the four visible option buttons (Option1
through Option4) located inside the frame control labeled # of Tickets (Figure
2-76 on Page VB93). The code for each option button is nearly identical. The following paragraphs describe the code for the Click event of the first option button
(Option1_Click subroutine). Later, the code will be copied for the other three
option buttons' Click events.

The Click subroutine for each option button must do the following:

1. Assign the number of tickets purchased to the num variable.
2. Determine the ticket price.
3. Calculate the amount due as num * price, and display it as dollars and cents
   in the Amount Due box.

The first code statement must set the variable (num) equal to the number of
tickets corresponding to that option button (selecting Option1 represents 1
ticket). The values assigned to num for the other three option buttons are 2, 3, and
4 respectively. Thus, for the first option button, the following statement sets the
variable num equal to 1:

```
num = 1
```

The second code statement will use a single-line If...Then...Else statement to
determine the price of the tickets purchased (based on whether the matinee discount is being given). In the Movie Box Office application, the regular price for all
movies is $5, and the matinee price for all movies is $3.50.

Single-line **If...Then...Else statements** are used to execute one statement or another conditionally. A partial flowchart and the form of the single-line If...Then...Else statement is shown in Figure 2-82. The condition follows the keyword If. A **condition** is made up of two expressions and a relational operator. Table 2-7 lists the **relational operators** and their meanings.

▸ **TABLE 2-7 RELATIONAL OPERATOR MEANINGS**

RELATIONAL OPERATOR	MEANING
=	is equal to
<	is less than
>	is greater than
<=	is less than or equal to
>=	is greater than or equal to
<>	is not equal to

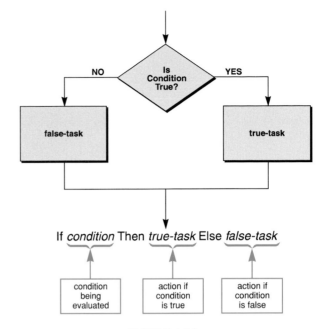

FIGURE 2-82

The statement to be executed when the condition is true follows the keyword Then. The statement to be executed when the condition is false follows the keyword Else. Figure 2-83 shows the logic and single-line If...Then...Else statement to determine the price of the ticket(s) purchased.

Recall that the Value property of a check box control is 1 when the box is checked and 0 when it is not checked. The chkMatinee.Value is equal to 1 or 0 depending on whether the user of the application has selected the option Matinee Discount. If the option Matinee Discount is selected, then the price of a ticket is \$3.50, else the price of a ticket is \$5.

The amount due is equal to the number of tickets purchased times the price. Thus, the formula num * price determines the amount due. The Movie Box Office application displays amount due as the caption of the lblAmtdue control, using dollars and cents. The following statement determines the amount due and formats the amount due as dollars and cents:

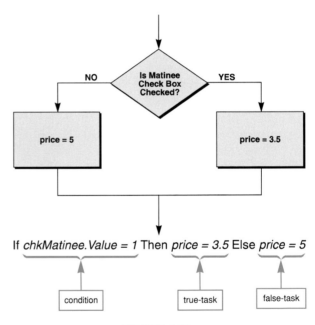

FIGURE 2-83

```
lblAmtdue.Caption = Format$(num * price, "currency")
```

lblAmtdue is the name of the Amount Due box. **Format\$** is a function that takes the first item in parentheses, num * price, and formats it to the second item in the parentheses, "currency". Currency is a **predefined format name**, which means Visual Basic will display the value num * price in a more readable fashion in the Amount Due box. The \$ character appended to Format instructs Visual Basic to change the numeric result of num * price to a string before it is assigned as the caption of the label control lblAmtdue.

Table 2-8 summarizes the most often used predefined formats in Visual Basic.

▶ **TABLE 2-8 PREDEFINED FORMATS IN VISUAL BASIC**

FORMAT	DESCRIPTION
General Number	Displays the number as is.
Currency	Displays number with a dollar sign, thousands separator with two digits to the right of the decimal. Negative numbers display enclosed in parentheses.
Fixed	Displays at least one digit to the left and two digits to the right of the decimal separator.
Standard	Displays number with thousands separator. If appropriate, displays two digits to the right of the decimal.
Percent	Displays number multiplied by 100 with percent (%) sign.
Yes/No	Displays No if number is 0; otherwise, displays Yes.

Perform the following steps to enter the code for the Option1_Click subroutine.

TO WRITE THE OPTION1_CLICK SUBROUTINE ▼

STEP 1 ▶

Click the arrow located next to the Object box in the Code window.

The Object drop-down list opens (Figure 2-84).

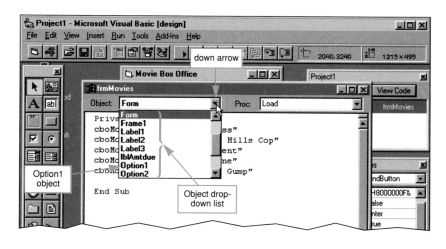

FIGURE 2-84

STEP 2 ▶

Click the Option1 choice in the Object drop-down list.

The Option1_Click subroutine appears in the Code window (Figure 2-85).

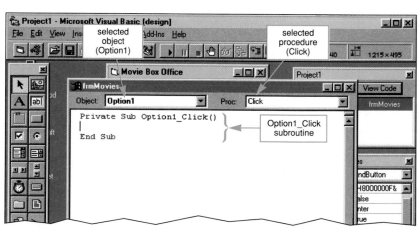

FIGURE 2-85

STEP 3 ▶

Drag the Code window's right border
to extend the Code window's width.
Enter the following three statements
in the Code window as shown in
Figure 2-86:

```
num = 1
If chkMatinee.Value = 1
  Then price = 3.5
  Else price = 5
lblAmtdue.Caption =
  Format$(num * price,
  "currency")
```

*The Code window appears as
shown in Figure 2-86.*

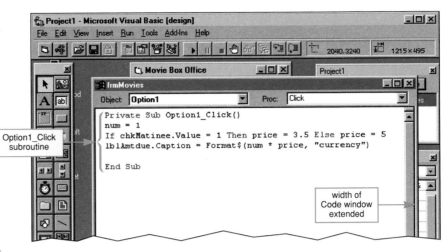

FIGURE 2-86

As mentioned earlier, the subroutines for the other three option button Click
events are very similar to this first one. Instead of typing all of the code statements
in all of the subroutines, you will copy the code from the first subroutine to the
other three and then make the minor changes necessary within the copied
subroutines. To copy code between subroutines, perform the following steps.

TO COPY CODE BETWEEN SUBROUTINES ▼

STEP 1 ▶

Position the mouse pointer to the
left of the first character in the
second line of code (Figure
2-87).

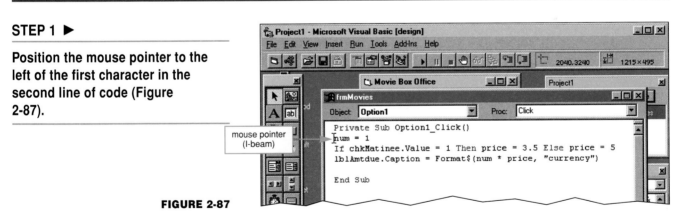

FIGURE 2-87

STEP 2 ▶

Drag the mouse downward through
the next to the last line of code.

*The code statements are high-
lighted (Figure 2-88).*

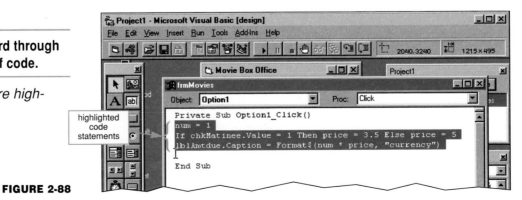

FIGURE 2-88

STEP 3 ▶

Release the left mouse button. Click the Copy command on the Edit menu (Figure 2-89).

The highlighted text is copied to the Clipboard.

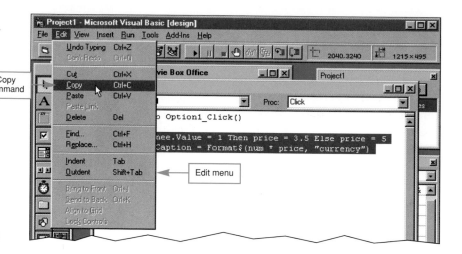

FIGURE 2-89

STEP 4 ▶

Select the Option2 control from the Object drop-down list in the Code window.

The Option2_Click subroutine appears with the cursor at the beginning of the second line (Figure 2-90).

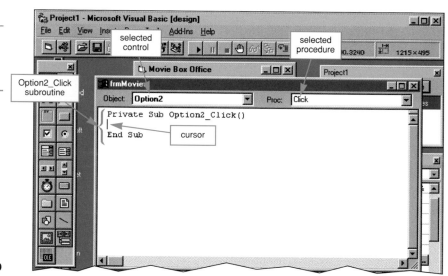

FIGURE 2-90

STEP 5 ▶

Click the Paste command on the Edit menu.

The code is copied from the Clipboard to the procedure in the Code window (Figure 2-91).

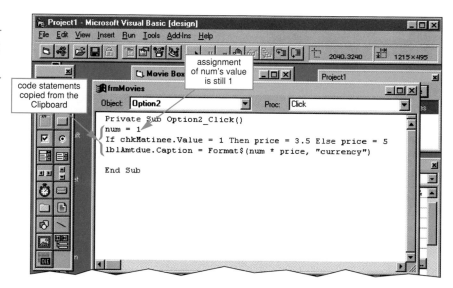

FIGURE 2-91

STEP 6 ▶

Edit the code to change the second line from num = 1 to num = 2.

This changes only what is different when 2 tickets are purchased (Figure 2-92).

STEP 7 ▶

Repeat Steps 4 through 6 to copy the code and edit it for the Option3_Click event and the Option4_Click event, changing the value of num to 3 and 4, respectively.

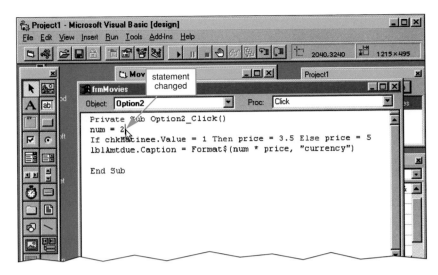

FIGURE 2-92

Once code has been copied to the Clipboard, it is not necessary to recopy it each time. You can continue to paste it as many times as is needed. Each time you copy code to the Clipboard, the previous contents of the Clipboard are erased.

The cmdEnter_Click Subroutine

The cmdEnter_Click event occurs when you click the Enter button (cmdEnter) on the form (Figure 2-93) or press the ENTER key on the keyboard. This event adds the number of tickets and the movie's name to the top of a scrollable list in the transaction record (txtRecord) and clears the movie name, number of tickets, and amount due. To accomplish this task, several functions involving the manipulation of string data are used.

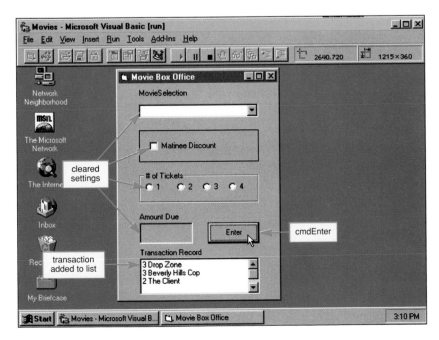

FIGURE 2-93

The value of a text box's Text property is a single string (group of characters). To have the transaction record behave the way it does, it is necessary to add special control code characters to the string that cause a new line to be started each time the cmdEnter event occurs. These characters are **chr$(13)** and **chr$(10).** The characters chr$(13) tell Visual Basic to return the cursor to the beginning of the line. The characters chr$(10) tell Visual Basic to move the cursor down one line.

Because the record must contain all of the previous sales information, it is necessary to add the new data to the old rather than replace it with the new data. This process of adding strings together is called **concatenation** and is done with the ampersand (&) character. The code statement to accomplish this is as follows:

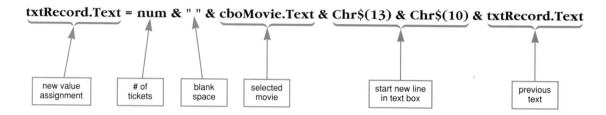

The code statements for the rest of the cmdEnter_Click subroutine are explained as follows:

▸ The list box is returned to an empty state by selecting a blank list item:

    cboMovie.Listindex = -1

▸ The matinee check box is unchecked by setting its Value property:

    chkMatinee.Value = 0

▸ The selected option button is deselected by selecting the Option5 (invisible) option button:

    Option5.Value = True

▸ The amount due is cleared by setting the value of its Caption property equal to the **null string** (two consecutive quotation marks):

    lblAmtdue.Caption = ""

Perform the following steps to write the cmdEnter_Click subroutine.

TO WRITE THE CMDENTER_CLICK SUBROUTINE ▼

STEP 1 ▸

Select the cmdEnter control from the Object drop-down list in the Code window.

The cmdEnter_Click subroutine appears in the Code window (Figure 2- 94).

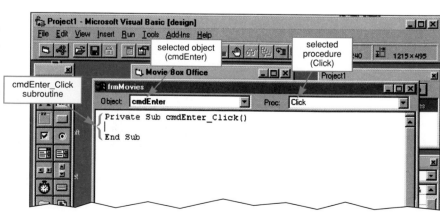

FIGURE 2-94

STEP 2 ▶

Enter the following statement in the Code window:

```
txtRecord.Text = num & " "
  & cboMovie.Text &
  Chr$(13) & Chr$(10) &
  txtRecord.Text
```

As you type the code, the Code window scrolls. Pressing the ENTER *key advances the cursor to the beginning of the next line (Figure 2-95).*

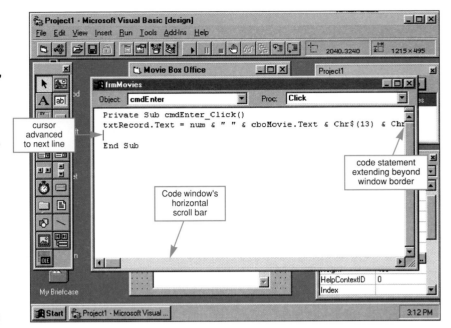

FIGURE 2-95

STEP 3 ▶

Enter the following four statements in the Code window:

```
cboMovie.ListIndex = -1
chkMatinee.Value = 0
Option5.Value = True
lblAmtdue.Caption = ""
```

The Code window appears as shown in Figure 2-96.

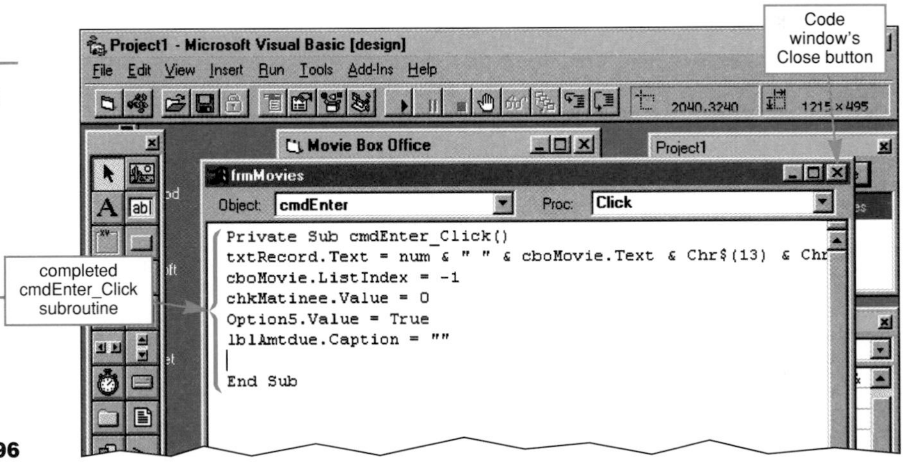

FIGURE 2-96

STEP 4 ▶

Click the Code window's Close button.

The Code window closes (Figure 2-97).

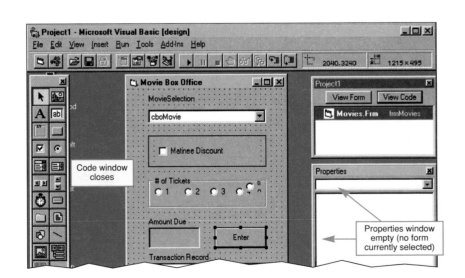

FIGURE 2-97

▶ SAVING AND RUNNING THE APPLICATION

The Movie Box Office application is now complete. Before running the application, the form and the project should be saved to a formatted diskette in the 3½ Floppy [A:] drive. The form was saved previously, before the subroutines were written. Saving the project will automatically re-save the form with the code included. The following steps save the project as movies.vbp and save the amended form as movies.frm.

TO SAVE THE PROJECT

Step 1: Choose the Save Project command from the File menu.
Step 2: Type Movies in the File name box in the Save Project As dialog box.
Step 3: Click the Save button.

The application is saved to the disk in the 3½ Floppy [A:] drive as two files, one for the form (Movies.frm) and one for the project (Movies.vbp).

Perform the following steps to test your Movie Box Office application. After Step 13, your application should appear as shown in Figure 2-98.

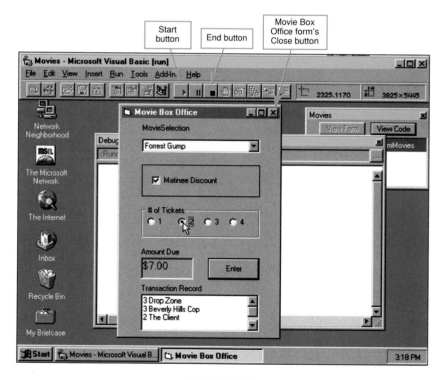

FIGURE 2-98

TO RUN THE APPLICATION

Step 1: Click the Start button on the toolbar, or choose the Start command from the Run menu.

Step 2: Select *The Client* from the MovieSelection list.

Step 3: Choose the 2 tickets option button.

Step 4: Choose the Enter button.

Step 5: Select *Beverly Hills Cop* from the movies list.

Step 6: Choose the 3 tickets option button.

Step 7: Choose the Enter button.

Step 8: Select *Drop Zone* from the movies list.

Step 9: Choose the 3 tickets option button.

Step 10: Choose the Enter button.

Step 11: Select *Forrest Gump* from the movies list.

Step 12: Check the Matinee Discount box.

Step 13: Choose the 2 tickets option button. The application appears as shown in Figure 2-98.

Step 14: To close (end) the application, click the End button on the toolbar, or click the Movie Box Office form's Close button.

Step 15: To close Visual Basic, choose Exit from the File menu or click the Close button on the Visual Basic Menu Bar and Toolbar window.

▶ PROJECT SUMMARY

Project 2 introduced you to building more complex applications than those built in Project 1. You used additional properties of the controls you learned about in Project 1, as well as several additional controls. You learned more about writing code by writing six event subroutines and a declaration procedure. You learned how to copy controls and to copy code between subroutines. You used variables in code statements and used code statements to concatenate string data.

There is no single, correct interface for a given application, nor is there a single, correct way to write code. In building this application, you may have thought of different ways to design the interface. You may have realized the events and code could have been written in a number of ways. See if you can think of other ways to design the interface and to create the events. Building applications in a graphical environment is an exciting, creative enterprise.

▶ KEY TERMS AND INDEX

AddItem *(VB96)*
AutoSize property *(VB62)*
BorderStyle property *(VB88)*
check box *(VB70)*
combo box *(VB66)*
concatenation *(VB104)*
condition *(VB99)*
chr$(10) *(VB104)*
chr$(13) *(VB104)*
data type *(VB94)*
declaration *(VB95)*

Default property *(VB92)*
drop-down list *(VB66)*
FontSize property *(VB88)*
Format$ *(VB99)*
Form_Load event *(VB96)*
frame control *(VB71)*
If...Then...Else statement *(VB99)*
index *(VB97)*
list box *(VB66)*
ListIndex property *(VB97)*
MultiLine property *(VB86)*

Name property *(VB80)*
null string *(VB104)*
option button *(VB73)*
predefined format name *(VB99)*
relational operator *(VB99)*
ScrollBars property *(VB86)*
shape control *(VB68)*
string *(VB94)*
Style property *(VB84)*
variable *(VB94)*
Visible property *(VB91)*

In Visual Basic you can accomplish a task in a number of ways. The following table provides a quick reference to each of the major tasks presented for the first time in the project with some of the available options. The commands listed in the Menu column can be executed using either the keyboard or mouse.

Task	Mouse	Menu	Keyboard Shortcuts
Copy Code from the Clipboard to a Selected Code Window		From Edit menu, choose Paste	Press CTRL+V
Copy Highlighted Code to the Clipboard		From Edit menu, choose Copy	Press CTRL+C
Copy Selected Control to the Clipboard		From Edit menu, choose Copy	Press CTRL+C
Highlight (Select) Code Statements in the Code Window	Drag mouse across code block to be selected		Press SHIFT+ARROW key
Paste a Control from the Clipboard onto a Selected Form		From Edit menu, choose Paste	Press CTRL+V

S T U D E N T   A S S I G N M E N T S

STUDENT ASSIGNMENT 1
True/False

Instructions: Circle T if the statement is true or F if the statement is false.

T F 1. Only one command button on a form can have its default property set to True.
T F 2. The Copy and Paste commands are found on the Options menu.
T F 3. A drop-down list box always has a scroll bar.
T F 4. A frame control can have a circular shape.
T F 5. When you click an option button during run time, an X appears inside the control.
T F 6. When controls have been added inside a frame, you can move all of the controls on the form by dragging just the frame.
T F 7. During run time, only one check box can be "checked" at a time.
T F 8. Code statements can be used to change the value that a control's property has at design time.
T F 9. A common practice in naming controls is to use a three-letter prefix designating to which form the control belongs.

T F 10. A text box control does not have a Caption property.
T F 11. The Style property is used to determine what type of combo box is displayed.
T F 12. Scroll bars are added automatically to a text box when its text will not fit within its borders.
T F 13. There is no difference between a label control and a text box control whose BorderStyle is fixed single.
T F 14. A label is the only control that has a FontSize property.
T F 15. For a variable to be used in more than one subroutine, it must be declared.
T F 16. The ListIndex property can be set only during run time.
T F 17. Code statements can be cut, copied, and pasted from one subroutine to another.
T F 18. Format$ is a property of all controls that have either Text or Caption properties.
T F 19. When the MultiLine property of a text box is set to True, a scroll bar automatically is added to the text box.
T F 20. Concatenation is a process used to add strings to numbers.

STUDENT ASSIGNMENT 2
Multiple Choice

Instructions: Circle the correct response.

1. If a command button's default property is set to True, pressing the _____ key during run time will have the same effect as clicking the command button.
   a. SPACEBAR
   b. CTRL
   c. ENTER
   d. ALT
2. A shape control cannot appear on a form as a(n) _____.
   a. oval
   b. circle
   c. square
   d. diamond
3. When a control is copied, _____ have (has) the same values as those of the control that was copied.
   a. the Name property only
   b. all properties
   c. all properties except the name
   d. none of the properties
4. The _____ is not a style of combo box.
   a. drop-down list
   b. simple list
   c. drop-down combo box
   d. simple combo box
5. The _____ can be changed during run time by using the keyboard.
   a. Caption property of labels
   b. Text property of text boxes
   c. both a and b
   d. neither a nor b

(continued)

STUDENT ASSIGNMENT 2 (continued)

6. The code statement _____ will add the name John to a list that appears in a combo box with the control name of cboNames.
   a. cboNames.AddItem = "John"
   b. AddItem.cboNames = "John"
   c. AddItem."John".cboNames
   d. cboNames.AddItem "John"

7. The control code chr$(10) _____.
   a. moves the cursor to the beginning of a new line
   b. signals the end of a line
   c. always must be used with chr$(13)
   d. sets the MultiLine property to True

8. The syntax for a code statement that changes the value of a property of a control is _____.
   a. controlname.property.oldvalue = controlname.property.newvalue
   b. property.controlname.newvalue
   c. controlname.property = newvalue
   d. property.controlname = newvalue

9. The _____ property is used to make a control not visible on a form during run time.
   a. Invisible
   b. Default
   c. BorderStyle
   d. Visible

10. Code statements of the form Dim variablename as datatype are placed in the _____ subroutine.
    a. Form_Load
    b. Form_Declarations
    c. Form_General
    d. General_Declarations

STUDENT ASSIGNMENT 3
Understanding Visual Basic Tools and Control Name Prefixes

Instructions: Figure SA2-3 shows the Visual Basic Toolbox and lists the prefixes used in naming several controls. In the spaces provided, match the control name prefix to the tool used to add that control to a form.

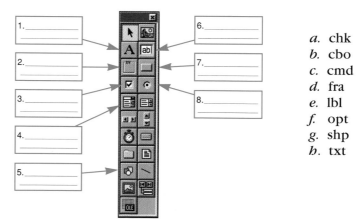

a. chk
b. cbo
c. cmd
d. fra
e. lbl
f. opt
g. shp
h. txt

FIGURE SA2-3

STUDENT ASSIGNMENT 4
Understanding Controls and Properties

Instructions: Figure SA2-4 lists the controls and properties you used in this project. Place an X in the spaces provided if the control has the property that follows. *Hint:* A control may have a property that you haven't used yet. If you're unsure, add the control to a form and look at the Properties drop-down list box in the Properties window or use online Help.

PROPERTIES	CONTROLS								
	Form	Check Box	Combo Box	Command Button	Frame	Label	Option Button	Shape	Text Box
AutoSize	[ ]	[ ]	[ ]	[ ]	[ ]	[ ]	[ ]	[ ]	[ ]
BorderStyle	[ ]	[ ]	[ ]	[ ]	[ ]	[ ]	[ ]	[ ]	[ ]
Caption	[ ]	[ ]	[ ]	[ ]	[ ]	[ ]	[ ]	[ ]	[ ]
Default	[ ]	[ ]	[ ]	[ ]	[ ]	[ ]	[ ]	[ ]	[ ]
FontSize	[ ]	[ ]	[ ]	[ ]	[ ]	[ ]	[ ]	[ ]	[ ]
MultiLine	[ ]	[ ]	[ ]	[ ]	[ ]	[ ]	[ ]	[ ]	[ ]
Name	[ ]	[ ]	[ ]	[ ]	[ ]	[ ]	[ ]	[ ]	[ ]
ScrollBars	[ ]	[ ]	[ ]	[ ]	[ ]	[ ]	[ ]	[ ]	[ ]
Shape	[ ]	[ ]	[ ]	[ ]	[ ]	[ ]	[ ]	[ ]	[ ]
Style	[ ]	[ ]	[ ]	[ ]	[ ]	[ ]	[ ]	[ ]	[ ]
Text	[ ]	[ ]	[ ]	[ ]	[ ]	[ ]	[ ]	[ ]	[ ]
Visible	[ ]	[ ]	[ ]	[ ]	[ ]	[ ]	[ ]	[ ]	[ ]

FIGURE SA2-4

STUDENT ASSIGNMENT 5
Understanding Code Statements

Instructions: Enter the correct answers.

1. Write a code statement that will display the characters *Hello* in a text box with a control name of txtGreeting.

Statement: _____

2. Write a code statement that will display the characters *Goodbye* in a label control with a control name of lblGreeting.

Statement: _____

3. Write a code statement that will create a variable named *Amount*. The variable should have an integer data type and should be able to be used in multiple subroutines.

Statement: _____

4. Write a code statement that will add *July* to a list that is displayed in a drop-down list with a control name of cboMonths.

Statement: _____

(continued)

5. Write a code statement that concatenates the contents of three text boxes (txt1, txt2, txt3) and displays the result in a fourth text box (txt4).

Statement: _____

6. Write a code statement that displays *Hello* in a label control (lblGreeting) if a check box (chkOne) is checked and displays *Goodbye* in the label if the check box is not checked.

Statement: _____

STUDENT ASSIGNMENT 6
Understanding Mathematical and Logical Operators

Instructions: Consider an application with the following controls, property settings and variable assignments.

```
txtAmount.Text = 45
rate = .1
price = 60
chkDiscount.Value = 1
```

Fill in the requested value after each of the following code statements.

1. `lblDue.Caption = txtAmount.Text * rate`
   lblDue.Caption: _____

2. `If chkDiscount.Value = 0 Then lblDue.Caption = rate * txtAmount.Text`
   lblDue.Caption: _____

3. `If rate <= .5 Then txtAmount.Text = txtAmount.Text - 10`
   txtAmount.Text: _____

4. `price = rate * txtAmount.Text / 5`
   price: _____

5. `lblDue.BorderStyle = 1`
   lblDue.Caption: _____

6. `If chkDiscount.Value = 1 Then price = txtAmount.Text * rate - 5 Else price = txtAmount.Text * rate`
   price: _____

COMPUTER LABORATORY EXERCISE 1
Changing Properties at Run Time with Check Boxes

Instructions: Start Visual Basic. Open project CLE2-1 from the VB4 folder on the Student Diskette that accompanies this book. Complete the tasks listed below Figure CLE2-1. When you run the application, you can see the effects of different Font properties by selecting those properties with check boxes, as shown in Figure CLE2-1.

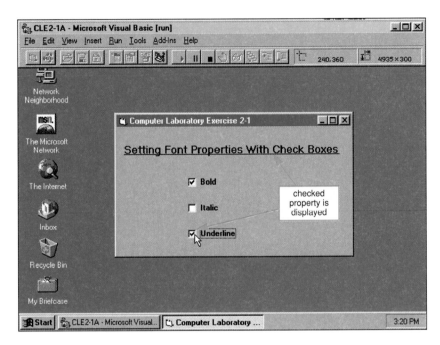

FIGURE CLE2-1

1. Click the View Form button in the Project window.
2. Click the View Code button in the Project window.
3. Select the chkBold control from the Object drop-down list in the Code window.
4. Type `lblDisplay.Fontbold = chkBold.Value` as the code statement.
5. Select the chkItalic control from the Object drop-down list in the Code window.
6. Type `lblDisplay.FontItalic = chkItalic.Value` as the code statement.
7. Select the chkUnderline control from the Object drop-down list in the Code window.
8. Type `lblDisplay.FontUnderline = chkUnderline.value` as the code statement.
9. Save the project using the form name CLE2-1A.FRM and the project name CLE2-1A.VBP.
10. Close the Code window by clicking its Close button.
11. Run the application. Click the form's Close button to stop the application.
12. Check with your instructor for directions on turning in the exercise.

COMPUTER LABORATORY EXERCISE 2
Mathematical Operators and Option Groups

Instructions: Start Visual Basic. Open project CLE2-2 from the VB4 folder on the Student Diskette that accompanies this book.

Perform the following steps. When you run the completed application, you will enter two numbers and click an option button that designates the operation to perform. The result of the operation then is displayed (Figure CLE2-2).

1. Click the View Form button in the Project window.
2. Use the Properties window to change the name of the Option1 control to optAdd.
2. Use the Properties window to change the name of the Option2 control to optSubtract.
3. Use the Properties window to change the name of the Option3 control to optMultiply.
4. Use the Properties window to change the name of the Option4 control to optDivide.
5. Use the Properties window to change the name of the Option5 control to optClear.
6. Choose the View Code button in the Project window.

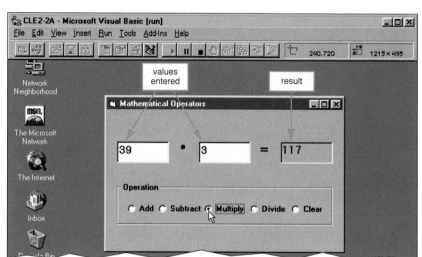

FIGURE CLE2-2

7. Select optAdd from the Object drop-down list in the Code window. Type the following two code statements:
```
lblOperation.Caption = "+"
lblResult.Caption = Val(txtNum1.Text) + Val(txtNum2.Text)
```
8. Select optSubtract from the Object drop-down list in the Code window. Type the following two code statements:
```
lblOperation.Caption = "-"
lblResult.Caption = Val(txtNum1.Text) - Val(txtNum2.Text)
```
9. Select optMultiply from the Object drop-down list in the Code window. Type the following two code statements:
```
lblOperation.Caption = "*"
lblResult.Caption = Val(txtNum1.Text) * Val(txtNum2.Text)
```
10. Select optDivide from the Object drop-down list in the Code window. Type the following two code statements:
```
lblOperation.Caption = "/"
lblResult.Caption = Val(txtNum1.Text) / Val(txtNum2.Text)
```
11. Select optClear from the Object drop-down list in the Code window. Type the following four code statements:
```
txtNum1.Text = ""
lblOperation.Caption = ""
txtNum2.Text = ""
lblResult.Caption = ""
```
12. Save the project using the form name CLE2-2A.FRM and the project name CLE2-2A.VBP.
13. Close the Code window. Run the application. Press the TAB key to move between text boxes. Double-click the form's Close button to stop the application.
14. Check with your instructor for directions on turning in the exercise.

COMPUTER LABORATORY EXERCISE 3
Relational Operators and Copying Code

Instructions: Start Visual Basic. Open project CLE2-3 from the VB4 folder on the Student Diskette that accompanies this book.

Perform the steps listed below Figure CLE2-3. When you run the completed application, you will enter two numbers and click a command button that designates the relational operation to perform. The result of the operation then is displayed (Figure CLE2-3).

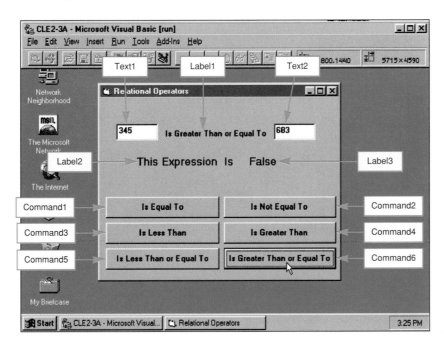

FIGURE CLE2-3

1. Click the View Form button in the Project window.
2. Click the View Code button in the Project window.
3. Select the Command1 control from the Object drop-down list in the Code window.
4. Type `Label1.Caption = Command1.Caption` and press the ENTER key.
5. Type `If Val(Text1.Text) = Val(Text2.Text) Then Label3.Caption = "True" Else Label3.Caption = "False"` as the entry and press the ENTER key.
6. Use the mouse to highlight the two code statements, as was done on page VB101.
7. Click Edit on the menu bar. Choose Copy from the Edit menu.
8. Select the Command3 control from the Object drop-down list in the Code window.
9. Click Edit on the menu bar. Choose Paste from the Edit menu. Change `Command1` in the first line to `Command3`. Change `If Val(Text1.Text) = Val(Text2.Text)` in the second line to `If Val(Text1.Text) < Val(Text2.Text)`
10. Repeat Steps 8 and 9 for each of the remaining command buttons, changing the name of the command button in the first code statement and the relational operator in the second code statement, so that the relational operators match the captions as shown in Figure CLE2-3. Refer to Table 2-7 on VB99.
11. Save the project using the form name CLE2-3A.FRM and the project name CLE2-3A.VBP.
12. Close the Code window.
13. Run the application. Try different combinations of values and relational operators. Click the form's Close button to stop the application.
14. Check with your instructor for directions on turning in the exercise.

COMPUTER LABORATORY ASSIGNMENT 1
Phone Drop-Down List

Purpose: To build an application that allows the addition of items to a drop-down list during run time.

Problem: In Project 2, you added items to a drop-down list using the AddItem method in the Form_Load procedure. In this application you would like to have a drop-down list of phone numbers (Figure CLA2-1), but you also want to be able to add persons to the list during run time. *Note:* Each time you start the application, the list is empty.

Instructions: Perform the following tasks:

1. Start Visual Basic, or open a new project if Visual Basic already is running.
2. Size and position the form as shown in Figure CLA2-1.

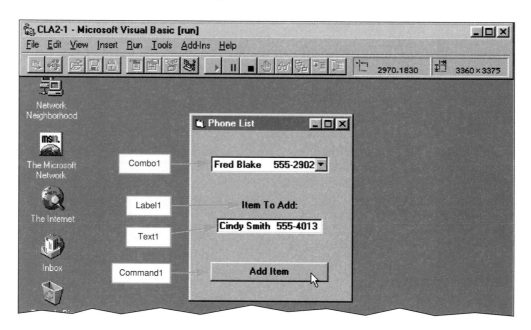

FIGURE CLA2-1

3. Add one text box, one label, one command button, and one combo box as shown in Figure CLA2-1.
4. Set the command buttons's caption to Add Item.
5. Set the label's caption to Item To Add.
6. Set the form's caption equal to Phone List.
7. Set the Text1.Text property equal to blank.
8. Double-click the command button to open the Command1_Click subroutine in the Code window.
9. Type these two statements:
```
Combo1.AddItem Text1.Text
Text1.Text = ""
```
10. Click File on the menu bar. Choose Save Project from the File menu.
11. Save the form as CLA2-1.FRM. Save the project as CLA2-1.VBP.
12. Run the application. Add several names and phone numbers to the drop-down list. Click the form's Close button to stop the application.
13. Check with your instructor for directions on turning in the assignment.

COMPUTER LABORATORY ASSIGNMENT 2
Shape Control Demonstration

Purpose: To build an application that incorporates multiple option groups.

Problem: You will build the application shown in Figure CLA2-2. The application has two option groups; one group is used to set the Shape property of the shape control on the form and the other group is used to set the BorderStyle property of the shape control.

Instructions: Perform the following tasks:

1. Start Visual Basic, or open a new project if Visual Basic is already running.
2. Size and position the form as shown in Figure CLA2-2.
3. Add the controls shown in Figure CLA2-2.
4. Set the Caption properties as shown in the table to the right.
5. Open the Code window by double-clicking the Option1 control. Type `Shape1.Shape = 0`
6. Select the Option2 control from the Object drop-down list in the Code window. Type `Shape1.Shape = 3`
7. Select the Option3 control from the Object drop-down list in the Code window. Type `Shape1.Shape = 2`
8. Select the Option4 control from the Object drop-down list in the Code window. Type `Shape1.BorderStyle = 1`
9. Select the Option5 control from the Object drop-down list in the Code window. Type `Shape1.BorderStyle = 2`

CONTROL	CAPTION
Form1	Shape Properties
Frame1	Shape
Frame2	BorderStyle
Option1	Rectangle
Option2	Circle
Option3	Oval
Option4	Solid
Option5	Dash
Option6	Dot

10. Select the Option6 control from the Object drop-down list in the Code window. Type `Shape1.BorderStyle = 3` and double-click the Code window's Close button.
11. Save the form as CLA2-2.FRM. Save the project as CLA2-2.VBP.
12. Run the application. Click the form's Close button to stop the application.
13. Check with your instructor for directions on turning in the assignment.

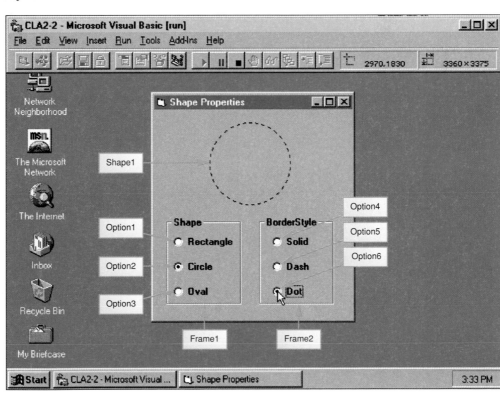

FIGURE CLA2-2

COMPUTER LABORATORY ASSIGNMENT 3
Currency Exchange

Purpose: To build an application that incorporates an option group.

Problem: In Project 1's Computer Laboratory Assignment 4, you built an application that converts an amount of dollars that you enter into one of four foreign currencies. You specified the foreign currency by clicking one of four command buttons. In this assignment you will improve the application by representing the currency choice with an option button group.

Instructions: Build the application with a user interface similar to the one shown in Figure CLA2-3. Name the controls according to Visual Basic conventions. Use a label control instead of a text box control for the amount in foreign currency. Use the option button Click event to change the name of the currency on the form and to perform the calculation and display the result.

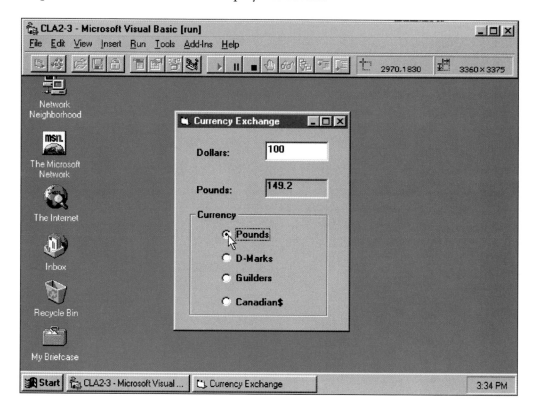

FIGURE CLA2-3

Use the following exchange rates. One dollar equals:

1.4920 pounds
1.6250 guilders
1.4506 marks
1.3757 Canadian dollars

Save the form as CLA2-3.FRM. Save the project as CLA2-3.VBP. Check with your instructor for directions on turning in the assignment.

COMPUTER LABORATORY ASSIGNMENT 4
Currency Exchange Revised

Purpose: To build an application that incorporates a drop-down list box and If...Then statements.

Problem: You would like the Currency Exchange application to be modified so that the foreign currency is selected from a drop-down list.

Instructions: Build an application with a user interface similar to the one shown in Figure CLA2-4. When you click the Convert button, the calculation depends on which item is selected from the drop-down list. Use the exchange rates listed in Computer Laboratory Assignment 3.

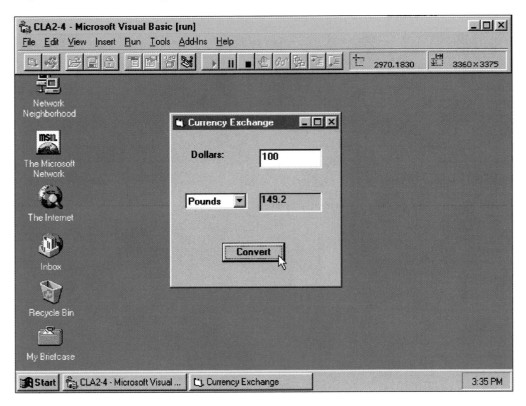

FIGURE CLA2-4

Hint #1: Use the ListIndex property of combo box controls to see which item is currently selected.
Hint #2: You can use a series of If...Then statements without the Else clause. For example:

If *condition1* Then *action1*
If *condition2* Then *action2*

Save the form as CLA2-4.FRM. Save the project as CLA2-4.VBP. Check with your instructor for directions on turning in the assignment.

MICROSOFT VISUAL BASIC 4 FOR WINDOWS

▼

APPLICATIONS WITH MULTIPLE FORMS AND WORKING WITH THE DEBUG WINDOW

OBJECTIVES You will have mastered the material in this project when you can:

▸ Add forms to a project
▸ Work with multiple forms' Code windows
▸ Specify a Startup Form
▸ Specify an icon for a form
▸ Build an About... form
▸ Add and remove forms from the desktop at run time
▸ Center forms on the desktop with code statements

▸ Use the MsgBox code statement
▸ Use an image control to display an icon
▸ Add a scroll bar control to a form and set its properties
▸ Add a line control to a form and set its properties
▸ Use the built-in financial functions
▸ Debug applications using the features of Visual Basic's Debug window

▶ INTRODUCTION

he applications built in Projects 1 and 2 consisted of several controls and one form. In this project, an application with additional controls and multiple forms will be built. Visual Basic's library of built-in financial functions and the use of dialog boxes within applications also will be introduced in this project. **Dialog boxes** are common in Windows applications and are used during run time to give information about the application to you or to prompt you to supply information to the application.

No matter how carefully you build a project, applications often do not work as planned and give erroneous results because of errors in the code. At the end of this project, the Debug window is explained and its features for finding code errors are demonstrated.

▶ PROJECT THREE – LOAN PAYMENT CALCULATOR

The application that will be built in this project calculates the amount of the monthly payment on a loan. This type of calculation is used frequently for home mortgages and car loans.

To carry out the calculation, you must supply the amount of the loan, the length of the loan repayment (in years), and the interest rate per year (APR) to the application. The loan amount is entered into a text box from the keyboard (Figure 3-1). The number of years and the APR are entered by using scroll bar controls. As you click the scroll arrows, the value supplied to the loan calculation changes and displays on the form. You can change the value more quickly by dragging the scroll box or by pointing to one of the scroll arrows and holding down the left mouse button.

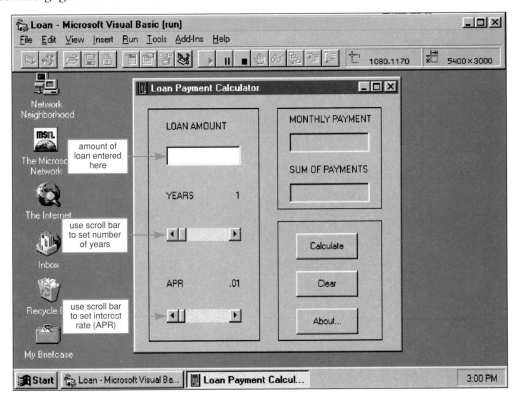

FIGURE 3-1

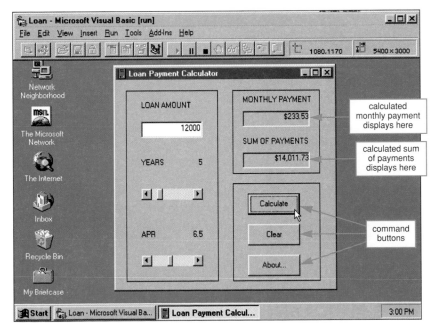

FIGURE 3-2

The Loan Payment Calculator window contains three command buttons, labeled Calculate, Clear, and About... . When you choose the Calculate button or press the ENTER key, the function is computed, and the monthly payment and the total amount to be repaid are displayed on the form (Figure 3-2 on the previous page). If the amount of the loan entered from the keyboard is not a valid numerical amount, the dialog box shown in Figure 3-3 displays to alert you to this input error. Choosing the OK button closes the dialog box and clears the text box so a new value can be entered.

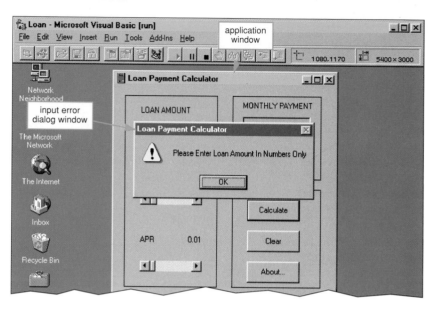

FIGURE 3-3

Choosing the Clear button in the Loan Payment Calculator window erases the loan amount, monthly payment, and sum of payments and returns the scroll bars to their lowest values. Choosing the About... button in the Loan Payment Calculator window displays the dialog box shown in Figure 3-4. Choosing the OK button in the About... dialog box closes the dialog box.

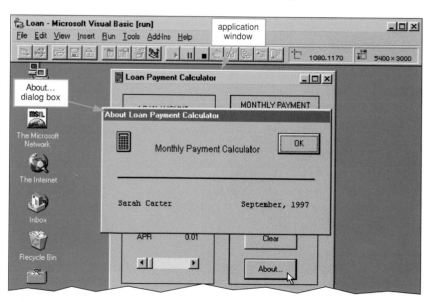

FIGURE 3-4

The Loan Payment Calculator window has a system menu (Figure 3-5) that is opened by clicking the system menu icon. The application can be minimized on the desktop by clicking Minimize on the system menu or by clicking the application's Minimize button. The window is closed by choosing Close from the system menu or by clicking the application's Close button.

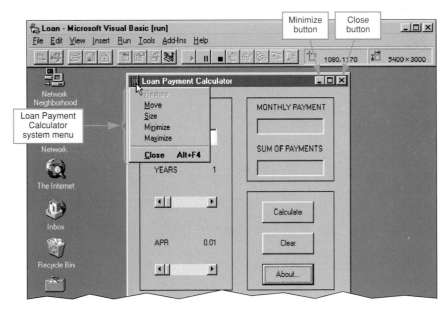

FIGURE 3-5

Starting Visual Basic

Begin this project by starting Visual Basic or by beginning a new project if Visual Basic is already running. If necessary, minimize or close other applications and adjust the sizes and locations of the Visual Basic windows to those shown in Figure 3-6. For more information on adjusting the Visual Basic windows, refer to page VB59.

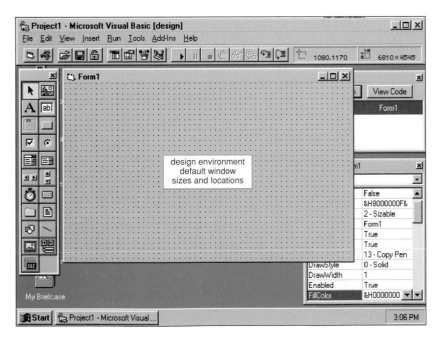

FIGURE 3-6

The application's interface (adding controls and setting properties) will be built one form at a time. After the interface is completed, the code for the application will be written.

▶ THE ABOUT... FORM AND ITS CONTROLS

T he About... dialog box shown in Figure 3-4 on page VB122 is created as a form within the project. The About... dialog box is common in Windows applications and is used to provide information about the application such as its version number, copyright date, and authors' names. Build the About... form as follows:

- ▶ set the size of the form
- ▶ add the controls
- ▶ set the properties of the form and its controls
- ▶ save the form as a file on diskette

Setting the Size of the Form

In Projects 1 and 2, the form's size was set by dragging the form's borders. The values of the form's Height property and Width property changed as the borders were dragged to new locations. In the following example, the size of the About... form will be changed by directly changing the values of the Height and Width properties in the Properties window.

TO SET THE SIZE OF THE FORM USING THE PROPERTIES WINDOW ▼

STEP 1 ▶

Click the Properties window.

The Properties window moves on top of the Form window (Figure 3-7).

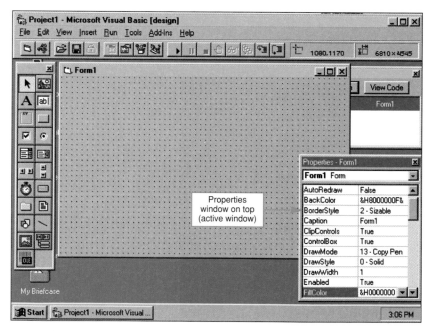

FIGURE 3-7

STEP 2 ►

Scroll through the Properties list, and then double-click the Height property. Type 3000 **and press the** ENTER **key.**

The form's bottom border moves to match the value entered in the Settings box (Figure 3-8).

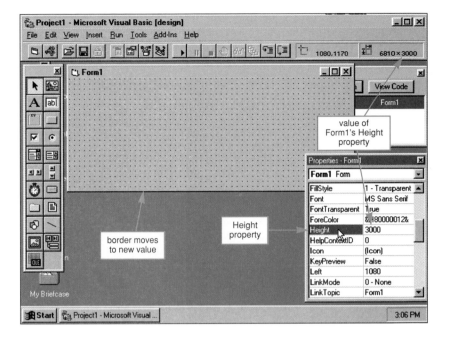

FIGURE 3-8

STEP 3 ►

Scroll through the Properties list, and then double-click the Width property. Type 5400 **and press the** ENTER **key.**

The form's right border moves to match the value entered in the Settings box (Figure 3-9).

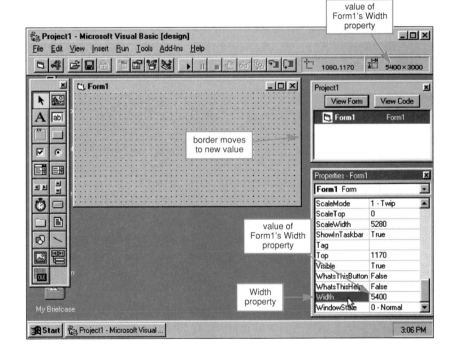

FIGURE 3-9

The form's **Top property** and **Left property** determine the position of the upper left corner of the form on the desktop. Because these properties were not changed, setting values of the form's height and width caused only the form's bottom and right borders to move. You can use this method to change a form's size during run time by writing code statements that, when executed, change the values of the form's Height and Width properties.

The form's location can be changed at run time in a similar manner by using code statements that change the values of a form's Top and Left properties. The Loan Payment Calculator application uses this method of locating the form at run time, so it is not necessary to locate the form at this time.

Adding the Command Button and Label Controls

The About... form contains three label controls and one command button control, as shown in Figure 3-10. Perform the following steps to add these controls to the form.

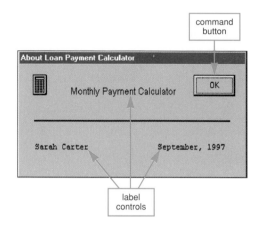

FIGURE 3-10

TO ADD THE COMMAND BUTTON AND LABEL CONTROLS ▼

STEP 1 ▶

Double-click the Label tool in the Toolbox. Drag the Label1 control to the position shown in Figure 3-11.

STEP 2 ▶

Double-click the Label tool in the Toolbox. Drag the Label2 control to the position shown in Figure 3-11.

STEP 3 ▶

Double-click the Label tool in the Toolbox. Drag the Label3 control to the position shown in Figure 3-11.

STEP 4 ▶

Double-click the CommandButton tool in the Toolbox. Drag the Command1 control to the position shown in Figure 3-11.

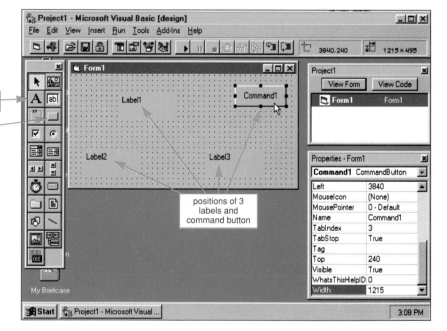

FIGURE 3-11

STEP 5 ▶

Drag the sizing handle on the left side of the Command1 control toward the right border of the form a distance of two grid marks (Figure 3-12). Release the left mouse button to resize the command button.

FIGURE 3-12

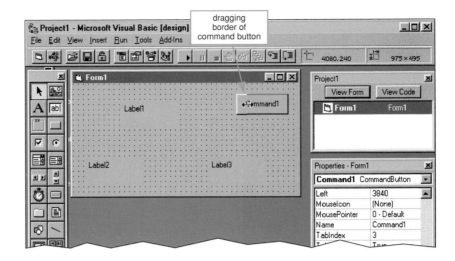

The Image Control

An **image control** can be used as a container for graphical images, such as icons or bitmapped graphics files. The image control acts like a command button, so it often is used to create custom buttons like those found in toolbars. An image control is used to add the Loan Payment Calculator application's icon to the About... form (Figure 3-13). Perform the following steps to add an image control to the About... form.

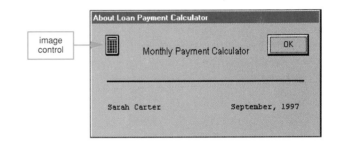

FIGURE 3-13

TO ADD AN IMAGE CONTROL ▼

STEP 1 ▶

Double-click the Image tool in the Toolbox.

An image control, Image1, is added to the center of the form (Figure 3-14).

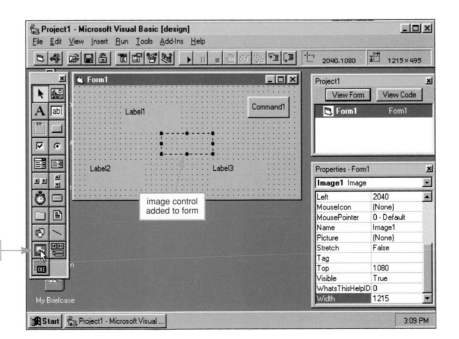

FIGURE 3-14

STEP 2 ▶

Drag the image control to the location shown in Figure 3-15.

Do not be concerned that the image control overlaps the Label1 control. This positioning will be adjusted later.

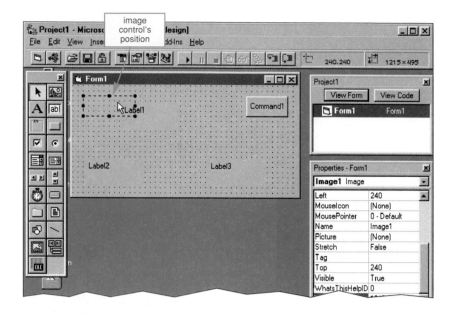

FIGURE 3-15

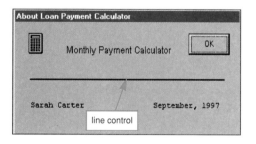

FIGURE 3-16

The Line Control

The **line control** is used to add straight lines between pairs of points on a form. The About... form contains a line control to visually separate the information on the form into two areas (Figure 3-16). Perform the following steps to add a line control to the About... form.

TO ADD A LINE CONTROL ▼

STEP 1 ▶

Click the Line tool in the Toolbox. Move the mouse pointer to where you want one end of the line to appear.

The mouse pointer changes to a cross hair (Figure 3-17).

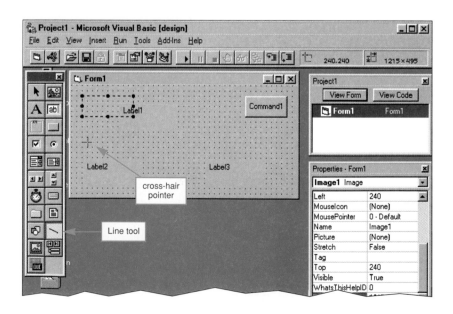

FIGURE 3-17

STEP 2 ▶

Drag the pointer to where you want the other end of the line to appear.

A gray outline of the line appears as you move the pointer (Figure 3-18).

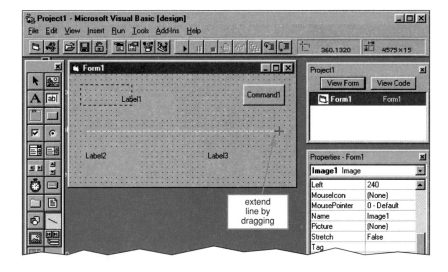

FIGURE 3-18

STEP 3 ▶

Release the left mouse button.

A solid line replaces the gray outline (Figure 3-19).

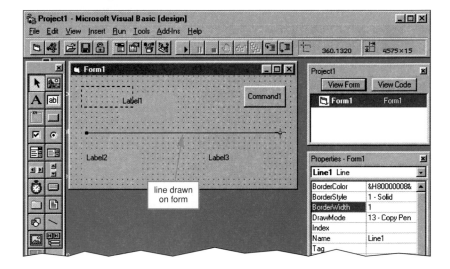

FIGURE 3-19

You can lengthen, shorten, or reposition line controls by dragging one end at a time to the new position desired.

▶ SETTING PROPERTIES FOR THE ABOUT... FORM AND ITS CONTROLS

he next step is to set the properties for the About... form and its controls. In addition to setting the Name and Caption properties presented in previous projects, the following properties will be set:

- ▶ the WindowState of forms
- ▶ the BorderStyle of forms
- ▶ the Font properties of controls
- ▶ the Picture property of image controls
- ▶ the BorderStyle and BorderWidth of line controls

The WindowState Property of Forms

The **WindowState** is a property of a form that corresponds with the window's size on the desktop during run time. The WindowState property takes one of three values, as listed in Table 3-1.

▶ **TABLE 3-1 WINDOWSTATE VALUES**

VALUE	WINDOW'S SIZE
0 - Normal	window open on desktop
1 - Minimized	window reduced to an icon
2 - Maximized	window enlarged to its maximum size

When the About... form appears on the desktop at run time, it has a WindowState value of 0 - Normal (Figure 3-20). If you look closely, you will see that its WindowState cannot be changed because it does not have a Minimize, Maximize or Close button in the upper right corner of the window. Also, the system menu icon is not present.

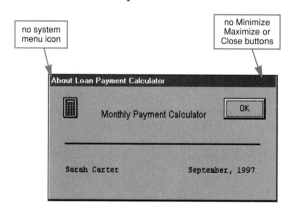

FIGURE 3-20

You control the ability to make run-time changes to the WindowState by including or removing Minimize and Maximize buttons from the form. This control is done by setting the values of the **MinButton property** and the **MaxButton property** of the form to True if you want to include the button or to False to exclude the button. Setting the value to False also removes the corresponding choice from the system menu. Setting the form's ControlBox property to False removes the system menu icon and the Minimize, Maximize and Close buttons. Perform the following steps to prevent the About... form from having its WindowState changed during run time.

TO SET THE CONTROL BOX

Step 1: Select the form object by clicking its name, Form1, in the Object drop-down list in the Properties window.
Step 2: Scroll through the Properties list until the ControlBox property is visible. Double-click the ControlBox property in the Properties list.

The new setting of False is shown in the Properties list (Figure 3-21).

When the ControlBox property is set to False, the form still contains a system menu icon and Minimize, Maximize, and Close buttons at design time (Figure 3-21). However, at run time the buttons will not appear on the form (Figure 3-20).

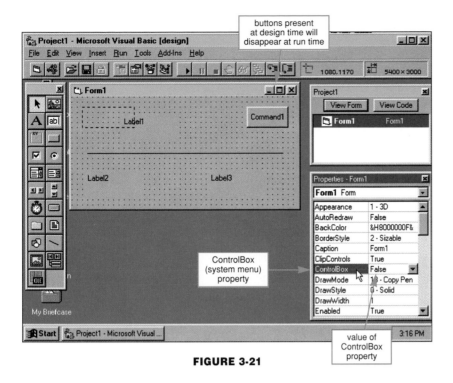

FIGURE 3-21

The BorderStyle Property of Forms

The ability to change the size of a window at run time by dragging its borders is determined by the value of the form's BorderStyle property. The **BorderStyle property** of a form affects the form's appearance and controls. A **sizable form** has borders that can be dragged to new positions. A form's BorderStyle property can take one of six values and affects whether certain controls appear on the form, as listed in Table 3-2.

▶ **TABLE 3-2 BORDERSTYLE PROPERTY VALUES**

CONTROL	BORDERSTYLE					
	0 - None	1 - Fixed Single	2 - Sizable	3 - Fixed Dialog	4 - Fixed Tool Window	5 - Sizable Tool Window
Minimize button	no	optional	optional	no	no	no
Maximize button	no	optional	optional	no	no	no
Control menu	no	optional	optional	optional	optional	optional
Title bar	no	optional	optional	optional	optional	optional
Sizable form	no	no	yes	no	no	yes

The About Loan Payment Calculator dialog box is typical of most dialog boxes. Generally, a dialog box's WindowState cannot be changed, and it is not sizable. Perform the steps on the next page to prevent the About... form from being resized during run time.

TO SET THE BORDERSTYLE PROPERTY

Step 1: Check to be certain the Form1 form object is selected. If it is not, click its name, Form1, in the Object drop-down list in the Properties window.

Step 2: Scroll through the Properties list until the BorderStyle property is visible. Select the BorderStyle property by clicking its name in the Properties list.

Step 3: Open the Settings drop-down list by clicking the arrow located next to the BorderStyle property.

Step 4: Click the 3 - Fixed Dialog choice in the Settings drop-down list.

The new value appears in the Properties window (Figure 3-22).

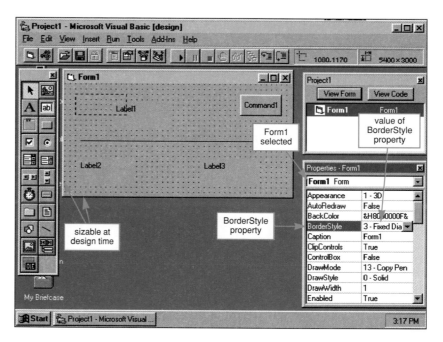

FIGURE 3-22

No matter what value of the BorderStyle is set, the form remains sizable at design time. At run time, however, the form displays with the selected value of the BorderStyle property.

Control Names and Captions

In Project 2, you learned that naming controls makes it easier for you to write code and makes your code easier for other people to understand. Not all of the controls in Project 2 were given names different from their default names. It is important to name forms, especially in projects that contain more than one form. If only one instance of a type of control is on a form, or if a control is not referred to by an event or procedure, it is not as important to have a name other than the default name Visual Basic assigns.

Perform the following steps to name the form and to assign captions to the controls on the About... form. In order to ensure the entire label captions fit inside the controls, set the labels' AutoSize property to True.

TO SET THE NAME AND CAPTIONS

Step 1: Check to be certain the Form1 form object is selected. If not, click its name in the Object drop-down list in the Properties window. Double-click the Name property in the Properties list.

Step 2: Type `frmLoanabt` and press the ENTER key.

Step 3: Double-click the Caption property in the Properties list.

Step 4: Type `About Loan Payment Calculator` and press the ENTER key.

Step 5: Select the Label1 control by clicking its name in the Object drop-down list in the Properties window. Double-click the AutoSize property in the Properties list.

Step 6: Double-click the Caption property in the Properties list. Type `Monthly Payment Calculator` and press the ENTER key.

Step 7: Select the Label2 control by clicking its name in the Object drop-down list in the Properties window. Double-click the AutoSize property in the Properties list.

Step 8: Double-click the Caption property in the Properties list. Type `Sarah Carter` (or your name) and press the ENTER key.

Step 9: Select the Label3 control by clicking its name in the Object drop-down list in the Properties window. Double-click the AutoSize property in the Properties list.

Step 10: Double-click the Caption property in the Properties list. Type `September, 1997` and press the ENTER key.

Step 11: Select the Command1 control by clicking its name in the Object drop-down list in the Properties window. Double-click the Caption property in the Properties list.

Step 12: Type `OK` and press the ENTER key.

The frmLoanabt form appears as shown in Figure 3-23.

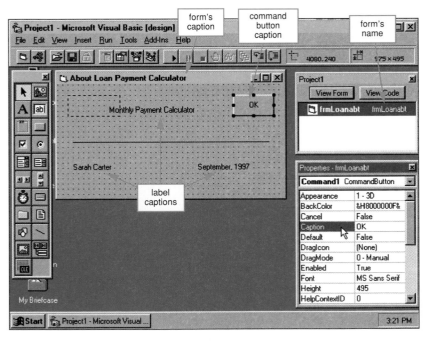

FIGURE 3-23

Font Properties

Project 2 showed how to change the size of text characters on controls by using the FontSize property. The Visual Basic controls containing text have several properties that affect the way text appears. For a detailed description of all the properties, use Visual Basic's online Help to search on the word *font*.

Four major **Font properties** are described in Table 3-3:

▸ **TABLE 3-3 FONT PROPERTIES**

PROPERTY	DESCRIPTION
FontName	the name of the selected font
FontSize	the size (in printer's points)
FontBold	a True value displays the selected font in bold
FontItalic	a True value displays the selected font in italics

As you can see in Figure 3-24, the labels and captions of controls on the frmLoanabt form have different Font properties. Perform the following steps to set these Font properties.

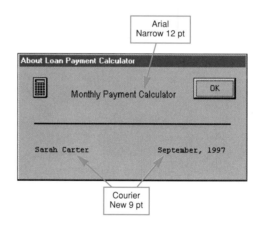

FIGURE 3-24

TO SET THE FONT PROPERTIES

Step 1: Select the Label1 control by clicking its name in the Object drop-down list in the Properties window.

Step 2: Double click Font in the properties list to open the Font dialog window (Figure 3-25).

Step 3: Click Arial Narrow in the Font list box. Click 12 in the Size list box.

Step 4: Click the OK button in the Font dialog window.

Step 5: Select the Label2 control by clicking its name in the Object drop-down list in the Properties window.

Step 6: Double click Font in the Properties list to open the Font dialog window.

Step 7: Click Courier New in the Font list box. Click 9 in the Size list box.

Step 8: Click the OK button in the Font dialog window.

Step 9: Repeat Steps 5 through 8 for the Label3 control.

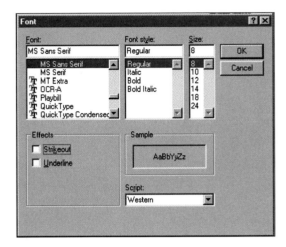

FIGURE 3-25

The list of available fonts (Step 2) depends on which fonts have been installed in your copy of Windows.

Bold and Italic properties can be used alone or in combination. For example, setting the value of the Font style to Bold Italic in the Font dialog window will display the selected font in boldface italics.

The Picture Property of Image Controls

You can add graphics to forms and controls at design time by setting the **Picture property** in the Properties window. The graphic image used on the frmLoanabt form comes from the set of icon files (.ICO) supplied as part of the Visual Basic system. When a form containing graphical data (such as an icon or picture) is saved, Visual Basic automatically creates an additional file with the same filename as the form but with an **.FRX** extension. Perform the steps on the next page to add an icon to the Image1 control.

TO ADD A GRAPHIC TO AN IMAGE CONTROL ▼

STEP 1 ►

Select the Image1 control by clicking its name in the Object drop-down list in the Properties window. Double-click the Picture property in the Properties list.

The Load Picture dialog box appears (Figure 3-26). The Load Picture dialog box is very similar to other common dialog boxes used in Windows applications.

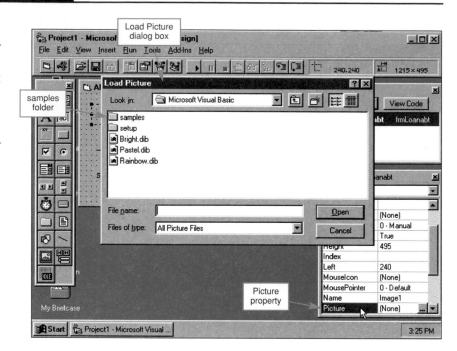

FIGURE 3-26

STEP 2 ►

Double-click the samples folder in the directory list box.

A list of the folders within the samples folder appears in the directory list box (Figure 3-27).

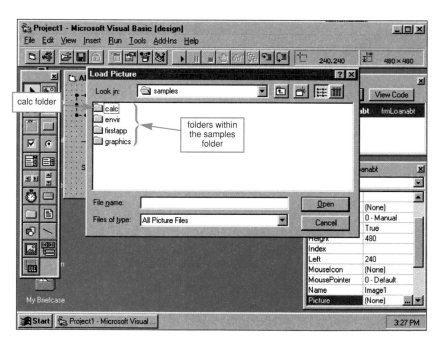

FIGURE 3-27

STEP 3 ▶

Double-click the calc folder.

A list of icon files (.ICO) displays in the File list box (Figure 3-28).

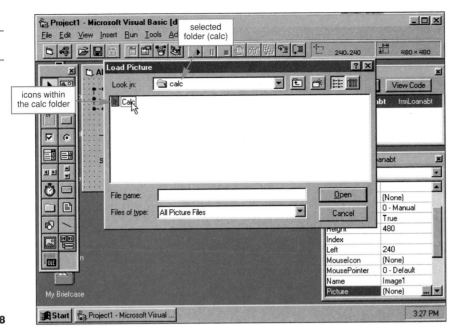

FIGURE 3-28

STEP 4 ▶

Select the calc icon by double-clicking its filename (Calc) in the File list box.

Visual Basic loads the calculator icon into the image control located in the upper left of the About... form (Figure 3-29).

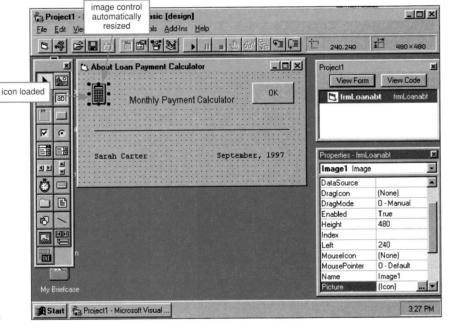

FIGURE 3-29

When Visual Basic loaded the icon, the size of the image control was adjusted automatically to the size of its contents (the calculator icon). This automatic sizing occurred because the default value of the image control's BorderStyle property is 0 - None. If you set the BorderStyle of the image control to 1 - Fixed Single, Visual Basic does not adjust its size automatically.

BorderStyle and BorderWidth Properties of Line Controls

The next step is to change the appearance of the horizontal line that runs across the center of the About... form. The **BorderStyle** property of the line control determines the appearance of the line, such as solid or dashed. The seven possible BorderStyles for the line control are listed in Table 3-4.

▶ **TABLE 3-4 BORDERSTYLE PROPERTIES OF LINE CONTROLS**

SETTING	DESCRIPTION
0	Transparent
1	(Default) Solid — The border is centered on the edge of the shape
2	Dash
3	Dot
4	Dash-Dot
5	Dash-Dot-Dot
6	Inside Solid — The outer edge of the border is the outer edge of the shape

The BorderStyle of the line on the frmLoanabt form is solid, which is the default value (Figure 3-30).

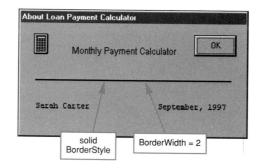

FIGURE 3-30

The **BorderWidth property** is used to set the width of the line. The values of the BorderWidth are integers from 1 to 8192. The line on the frmLoanabt form is wider than the default width of 1 (Figure 3-30). Perform the following steps to change the width of the line control located on the frmLoanabt form.

TO SET THE BORDERWIDTH PROPERTY OF THE LINE CONTROL

Step 1: Select the Line1 control by clicking its name in the Object drop-down list in the Properties window.
Step 2: Double-click the BorderWidth property in the Properties list.
Step 3: Type 2 and press the ENTER key.

The line control appears as shown in Figure 3-31.

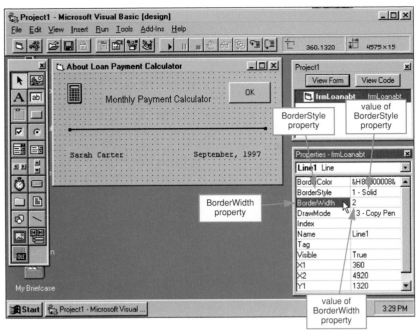

FIGURE 3-31

If the BorderWidth is set to a value greater than 1, the only effective settings of the BorderStyle are 1 - Solid and 6 - Inside Solid.

Saving the Form

The frmLoanabt form is now complete. Before proceeding with building the second form in the project, save the form. Perform the following steps to save the form to a formatted diskette in the 3½ Floppy [A:] drive.

TO SAVE A FORM ▼

STEP 1 ▶

Insert a formatted diskette in drive A. Click the File menu on the menu bar. Click Save File As from the File menu.

The Save File As dialog box appears, and the form's name appears in the File name box (Figure 3-32).

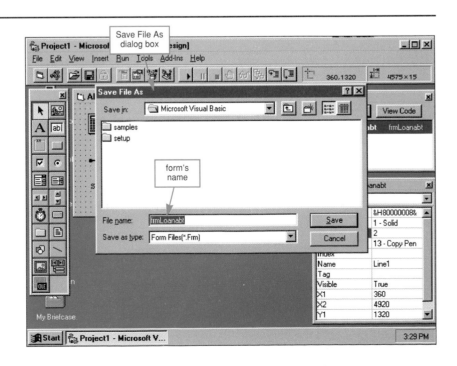

FIGURE 3-32

STEP 2 ▶

Type Loanabt **as the entry.**

The filename changes in the File name box (Figure 3-33).

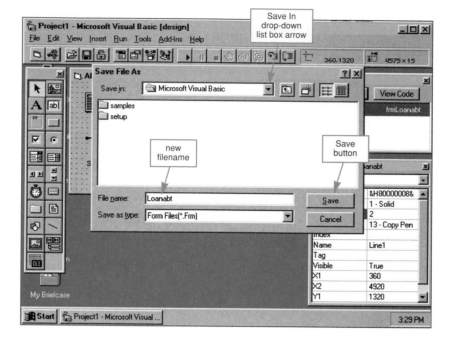

FIGURE 3-33

STEP 3 ▶

Open the Save In drop-down list box by clicking its arrow. Scroll through the list if necessary, and then click the 3½ Floppy [A:] drive. Click the Save button.

The form is saved as a file on the diskette, and the dialog box closes. The form's filename is shown preceding the Visual Basic name of the form in the Project window (Figure 3-34).

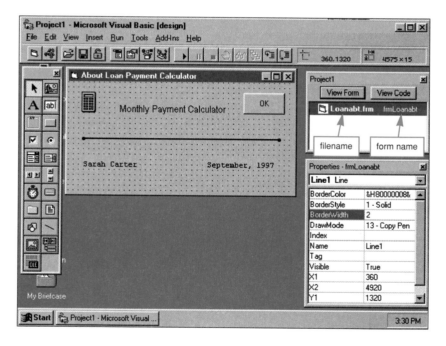

FIGURE 3-34

Because form files automatically have the .FRM file extension added when you save them, the FRM prefix in the form's name was not included in the filename. You can save a file with any name, and the filename can be different from Visual Basic's value of the Name property of the form.

▶ THE LOAN PAYMENT CALCULATOR FORM AND ITS CONTROLS

T he second form to construct in this project is the Loan Payment Calculator form shown in Figure 3-35. Because this form is the second one in the project, a new form must be added. The Loan Payment Calculator form is built following this sequence of activities:

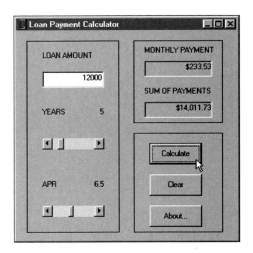

FIGURE 3-35

- ▶ add a new form to the project
- ▶ set the size of the form
- ▶ add the controls
- ▶ set the properties of the form and its controls
- ▶ save the form as a file on a diskette

Adding Additional Forms to the Project

You can have multiple Form windows open on the desktop at the same time. However, it reduces confusion if you minimize the windows of forms you are not currently using. Perform the following steps to minimize the About... form (frmLoanabt) and to add a new form to the project.

TO ADD A NEW FORM

Step 1: Click the About... form's (frmLoanabt's) Minimize button.
Step 2: Click the Form button on the toolbar.

The About... form's (frmLoanabt's) window is reduced to a button on the lower-left corner of the desktop. A new form with the default name Form1 is added to the project, and its window opens on the desktop (Figure 3-36).

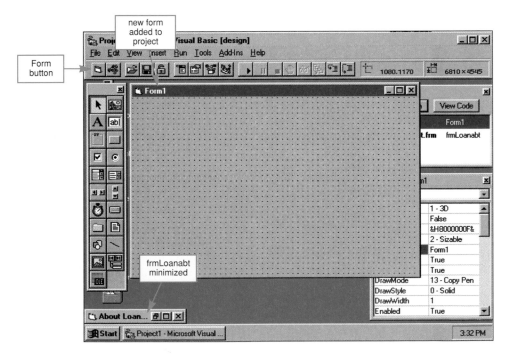

FIGURE 3-36

Setting the Form Size and Position

Perform the following steps to change the size of the Loan Payment Calculator form by directly changing the values of the Height and Width properties in the Properties window, as was done with the About... form.

TO SET THE SIZE OF THE FORM USING THE PROPERTIES WINDOW

Step 1: Make the Properties window the active window by clicking it.
Step 2: Scroll through the Properties list, and then double-click the Height property. Type 5265 and press the ENTER key.
Step 3: Scroll through the Properties list and double-click the Width property. Type 5265 and press the ENTER key.

The form (Form1) appears as shown in Figure 3-37.

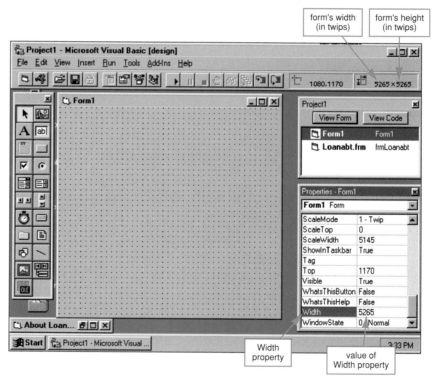

FIGURE 3-37

It is not necessary to locate the second form at this time. The form's location will be changed at run time by using code statements that change the values of the form's Top and Left properties.

Adding Shape Controls

The Loan Payment Calculator form has three shape controls, as shown in Figure 3-38. These controls are not functional within the application because no events or code statements are associated with them. However, they do serve an important purpose.

Shape controls are used in the Loan Payment Calculator application to visually group related controls on the form. All the controls within the shape on the left of the form are related to the **inputs**, or data needed by the application to carry out its function. The shape on the top, right of the form groups all of the controls related to the results of the application's function, called **outputs**. The shape control located on the bottom, right contains all of the controls used to initiate different actions within the application. Perform the following steps to add three shape controls to the form.

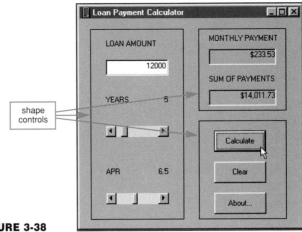

FIGURE 3-38

TO ADD THE SHAPE CONTROLS ▼

STEP 1 ▶

Click the Shape tool in the Toolbox, and move the mouse to the location where the top left corner of the shape will appear.

The Shape tool is highlighted in the Toolbox. The mouse pointer changes to a cross hair (Figure 3-39).

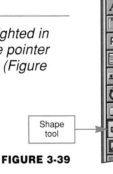
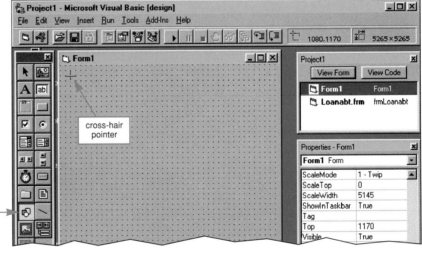

FIGURE 3-39

STEP 2 ▶

Drag the mouse pointer down and to the right as shown in Figure 3-40. Release the left mouse button.

As you drag the mouse, a gray outline of the control appears on the form (Figure 3-40). When you release the left mouse button, the shape control is redrawn in the position of the outline.

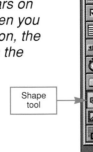
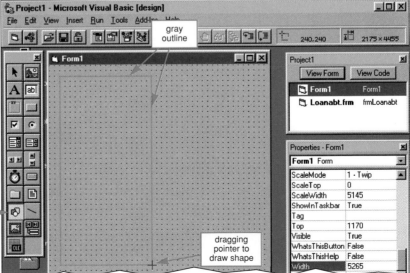

FIGURE 3-40

STEP 3 ▶

Repeat Steps 1 and 2 to draw a
second shape control (Figure 3-41).

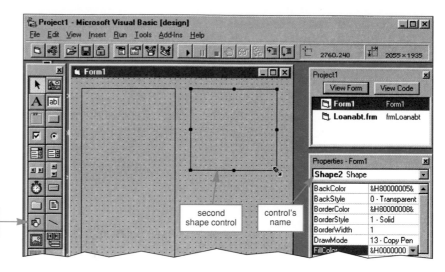

FIGURE 3-41

STEP 4 ▶

Repeat Steps 1 and 2 to draw a third
shape control (Figure 3-42).

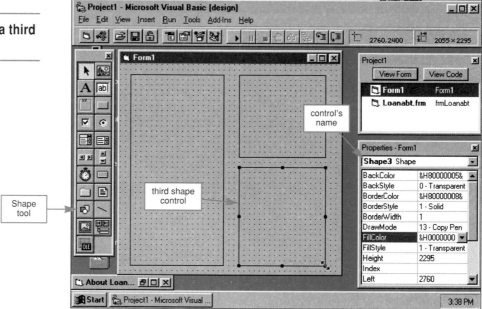

FIGURE 3-42

Adding and Copying Label Controls

The Loan Payment Calculator form contains nine labels, as identified in Figure
3-43. The two labels used to display the outputs of the loan calculation have
borders around them. At run time, their contents (captions) are blank until you
click the Calculate button. The reason for displaying the outputs in this way is that
an empty box visually communicates "something goes here." The labels above the
boxes communicate what that "something" is.

Project 2 showed how to copy controls using the mouse and the Edit menu. In the following example, controls are copied using the keyboard. Perform the following steps to add the seven borderless labels and then to add the two labels with borders.

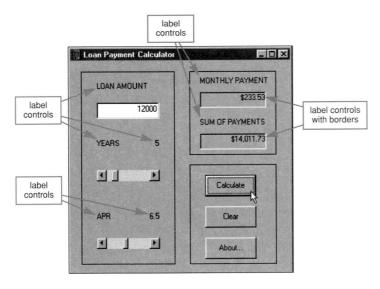

FIGURE 3-43

TO ADD THE BORDERLESS LABEL CONTROLS ▼

STEP 1 ▶

Add a default-sized label control to the center of the form by double-clicking the Label tool in the Toolbox. Use the mouse to drag the control to the position shown in Figure 3-44.

STEP 2 ▶

Set the label's AutoSize property to True by double-clicking the AutoSize property in the Properties window.

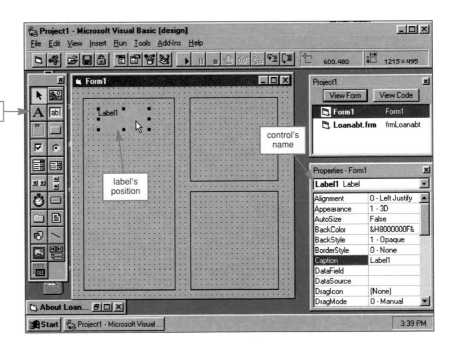

FIGURE 3-44

STEP 3 ▶

Press CTRL+C. Press CTRL+V. In response to the dialog box that appears, type N for No.

An additional label control with its AutoSize property set to True appears on the form. When you copy a control, all of its property settings also are copied. Thus, the second label control has the caption Label1 (Figure 3-45).

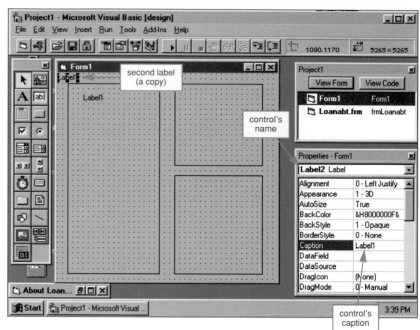

FIGURE 3-45

STEP 4 ▶

Drag the label to the position shown in Figure 3-46.

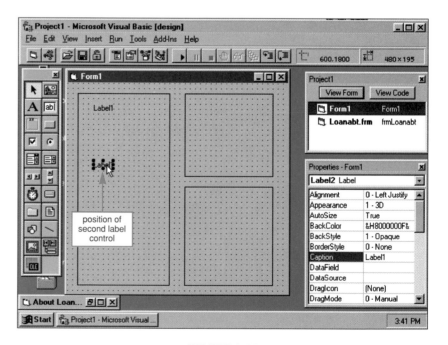

FIGURE 3-46

STEP 5 ▶

Press CTRL+V. In response to the
dialog box that appears, type N for
No. Drag the control to the position
shown in Figure 3-47.

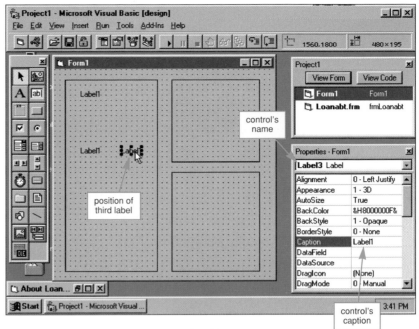

FIGURE 3-47

STEP 6 ▶

Repeat Step 5 four times to add the
remaining labels to the positions
shown in Figure 3-48. Be careful to
locate the labels in the order shown.

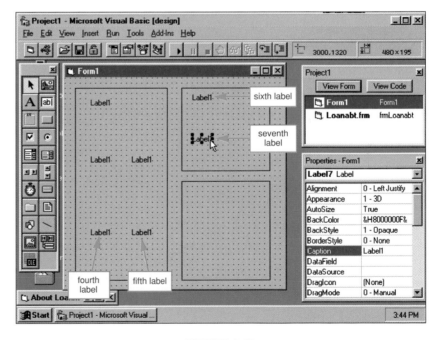

FIGURE 3-48

CTRL+C copies the selected control to the Clipboard. CTRL+V pastes the
control from the Clipboard to the form. Seven similar labels have been added to
the form. Perform the steps on the next page to add the remaining two labels used
to contain the application's outputs.

TO ADD THE REMAINING LABELS ▼

STEP 1 ►

Add a default-sized label control to the center of the form by double-clicking the Label tool in the Toolbox. Use the mouse to drag the control to the position shown in Figure 3-49.

STEP 2 ►

Change the label's BorderStyle property from 0 - No Border to 1 - Fixed Single by double-clicking the BorderStyle property in the Properties window.

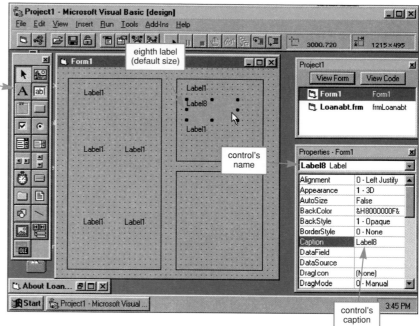

FIGURE 3-49

STEP 3 ►

Drag the control's lower, right sizing handle up and to the right, as shown in Figure 3-50. Release the left mouse button.

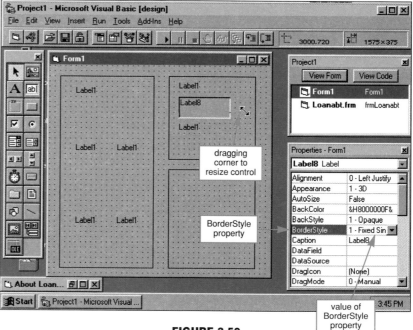

FIGURE 3-50

STEP 4 ▶

Press CTRL+C. Press CTRL+V. In response to the dialog box that appears, type N for No.

An identically sized label control with its BorderStyle property set to 1 appears on the form (Figure 3-51).

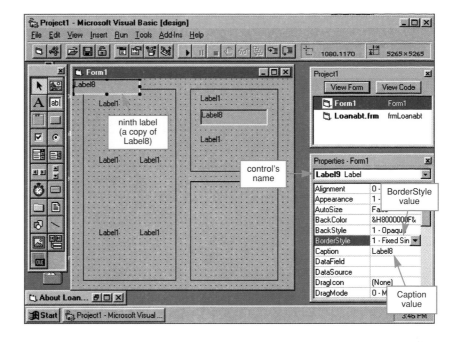

FIGURE 3-51

STEP 5 ▶

Drag the label to the position shown in Figure 3-52.

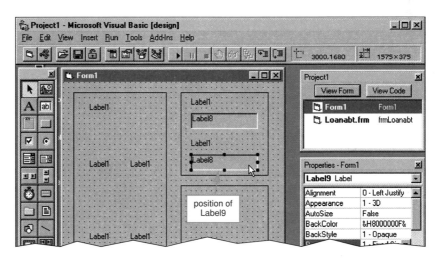

FIGURE 3-52

All of the label controls now have been added to the form. Compare the positions and appearance of the label controls in Figure 3-52 to the completed form shown in Figure 3-53.

Generally, all of the form's controls are added before setting properties. In the preceding example, you set the AutoSize and BorderStyle properties immediately so that you could take advantage of the fact that property values are copied when a control is copied.

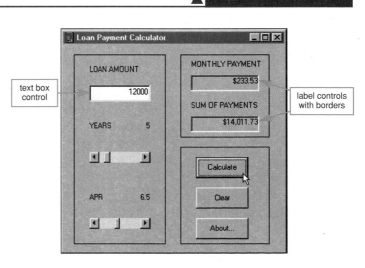

FIGURE 3-53

Copying the labels with the property already set will save you time because you won't have to set each label's AutoSize or BorderStyle property when you set the rest of the properties later. By copying the first output label (Label8), you did not have to draw or resize the second output label (Label9) to match the size of the first.

Adding the Text Box Control

The Loan Payment Calculator form contains one text box control, which is used at run time to accept the loan amount (Figure 3-53 on the previous page). A text box is used for you to enter the loan amount instead of a label because a label's contents can be changed during run time only with a code statement. Perform the following steps to add the text box control to the form.

TO ADD THE TEXT BOX CONTROL ▼

STEP 1 ▶

Add a default-sized text box control to the center of the form by double-clicking the TextBox tool in the Toolbox. Use the mouse to drag the control to the position shown in Figure 3-54.

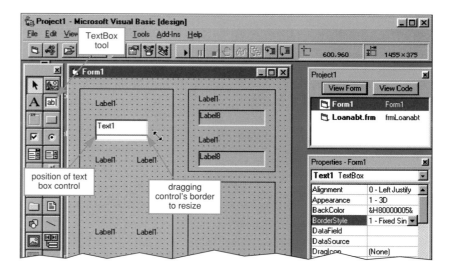

FIGURE 3-54

STEP 2 ▶

Drag the control's lower, right sizing handle up and to the right (Figure 3-54). Release the left mouse button. The control appears as shown in Figure 3-55.

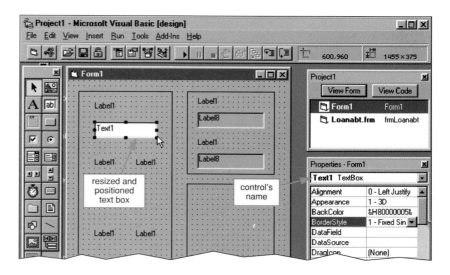

FIGURE 3-55

Adding Scroll Bar Controls

Scroll bars commonly are used to view the contents of a control when the contents cannot fit within the control's borders. An example is the scroll bar on the Properties list in the Properties window. Visual Basic has two different scroll bar controls; the **horizontal scroll bar** and the **vertical scroll bar**. Their names reflect the orientation of the control on the form, not its use. You control its use. For example, you can use a vertical scroll bar to control the horizontal scrolling of a control on a form.

Another use of the scroll bar control is to give a value to an input. One benefit of using a scroll bar for input is that it prevents you from entering an improper value by mistake, such as a letter instead of a number. The two horizontal scroll bar controls shown in Figure 3-56 are used as input controls for the number of years of the loan and for the annual interest rate. Perform the following steps to add the two scroll bar controls.

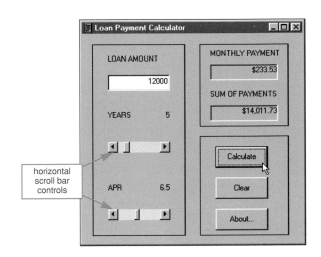

FIGURE 3-56

TO ADD SCROLL BAR CONTROLS ▼

STEP 1 ▶

Double-click the HScrollBar tool in the Toolbox. Extend the scroll bar's width by dragging its sizing handle the distance of two grid marks on the form. Drag the scroll bar to the position shown in Figure 3-57.

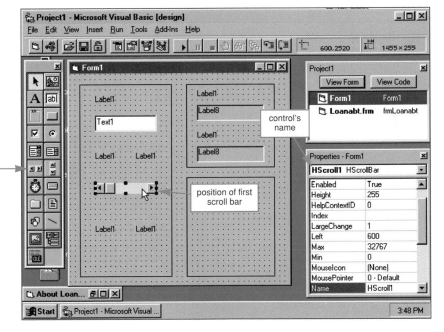

FIGURE 3-57

STEP 2 ▶

Double-click the HScrollBar tool in the Toolbox. Extend the new scroll bar's width by dragging its sizing handle the distance of two grid marks on the form. Drag the scroll bar to the position shown in Figure 3-58.

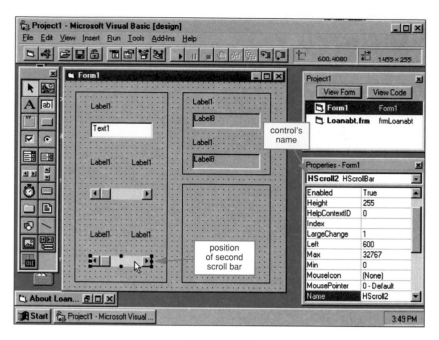

FIGURE 3-58

In the Loan Payment Calculator application, the caption of the label located above the right end of the scroll bar is used to display the current value of the input controlled by that scroll bar. When you click a scroll arrow or drag the scroll box, the scroll bar's **Change event** is triggered. A code statement will be written later in this project that will link the caption of the label to the Change event.

Adding Command Buttons

The last three controls to be added to the Loan Payment Calculator form are the three command buttons identified in Figure 3-59. The command buttons used in this application are the default size, so you can add them to the form by using the double-click method instead of drawing them with the mouse.

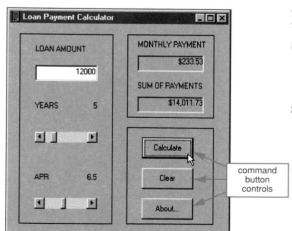

FIGURE 3-59

TO ADD THE COMMAND BUTTONS

Step 1: Double-click the CommandButton tool in the Toolbox. Drag the Command1 command button inside and to the top, center of the shape control located on the lower right of the Form window.

Step 2: Double-click the CommandButton tool in the Toolbox. Drag the Command2 button inside and to the center of the shape control located on the lower right of the Form window.

Step 3: Double-click the CommandButton tool in the Toolbox. Drag the Command3 button inside and to the bottom, center of the shape control located on the lower right of the Form window.

The command buttons appear as shown in Figure 3-60.

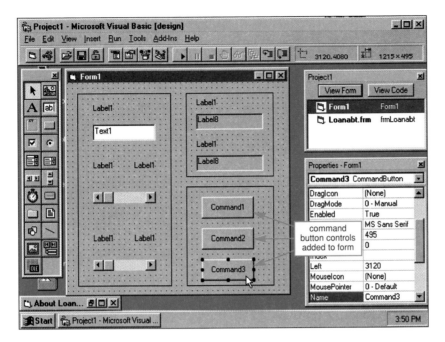

FIGURE 3-60

You now have completed the design of the Loan Payment Calculator form. The next step in the development process is to set the properties for the form and its controls.

▶ SETTING PROPERTIES OF THE LOAN PAYMENT CALCULATOR FORM AND ITS CONTROLS

 n addition to setting the Caption and Name properties of the controls on the Loan Payment Calculator form, you will set the following properties:

▶ the Alignment property of text boxes and labels
▶ the Min and Max properties of scroll bars
▶ the SmallChange and LargeChange properties of scroll bars
▶ the Icon property of forms

Setting the Alignment Property of Text Boxes and Labels

The **Alignment property** specifies where the caption will appear within the borders of a control, regardless of whether the borders are visible. The values of the Alignment property are listed in Table 3-5.

▶ **TABLE 3-5 ALIGNMENT PROPERTY**

VALUE	EXAMPLE	
0 - Left Justify	loan	
1 - Right Justify	loan	
2 - Center	loan	

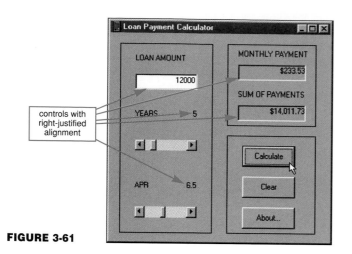

controls with
right-justified
alignment

FIGURE 3-61

The default value of the Alignment property is left justified. Because the values appear in the Properties drop-down list in the same order as in Table 3-5, you can change from left justify to right justify by double-clicking the Alignment property in the Properties list instead of opening the Settings list and then selecting 1 - Right Justify. The five controls with right-justified alignment are identified in Figure 3-61.

The text box control is among the five right-justified controls. To change a text box's alignment, the value of its MultiLine property must be equal to True. Perform the following steps to set the Alignment property.

TO SET THE ALIGNMENT PROPERTY

Step 1: Select the Text1 control by clicking it on the form or by clicking its name in the Object drop-down list in the Properties window. Double-click the Alignment property in the Properties list in the Properties window.

Step 2: Scroll down the Properties list and double-click the MultiLine property in the Properties list.

Step 3: Select the Label3 control by clicking its name in the Object drop-down list in the Properties window. Double-click the Alignment property in the Properties list.

Step 4: Select the Label5 control by clicking its name in the Object drop-down list in the Properties window. Double-click the Alignment property in the Properties list.

Step 5: Select the Label8 control by clicking it on the form or by clicking its name in the Object drop-down list in the Properties window. Double-click the Alignment property in the Properties list.

Step 6: Select the Label9 control by clicking it on the form or by clicking its name in the Object drop-down list in the Properties window. Double-click the Alignment property in the Properties list.

Setting the Caption and Text Properties

Figure 3-62 shows the Loan Payment Calculator form as it appears at the current stage of development and as it will appear when completed. The differences between these two figures relate to the Caption property of the form, labels, and command buttons and to the Text property of the one text box control. At run time, the text box should start out empty. This text box is made empty by setting the initial value of its Text property to be blank. Perform the following steps to set the Caption property and Text property.

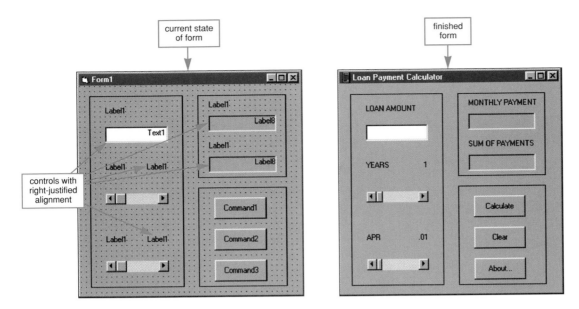

FIGURE 3-62

TO SET THE CONTROLS' CAPTIONS AND TEXT

Step 1: Select the Form1 form control by clicking its name in the Object drop-down list in the Properties window. Double-click the Caption property in the Properties list. Type Loan Payment Calculator and press the ENTER key.

Step 2: Select the Label1 control by clicking its name in the Object drop-down list in the Properties window. Double-click the Caption property in the Properties list. Type LOAN AMOUNT and press the ENTER key.

Step 3: Select the Text1 control by clicking its name in the Object drop-down list in the Properties window. Double-click the Text property in the Properties list. Drag the cursor over the text to highlight it. Press the DELETE key.

Step 4: Select the Label2 control by clicking its name in the Object drop-down list in the Properties window. Double-click the Caption property in the Properties list. Type YEARS and press the ENTER key.

Step 5: Select the Label3 control by clicking its name in the Object drop-down list in the Properties window. Double-click the Caption property in the Properties list. Type 1 and press the ENTER key.

Step 6: Select the Label4 control by clicking its name in the Object drop-down list in the Properties window. Double-click the Caption property in the Properties list. Type APR and press the ENTER key.

Step 7: Select the Label5 control by clicking its name in the Object drop-down list in the Properties window. Double-click the Caption property in the Properties list. Type .01 and press the ENTER key.

Step 8: Select the Label6 control by clicking its name in the Object drop-down list in the Properties window. Double-click the Caption property in the Properties list. Type MONTHLY PAYMENT and press the ENTER key.

Step 9: Select the Label7 control by clicking its name in the Object drop-down list in the Properties window. Double-click the Caption property in the Properties list. Type SUM OF PAYMENTS and press the ENTER key.

Step 10: Select the Label8 control by clicking its name in the Object drop-down list in the Properties window. Double-click the Caption property in the Properties list. Press the DELETE key.

Step 11: Select the Label9 control by clicking its name in the Object drop-down list in the Properties window. Double-click the Caption property in the Properties list. Press the DELETE key.

Step 12: Select the Command1 control by clicking its name in the Object drop-down list in the Properties window. Double-click the Caption property in the Properties list. Type `Calculate` and press the ENTER key.

Step 13: Select the Command2 control by clicking its name in the Object drop-down list in the Properties window. Double-click the Caption property in the Properties list. Type `Clear` and press the ENTER key.

Step 14: Select the Command3 control by clicking its name in the Object drop-down list in the Properties window. Double-click the Caption property in the Properties list. Type `About...` and press the ENTER key.

The Loan Payment Calculator form appears as shown in Figure 3-63.

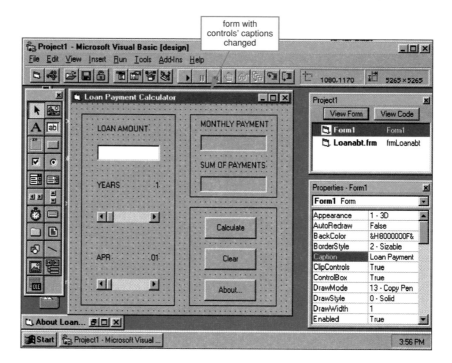

FIGURE 3-63

Naming the Controls

In addition to the form control itself, four labels, two scroll bars, three command buttons, and one text box on the Loan Payment Calculator form will be referred to in the events and code statements that will be written later. These controls, with their current (default) names, are shown in Figure 3-64. It would be confusing to write events and code statements using the default names of these controls. Perform the following steps to rename the controls that will be referred to in code statements.

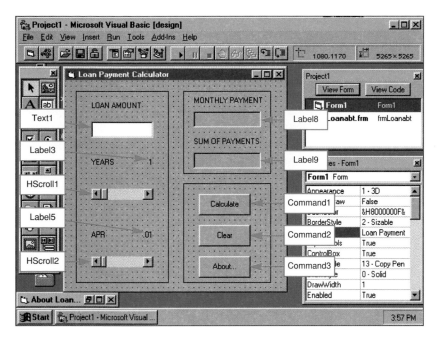

FIGURE 3-64

TO NAME CONTROLS

Step 1: Select the Form1 control by clicking its name in the Object drop-down list in the Properties window. Double-click the Name property in the Properties list. Type the control name `frmLoanpmt` and press the ENTER key.

Step 2: Select the Text1 control by clicking its name in the Object drop-down list in the Properties window. Double-click the Name property in the Properties list. Type the control name `txtAmount` and press the ENTER key.

Step 3: Select the Label3 control by clicking its name in the Object drop-down list in the Properties window. Double-click the Name property in the Properties list. Type the control name `lblYears` and press the ENTER key.

Step 4: Select the HScroll1 control by clicking its name in the Object drop-down list in the Properties window. Double-click the Name property in the Properties list. Type the control name `hsbYears` and press the ENTER key.

Step 5: Select the Label5 control by clicking its name in the Object drop-down list in the Properties window. Double-click the Name property in the Properties list. Type `lblRate` as the control name and press the ENTER key.

Step 6: Select the HScroll2 control by clicking its name in the Object drop-down list in the Properties window. Double-click the Name property in the Properties list. Type `hsbRate` and press the ENTER key.

Step 7: Select the Label8 control by clicking its name in the Object drop-down list in the Properties window. Double-click the Name property in the Properties list. Type `lblPayment` as the control name and press the ENTER key.

Step 8: Select the Label9 control by clicking its name in the Object drop-down list in the Properties window. Double-click the Name property in the Properties list. Type `lblSumpmts` as the control name and press the ENTER key.

Step 9: Select the Command1 control by clicking its name in the Object drop-down list in the Properties window. Double-click the Name property in the Properties list. Type `cmdCalculate` as the control name and press the ENTER key.

Step 10: Select the Command2 control by clicking its name in the Object drop-down list in the Properties window. Double-click the Name property in the Properties list. Type `cmdClear` as the control name and press the ENTER key.

Step 11: Select the Command3 control by clicking its name in the Object drop-down list in the Properties window. Double-click the Name property in the Properties list. Type `cmdAbout` as the control name and press the ENTER key.

The controls are identified by their new names in Figure 3-65.

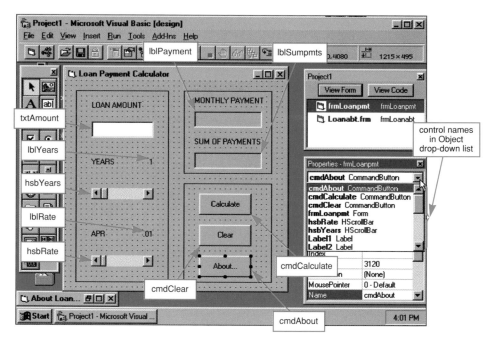

FIGURE 3-65

Setting the Scroll Bar Properties

The **Value property** of a scroll bar is an integer number that changes in relation to the position of the scroll box within the scroll bar. The lowest and highest numbers that the Value property can take are set with the **Min** and **Max properties** of the scroll bar. In a horizontal scroll bar control, these values correspond to the farthest left and farthest right positions of the scroll box.

The amount that the value changes each time you click one of the scroll arrows is set by the **SmallChange property** of the scroll bar. The amount that the value changes by clicking the area between the scroll box and one of the two scroll arrows is set with the **LargeChange property** of the scroll bar. Perform the following steps to set the properties of the scroll bar controls.

TO SET THE SCROLL BAR PROPERTIES

Step 1: Select the Years scroll bar by clicking it on the form or by clicking its name, hsbYears, in the Object drop-down list in the Properties window.

Step 2: Double-click the Max property in the Properties list. Type 30 and press the ENTER key.

Step 3: Double-click the Min property in the Properties list. Type 1 and press the ENTER key.

Step 4: Double-click the LargeChange property in the Properties list. Type 5 and press the ENTER key.

Step 5: Select the APR scroll bar by clicking it on the form or by clicking its name, hsbRate, in the Object drop-down list in the Properties window.

Step 6: Double-click the Max property in the Properties list. Type 1500 and press the ENTER key.

Step 7: Double-click the Min property in the Properties list. Type 1 and press the ENTER key.

Step 8: Double-click the LargeChange property in the Properties list. Type 10 and press the ENTER key.

The new values of these properties are visible by scrolling through the Properties list.

The preceding steps set properties of the scroll bars so that the value of the scroll bar used to set years (hsbYears) will range from 1 to 30 and the value of the scroll bar used to set the APR (hsbRate) will range from 1 to 1500. It was not necessary to set the SmallChange property because its default value is 1. The caption of the label (lblYears), located above the scroll bar, will be the value of the scroll bar hsbYears, representing the number of years to repay the loan (from 1 to 30).

The annual interest rate displayed as the caption of the label (lblRate), located above the lower scroll bar (hsbRate), will work differently. Percentage rates on loans usually are expressed as a one or two digit number followed by a decimal point and a two digit decimal fraction, such as 12.25 percent or 6.30 percent. Because the value of a scroll bar cannot include a fraction, you will multiply the value of the scroll bar hsbRate by .01 to get the value of the caption of the label (lblRate), located above the scroll bar. For example, a scroll bar value of 678 will represent an APR of 6.78 percent, and a scroll bar value of 1250 will represent an APR of 12.50 percent. Multiplying a scroll bar value by a decimal is a common way to make scroll bars able to represent numbers with fractional parts. You set the range of the APR scroll bar (hsbRate) values from 1 to 1500 so that it can be used as described above to represent .01 to 15.00 percent.

The Icon Property of Forms

When a window is minimized, it appears on the taskbar as a button with a small graphical image called an icon. You can specify the graphical image used to represent the form by setting the form's **Icon property.** In the example on the next page, an icon for the Loanpmt form will be selected.

TO SELECT AN ICON ▼

STEP 1 ▶

Select the Loanpmt form by clicking an empty area of the form. Scroll through the Properties list until the Icon property is visible (Figure 3-66).

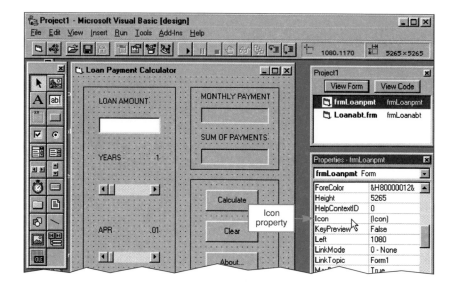

FIGURE 3-66

STEP 2 ▶

Double-click the Icon property in the Properties list.

The Load Icon dialog box appears (Figure 3-67). The Load Icon dialog box is similar to other common dialog boxes such as the Save File As dialog box. The current folder is the one last selected when you added the icon to the image control in Figure 3-28 on page VB137.

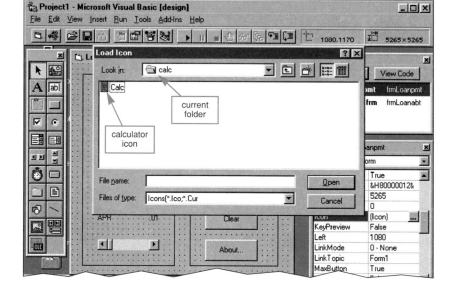

FIGURE 3-67

STEP 3 ▶

Select the calculator icon by double-clicking its filename (Calc) in the File list box.

The Load Icon dialog box closes, and the icon is added to form (Figure 3-68).

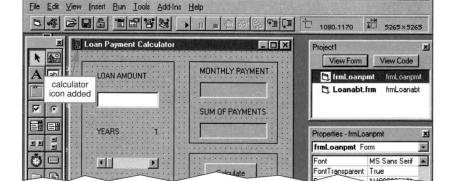

FIGURE 3-68

In the preceding example, an icon was selected from the set of sample files provided with the Visual Basic 4 Working Model. The other editions of Visual Basic 4 contain a libary of icons and also include a sample application called IconWorks, which you can use to view, edit, or create icons.

Saving the Form

The frmLoanpmt form is now complete. Before proceeding, you should save the form to a formatted diskette in the 3½ Floppy [A:] drive.

TO SAVE THE FORM

Step 1: Select the File menu on the menu bar. Click Save File As from the File menu.

Step 2: Type Loanpmt and with the Save In box set to the 3½ Floppy [A:] drive, click the Save button.

Step 3: Minimize the frmLoanpmt window by clicking the Form window's Minimize button.

The frmLoanpmt's filename appears in the Project window, followed by its name (Figure 3-69).

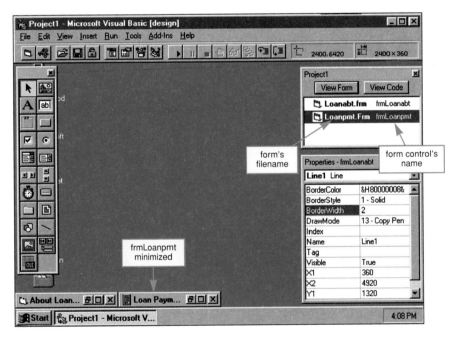

FIGURE 3-69

▶ WRITING CODE

vent procedures (subroutines) must be written for seven events in the Loan Payment Calculator application. These events and their actions are listed in Table 3-6 on the next page.

▸ **TABLE 3-6 LOAN PAYMENT CALCULATOR APPLICATION EVENT PROCEDURES**

FORM	CONTROL	EVENT	ACTIONS
frmLoanpmt	Form	Load	Position the form in the center of the desktop
frmLoanpmt	hsbYears	Change	Update the caption of lblYears
frmLoanpmt	hsbRate	Change	Update the caption lblRate
frmLoanpmt	cmdCalculate	Click	Perform the monthly payment and sum of payments calculations, and display results in lblPayment and lblSumpmts
frmLoanpmt	cmdClear	Click	Clear the contents of txtAmount, lblPayment, and lblSumpmts; reset hsbYears and hsbRate to lowest values
frmLoanpmt	cmdAbout	Click	Add About... dialog box to desktop
frmLoanabt	Command1	Click	Remove About... dialog box from desktop

The code for the Loan Payment Calculator application will be written one event at a time using the Visual Basic Code window in the same manner as in Projects 1 and 2. However, in a project that has more than one form, each form has its own Code window. Before writing the subroutines, a Startup Form for the project will be specified.

The Startup Form

At run time, the **Startup Form** is the first form in a project loaded into the computer's memory and added to the desktop. By default, the Startup Form is the first form you create in a project. The Loan Payment Calculator application begins by displaying the frmLoanpmt form on the desktop. Because frmLoanpmt was not the first form created, it must be specified as the Startup Form.

TO SPECIFY A STARTUP FORM ▼

STEP 1 ▶

Click Tools on the menu bar.

The Tools menu opens (Figure 3-70).

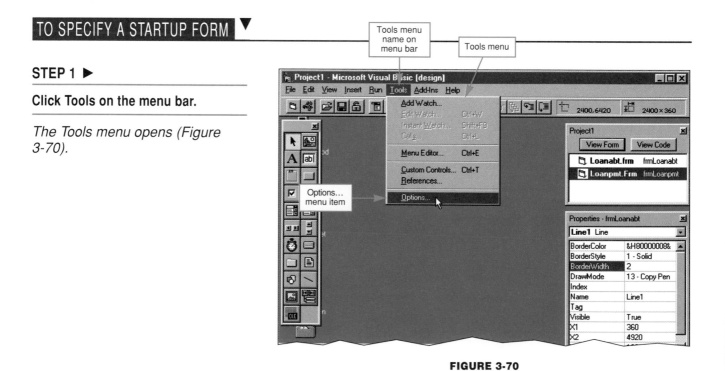

FIGURE 3-70

STEP 2 ▶

Click the Options menu choice. Click the Project tab on the Options dialog box.

The Options dialog box appears (Figure 3-71).

FIGURE 3-71

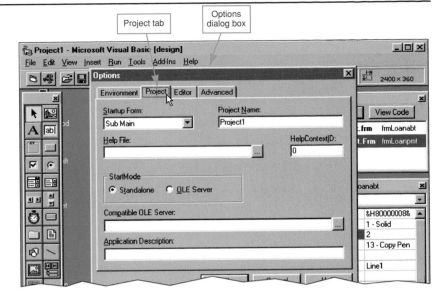

STEP 3 ▶

Click the arrow next to the Startup Form drop-down list.

A drop-down list of possible values is displayed (Figure 3-72).

FIGURE 3-72

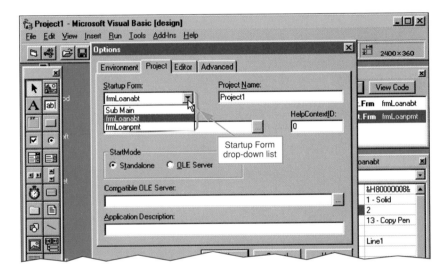

STEP 4 ▶

Select frmLoanpmt by clicking its name in the list.

frmLoanpmt is now the Startup Form (Figure 3-73).

STEP 5 ▶

Click the OK button to close the dialog box.

FIGURE 3-73

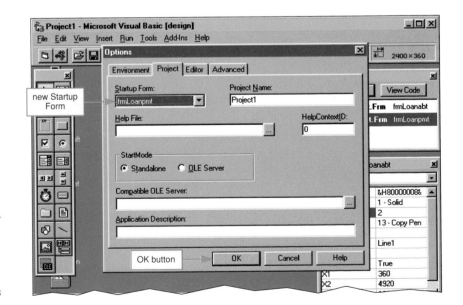

In Projects 1 and 2, a Startup Form was not specified explicitly because when a project consists of just one form (as those projects did), the form is automatically set as the Startup Form.

The frmLoanpmt Form_Load Subroutine

In Project 2, the Form_Load event was presented and used to add items to a drop-down list. Project 3 uses the Form_Load event to set the location of the form on the desktop by specifying its Top and Left properties. Recall that control properties are set at run time by using a code statement consisting of the control's name, a period, the name of the property you want to change (with no blank spaces) followed by an equal sign, and the new value of the property, such as

```
Label1.Caption = "John" or chkMatinee.Value = True
```

A simple procedure exists for placing any form in the center of the desktop, regardless of its dimensions. The total height and width of the desktop (in twips) are kept by Visual Basic as the values of Screen.Height and Screen.Width, respectively. A form is centered top to bottom by placing its top at a position that is half the difference between the total height of the desktop and the height of the form. A form is centered left to right on the desktop in a similar way by placing its left border at a position that is half the difference between the total width of the desktop and the width of the form. Perform the following steps to open the frmLoanpmt Code window and to write the Form_Load event subroutine.

TO WRITE THE FORM_LOAD SUBROUTINE

Step 1: Be certain the frmLoanpmt form is selected. If not, click its name, frmLoanpmt, in the Project window. Click the View Code button.

Step 2: Drag the Code window's right border to the right to increase its width.

Step 3: Select the Form object from the Object drop-down list in the Code window.

Step 4: Enter the following statements in the Code window:
```
frmLoanpmt.Top = (Screen.Height - frmLoanpmt.Height) / 2
frmLoanpmt.Left = (Screen.Width - frmLoanpmt.Width) / 2
```

The code appears as shown in Figure 3-74.

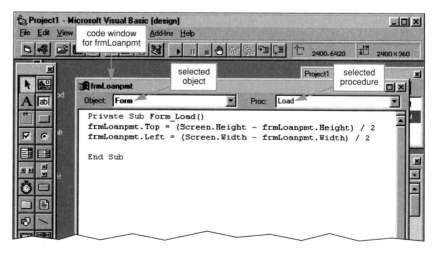

FIGURE 3-74

The frmLoanpmt hsbYears_Change Subroutine

A scroll bar control's **Change event** is triggered any time the control's scroll box is moved by clicking a scroll arrow, dragging the scroll box, or clicking the space between the scroll box and scroll arrow. Each of these three movements also changes the Value property of the scroll bar.

In the Loan Payment Calculator application, a movement of the scroll box must be linked to a new number displayed in the caption located above the scroll bar. Perform the following steps to establish this link by setting the Caption property of the label used to display the years (lblYears) to equal the Value property of the scroll bar located beneath it on the form (hsbYears).

TO WRITE THE HSBYEARS_CHANGE SUBROUTINE

Step 1: Select the hsbYears control from the Object drop-down list in the frmLoanpmt Code window. The Change procedure is already selected.
Step 2: Enter the following statement in the Code window:

```
lblYears.Caption = hsbYears.Value
```

The Code window appears as shown in Figure 3-75.

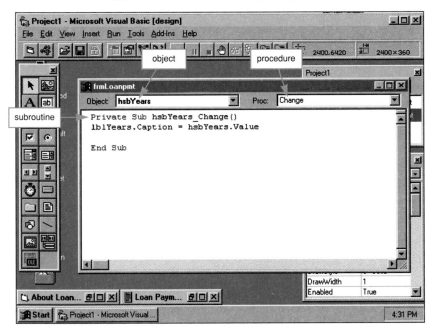

FIGURE 3-75

The frmLoanpmt hsbRate_Change Event

This event is very similar to the Change event for hsbYears. The only difference is the interest rate displayed as the caption of lblApr must be converted from the value of hsbRate by multiplying it by .01. Perform the following steps to write the hsbRate_Change subroutine.

TO WRITE THE HSBRATE_CHANGE SUBROUTINE

Step 1: Select the hsbRate control from the Object drop-down list in the frmLoanpmt Code window. The Change procedure is already selected.

Step 2: Enter the following statement in the Code window:
```
lblRate.Caption = hsbRate.Value * 0.01
```

The Code window appears as shown in Figure 3-76.

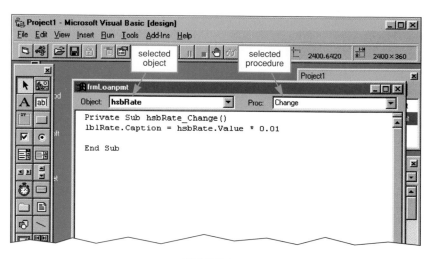

FIGURE 3-76

The frmLoanpmt cmdCalculate_Click Subroutine

The cmdCalculate_Click subroutine is used to perform the loan payment calculation and to display the results. The actual computation is performed by one of Visual Basic's financial functions, the Pmt function. For a complete list and descriptions of all the Visual Basic financial functions, use online Help to search on the words, *financial functions*. The **Pmt function** returns the payment for a loan based on periodic, constant payments and a constant interest rate. The function is used in a code statement in the following manner:

Pmt(*rate, nper, pv, fv, due*)

The entries within parentheses are called **arguments**. Arguments within the Pmt function are described in Table 3-7.

▶ **TABLE 3-7 PMT FUNCTION ARGUMENTS**

ARGUMENT	DESCRIPTION
rate	Interest rate per period. For example, if you get a car loan at an annual percentage rate of 9 percent and make monthly payments, the rate per period is 0.09/12 or 0.0075.
nper	Total number of payment periods in the loan. For example, if you make monthly payments on a five-year car loan, your loan has a total of 5 * 12 (or 60) payment periods.
pv	Present value that a series of payments to be paid in the future is worth now (to the lender). For example, if you borrow $10,000 to buy a car its pv is -10,000.
fv	Future value or cash balance you want after you've made the final payment. The future value of a loan is $0.
due	Number indicating when payments are due. Use 0 if payments are due at the end of the payment period, and use 1 if payments are due at the beginning of the period. In the Loan Payment Calculator application you will use 1 to indicate payments are due on the first day of the month.

In the cmdCalculate_Click subroutine, the inputs of the Loan Payment Calculator application are substituted for the arguments of the Pmt function described in Table 3-7. Remember that the value of hsbRate runs from 1 to 1500 and that the decimal interest rate is .0001 times that value. The Pmt function arguments and values assigned in this project are listed in Table 3-8.

▶ **TABLE 3-8 ARGUMENTS IN LOAN PAYMENT CALCULATOR APPLICATION**

ARGUMENT	VALUE
rate	.0001 * hsbRate.Value / 12
nper	hsbYears.Value * 12
pv	-1 * txtAmount.Text
fv	0
due	1

When you use the Pmt function, all of the arguments must be numbers (or variables whose value is a number). What if you typed Hello as the amount of the loan in the txtAmount text box at run time and then chose the Calculate button? The function would be unable to calculate a value, and the program would end abruptly. It is possible for you to make an error when typing the loan amount, so you want some way to trap this error and to correct it without the program ending abruptly.

Because the Text property of a text box can be either numbers (numeric) or text (string), you need to write some additional code that checks to see if the contents are numeric. This checking is done with the Visual Basic **IsNumeric** function. The function is used within code statements as follows:

IsNumeric(txtAmount.Text)

The function will return a True value if the contents are a number and a False value if the contents are not a valid number. The logical flow of actions within the cmdCalculate_Click subroutine is shown in Figure 3-77.

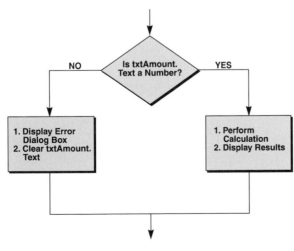

FIGURE 3-77

In Project 2, this type of logical structure was represented in code by using an If...Then statement. This project uses an extension to the If...Then statement called an **If...Then block**. The If...Then block evaluates a condition like the If...Then statement. However, the block allows you to have multiple code statements executed, as illustrated in Figure 3-78.

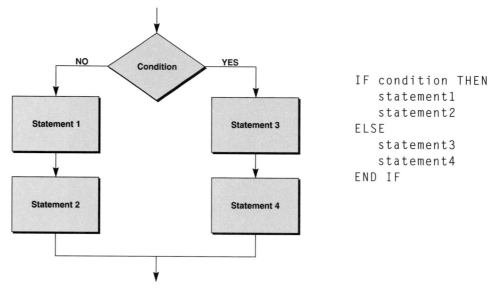

```
IF condition THEN
     statement1
     statement2
ELSE
     statement3
     statement4
END IF
```

FIGURE 3-78

If the value is not a number, you want to first display a dialog box that alerts you to the error, and then erase the contents of txtAmount. Creating customized forms is one way that you can add dialog boxes to your applications (as you did with the About... dialog box). Another way is to use the Visual Basic **MsgBox** statement to display message dialog boxes.

The dialog box shown in Figure 3-79 is used to alert you when an error has been made in entering a value for the loan amount. The dialog box is created with a MsgBox statement in the application's code. The generalized form of the MsgBox code statement consists of three parts: MsgBox *text, type, title,* which are described in Table 3-9.

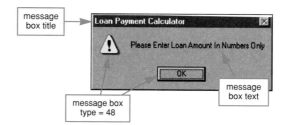

FIGURE 3-79

▶ **TABLE 3-9 MESSAGE BOX CODE STATEMENT ARGUMENTS**

ARGUMENT	DESCRIPTION
text	The text that appears in the body of the message box. It is enclosed in quotes.
type	A number that represents the type of button displayed, the icon displayed, and whether or not the dialog box is modal.
title	The text that appears in the title bar of the dialog box. It is enclosed in quotes.

For a detailed description of how to use different values of *type* for various combinations of buttons, icons, and modality, use Visual Basic online Help to search for help on the MsgBox topic.

After these actions are completed, you want to place the cursor back in the txtAmount control for a new loan amount to be entered. You could select the textAmount control during run time by clicking it, which would place the cursor in the text box. However, you can cause this event to occur through code using the **SetFocus statement**. The syntax of the statement is:

> *controlname*.SetFocus

The single argument *controlname* is the name of the control that you want to select.

The code statements that make up the cmdCalculate_Click subroutine are shown in Figure 3-80.

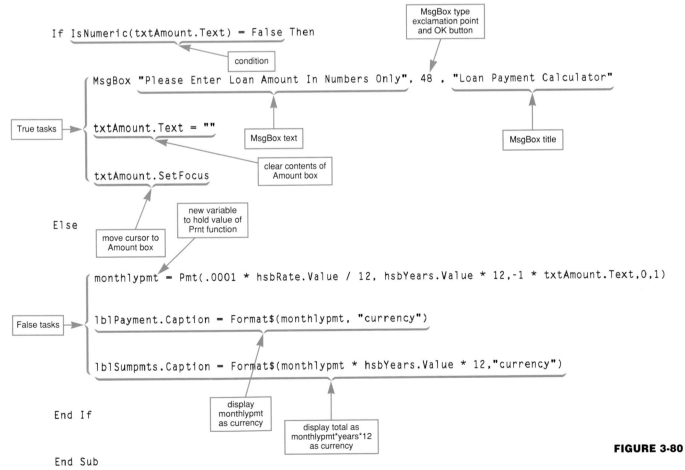

FIGURE 3-80

Perform the following steps to write the cmdCalculate_Click subroutine.

TO WRITE THE CMDCALCULATE_CLICK SUBROUTINE

Step 1: Select cmdCalculate from the Object drop-down list in the Code window.
Step 2: Enter the following statements in the Code window:

```
If IsNumeric(txtAmount.Text) = False Then
    MsgBox "Please Enter Loan Amount In Numbers Only", 48,"Loan Payment Calculator"
    txtAmount.Text = ""
    txtAmount.SetFocus
Else
    monthlypmt = Pmt(0.0001 * hsbRate.Value / 12, hsbYears.Value * 12,-1 *
txtAmount.Text,0,1)
    lblPayment.Caption = Format$(monthlypmt,"currency")
    lblSumpmts.Caption = Format$(monthlypmt * hsbYears.Value *12, "currency")
End If
```

The Code window should appear as shown in Figure 3-81.

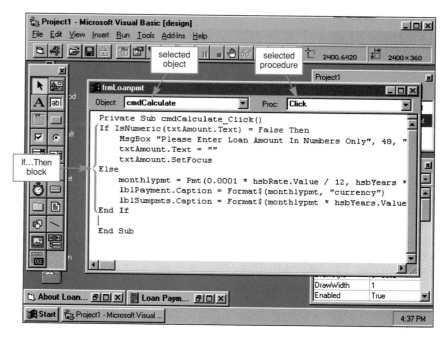

FIGURE 3-81

Line 6 in Step 2 (above) creates a variable named monthlypmt to hold the value returned by the Pmt function. This step makes the statement in Line 7 easier to read, where that value (monthlypmt), formatted as currency, is assigned to the Caption property of the lblPayment control. In Line 8, the sum of payments is calculated as the monthly payment times the number of years times 12 months in a year, and it also is formatted as currency.

The frmLoanpmt cmdClear_Click Subroutine

During run time, you choose the Clear button (cmdClear) to remove any currently displayed inputs or outputs from the form. These include the loan amount (txtAmount.Text), length of loan period (lblYears.Caption), APR (lblRate.Caption), monthly payment (lblPayment.Caption), and sum of payments (lblSumpmts. Caption). You also want the scroll bars (hsbYears and hsbRate) to return to their farthest left positions. Each of these actions will be accomplished by a statement that changes the value of the appropriate property of each control.

You do not need to directly change the number of years (the caption of lblYears) or the APR (the caption of lblRate). A code statement that changes the Value property of the scroll bar controls activates their Change event, which sets the captions of those labels.

After these actions are completed, you want the cursor to move back to the Loan Amount box (txtAmount control) for a new amount to be entered. This procedure will be accomplished using the SetFocus method described on page VB169. Perform the following steps to write the subroutine.

TO WRITE THE CMDCLEAR SUBROUTINE

Step 1: Select cmdClear from the Object drop-down list in the Code window.

Step 2: Enter the following statements in the Code window:

```
txtAmount.Text = ""
hsbYears.Value = 1
hsbRate.Value = 1
lblPayment.Caption = ""
lblSumpmts.Caption = ""
txtAmount.SetFocus
```

The Code window appears as shown in Figure 3-82.

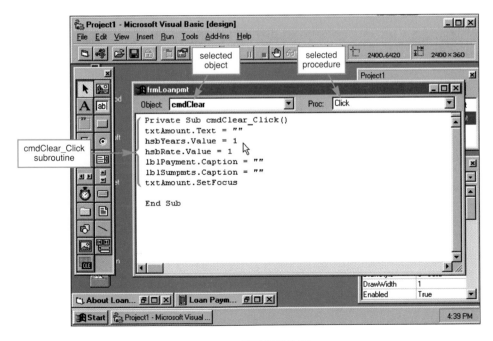

FIGURE 3-82

The frmLoanpmt cmdAbout_Click Event

This event is triggered at run time when you click the About... command button. This event is used to display the frmLoanabt form. In Windows applications, a dialog box usually appears on top of all other open windows on the desktop, and you cannot work with any other window until the dialog box is closed. A form or window with these characteristics is called a **modal** form. Forms without these properties are called **modeless**.

You make forms visible on the desktop and control their modality at run time with the **Form.Show code statement**. The statement has these parts (as described in Table 3-10):

form.SHOW *style*

▶ **TABLE 3-10 ARGUMENTS OF SHOW STATEMENT**

ARGUMENT	DESCRIPTION
form	Name of form to display
style	Integer value that determines if the form is modal or modeless. If style is 0, the form is modeless; if style is 1, then form is modal; if a value for style is not included, the form is modeless.

In addition to being modal, you want the About... dialog box to appear in the center of the desktop. This project uses the method presented earlier to center the About... dialog box when it appears during run time. Perform the following steps to write the cmdAbout_Click subroutine.

TO WRITE THE CMDABOUT_CLICK SUBROUTINE

Step 1: Select the cmdAbout control from the Object drop-down list in the frmLoanpmt Code window.
Step 2: Enter the following statements in the Code window:
```
frmLoanabt.Top = (Screen.Height - frmLoanabt.Height) / 2
frmLoanabt.Left = (Screen.Width - frmLoanabt.Width) / 2
frmLoanabt.Show 1
```

The Code window appears as shown in Figure 3-83.

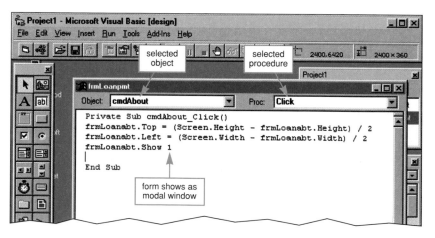

FIGURE 3-83

The frmLoanabt Command1_Click Subroutine

This event is triggered when you click the command button labeled OK. The action of this event removes the About... dialog box from the desktop. You remove forms from the desktop during run time by using the **Unload code statement**. Perform the following steps to minimize the frmLoanpmt Code window, to open the frmLoanabt Code window, and to write the subroutine.

TO WRITE THE COMMAND1_CLICK SUBROUTINE

Step 1: Click the Close button on the frmLoanpmt Code window.
Step 2: Select the frmLoanabt form by clicking its name in the Project window. Choose the View Code button.
Step 3: Select the Command1 control from the Object drop-down list in the Code window.
Step 4: Enter the following statement in the Code window:
```
Unload frmLoanabt
```

The Code window appears as shown in Figure 3-84.

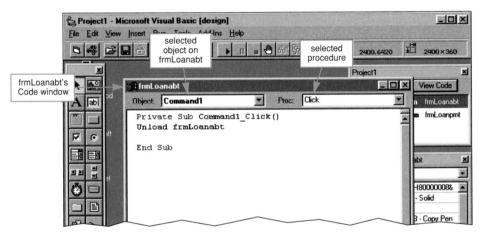

FIGURE 3-84

Saving the Project

The Loan Payment Calculator project is complete. When you save a form, the subroutines you wrote for that form are saved as part of that form's .frm file. The forms were saved earlier, before the code had been written. Before running the project, the form files should be re-saved and the project should be saved as a .vbp file.

The Visual Basic 4 Working Model limits projects to a total of two forms and modules. If you attempt to add an additional form to the Loan Payment Calculator application, an error dialog window will appear. This dialog window also will appear in the Working Model if you attempt to open a project that contains more than two forms and modules. In order to save the Loan Payment Calculator project as just two forms, you must first remove an additional module that is not required for this project. Perform the steps on the next page to save the project.

TO SAVE THE PROJECT

Step 1: Close the Loanabt Code window. Click Tools on the menu bar.

Step 2: Click References... on the Tools menu. The References dialog box appears (Figure 3-85).

Step 3: Click the Standard OLE Types check box to remove the check mark. Click the OK button.

Step 4: Click the Save Project tool on the toolbar.

Step 5: Type LOAN in the File name box and click the Save button.

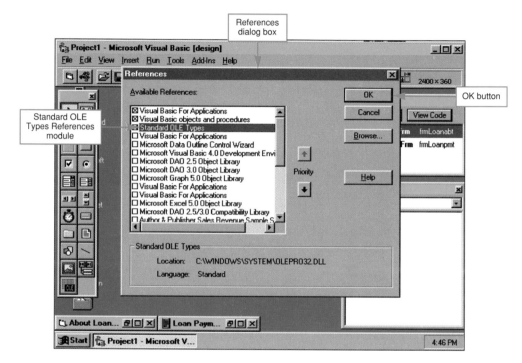

FIGURE 3-85

In the preceding steps, the Standard OLE Types References module was removed from the project. The Loan Payment Calculator application then could be saved with just two forms, allowing the project to be re-opened later without an error dialog window appearing.

▶ WORKING WITH THE DEBUG WINDOW

N o matter how carefully you build a project, applications often do not work as planned and give erroneous results because of errors in the code, called **bugs**. The process of isolating and correcting these errors is called **debugging**. When you run an application, Visual Basic opens a special window, called the **Debug window**, that can be used to help debug your application.

You can temporarily halt the execution of your application by clicking the Break button on the toolbar, and then resume execution by clicking the Continue button. During the period of time when execution is stopped, the application is said to be in **break mode**.

Debugging features available through Visual Basic include:

1. viewing the values of variables and properties (setting and viewing watch expressions)

2. halting execution at a particular point (setting a breakpoint)
3. executing your code one line at a time (stepping through the code)
4. execute code immediately (the immediate pane)

Setting and Viewing Watch Expressions

In break mode, you can isolate and view the values of particular variables and properties as a way of checking for errors. You specify which variables and properties you want to monitor by setting **watch expressions**. You can set a watch expression in advance of running the application and then cause the application to break when that expression's value changes. You can also check the value of any variable or property in break mode by setting an **immediate watch**. You can specify a particular point at which you want to break execution by setting a breakpoint. Perform the following steps to set a breakpoint and then perform an immediate watch during break mode.

TO SET A BREAKPOINT AND IMMEDIATE WATCH ▼

STEP 1 ▶

Click frmLoanpmt in the Project window. Click the View Code button in the Project window. Select cmdCalculate from the Object drop-down list in the Code window. Position the cursor at the beginning of the eighth line of code and click.

The cursor displays at the beginning of the selected code line in the cmdCalculate_Click procedure in the frmLoanpmt Code window (Figure 3-86).

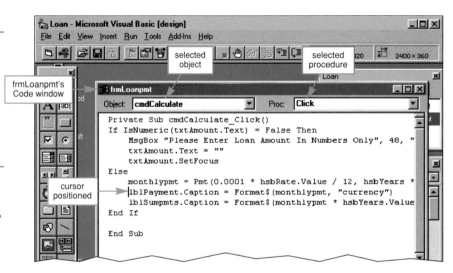

FIGURE 3-86

STEP 2 ▶

Click the Toggle Breakpoint button on the toolbar.

The code statement is highlighted in red (Figure 3-87).

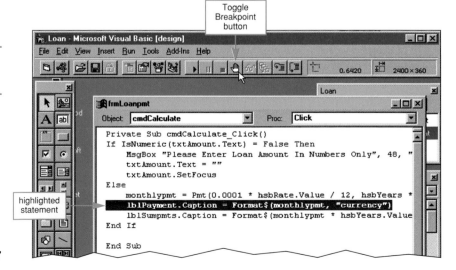

FIGURE 3-87

STEP 3 ▶

Click Start. Enter 12000 for the loan amount, 5 for the number of years, and 6.5 as the APR. Click the Calculate button.

The program executes up to the highlighted code statement and then enters break mode. The Code window displays and the next code line to be executed has a box around it (Figure 3-88).

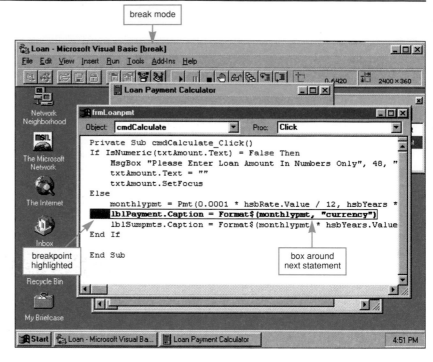

FIGURE 3-88

STEP 4 ▶

Use the mouse to highlight monthlypmt as shown in Figure 3-89 and point to the Instant Watch button on the toolbar.

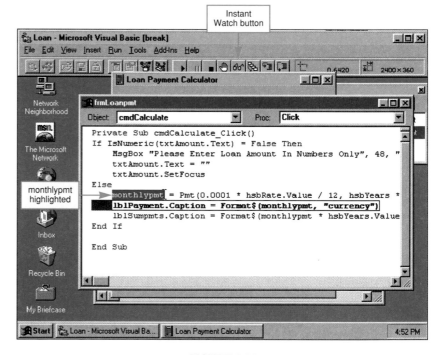

FIGURE 3-89

STEP 5 ▶

Click the Instant Watch button.

The Instant Watch dialog window displays the current value of the monthlypmt variable (Figure 3-90).

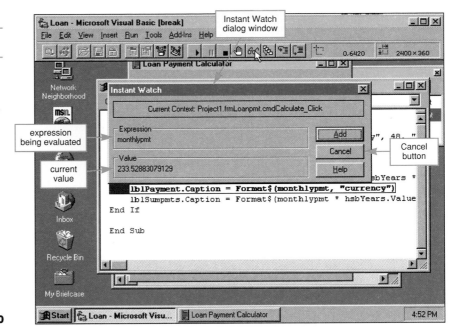

FIGURE 3-90

STEP 6 ▶

Click the Cancel button. Click the Continue button on the toolbar.

The application resumes execution and displays as shown in Figure 3-91.

STEP 7 ▶

Click the End button to stop the application.

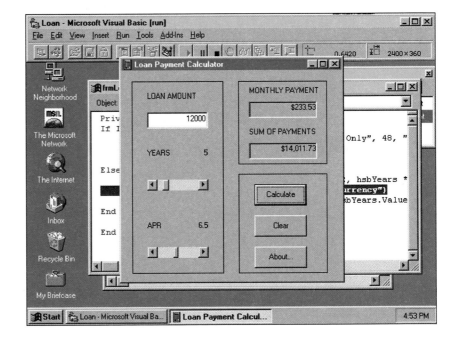

FIGURE 3-91

Setting a Watch Expression and Stepping Through Code

You also can set watch expressions in advance of running the application, and also can step through code statements one at a time as additional ways to help isolate errors.

TO SET A WATCH EXPRESSION AND STEP THROUGH CODE ▼

STEP 1 ▶

Position the cursor and click the code statement highlighted in red. Click the Toggle Breakpoint button on the toolbar. Position the cursor and click in front of the IF statement. Click the Toggle Breakpoint button.

The breakpoint is changed to the If statement now highlighted in red (Figure 3-92).

FIGURE 3-92

STEP 2 ▶

Highlight IsNumeric(txtAmount.Text). Click Tools on the menu bar. Click Add Watch on the Tools menu.

The Add Watch dialog window opens (Figure 3-93).

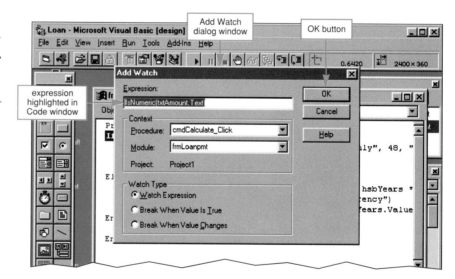

FIGURE 3-93

STEP 3 ▶

Click OK. Click Start. Enter 12000 for the loan amount, 5 for the number of years, and 6.5 as the APR. Click the Calculate button.

Execution halts at the new breakpoint (Figure 3-94).

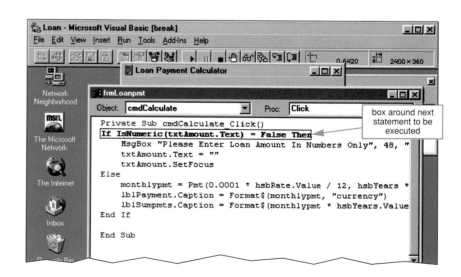

FIGURE 3-94

STEP 4 ▶

Click the Debug window.

The current value of the IsNumeric function is displayed (Figure 3-95).

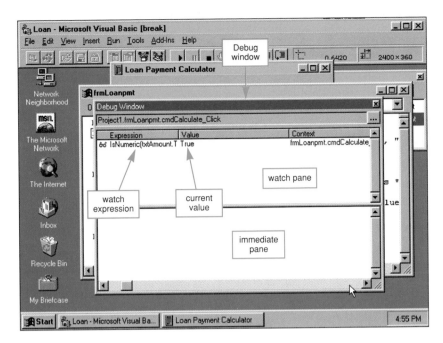

FIGURE 3-95

STEP 5 ▶

Click the Code window. Click the Step Into button on the toolbar.

The previously boxed line of code is executed (testing IsNumeric) and the next line of code to be executed is boxed (Figure 3-96).

STEP 6 ▶

Click the Step Into button six more times to see line by line execution. Click the End button on the toolbar.

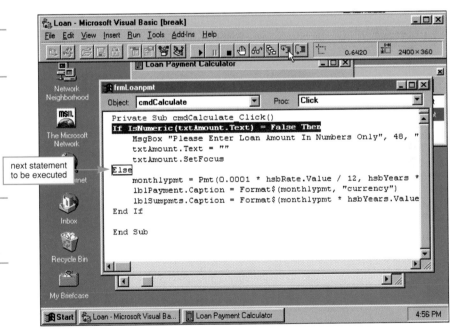

FIGURE 3-96

In the preceding steps, you set a watch expression, a breakpoint, and then stepped through code. In the step by step execution, the code statements for the input error message box were skipped because the preceding IsNumeric condition was True. A watch expression can be removed by highlighting it in the Debug window and pressing the DELETE key.

Using the Immediate Pane

The immediate pane of the Debug window allows you to test out code statements without changing any of your procedures. You can cut and paste code to and from the immediate pane.

TO USE THE IMMEDIATE PANE

STEP 1 ▶

Click Start. Enter 12000 for the loan amount, 5 for the number of years, and 6.5 as the APR. Click the Calculate button. Click the Debug window. Click the lower pane of the Debug window and type `Print txtAmount.Text` as the entry.

The Debug window appears as shown in Figure 3-97.

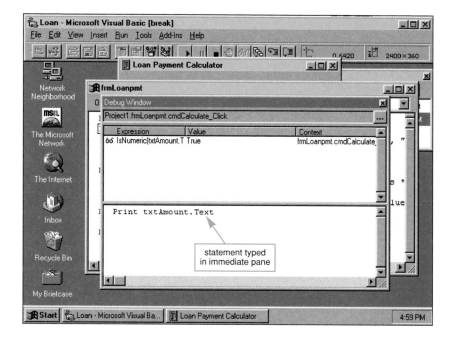

FIGURE 3-97

STEP 2 ▶

Press the ENTER key.

The result of executing the code statement is displayed in the immediate pane (Figure 2-98).

STEP 3 ▶

Click the End button on the toolbar.

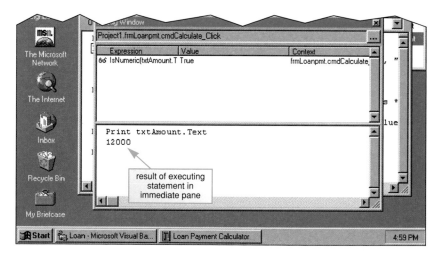

FIGURE 3-98

In the immediate pane, you can type or paste a line of code and press ENTER to run it. However, you can execute only one line of code at a time.

▶ PROJECT SUMMARY

Project 3 extended the basics of building an application that were presented in Projects 1 and 2. You built an application by designing the interface and then writing code. The application in this project consisted of multiple forms and dialog boxes. You learned more about the form control's properties, WindowState, and modality. You also learned how to add an icon to a form.

Several new properties of familiar controls were presented. You also learned about image, line, and scroll bar controls. At the end of the project, you learned how to use Visual Basic's Debug window to isolate and correct errors in code.

▶ KEY TERMS AND INDEX

About... dialog box *(VB122)*
Alignment property *(VB153)*
arguments *(VB166)*
BorderStyle property
    (VB131, VB138)
BorderWidth property *(VB138)*
break mode *(VB174)*
breakpoint *(VB175)*
bugs *(VB174)*
Change event *(VB152, VB165)*
debugging *(VB174)*
Debug window *(VB174)*
dialog box *(VB120)*
Font properties *(VB134)*
FontBold property *(VB134)*
FontItalic property *(VB134)*
FontName property *(VB134)*
FontSize property *(VB134)*

Form.Show code statement
    (VB172)
.FRX *(VB135)*
horizontal scroll bar *(VB151)*
Icon property *(VB159)*
If... Then block *(VB168)*
inputs *(VB143)*
image control *(VB127)*
immediate watch *(VB175)*
IsNumeric function *(VB167)*
LargeChange property *(VB158)*
Left property *(VB125)*
line control *(VB128)*
Max property *(VB158)*
MaxButton property *(VB130)*
Min property *(VB158)*
MinButton property *(VB130)*
modal *(VB172)*

modeless *(VB172)*
MsgBox statement *(VB168)*
outputs *(VB143)*
Picture property *(VB135)*
Pmt function *(VB166)*
scroll bars *(VB151)*
shape controls *(VB143)*
SetFocus statement *(VB169)*
sizable form *(VB131)*
SmallChange property *(VB158)*
Startup Form *(VB162)*
Top property *(VB125)*
Unload code statement *(VB173)*
Value property *(VB158)*
vertical scroll bar *(VB151)*
watch expressions *(VB175)*
WindowState *(VB130)*

Q U I C K   R E F E R E N C E

In Visual Basic you can accomplish a task in a number of ways. The following table provides a quick reference to each of the major tasks presented for the first time in the project with some of the available options. The commands listed in the Menu column can be executed using either the keyboard or mouse.

Task	Mouse	Menu	Keyboard Shortcuts
Add an Additional Form to a Project	Click the New Form button on the toolbar	From File menu, choose New Form	
Copy a Selected Control to the Clipboard		From Edit menu, choose Copy	Press CTRL+C
Open the Project Options Dialog Box		From Tools menu, choose Options	
Paste a Control from the Clipboard onto a Selected Form		From Edit menu, choose Paste	Press CTRL+V

STUDENT ASSIGNMENT 1
True/False

Instructions: Circle T if the statement is true or F if the statement is false.

T   F   1. Dialog boxes rarely are used in Windows applications.
T   F   2. A form's width can be changed only by dragging its borders.
T   F   3. Top and Left properties determine the position of the upper left corner of the form on the desktop.
T   F   4. A shape control can be displayed as a circle.
T   F   5. Label controls cannot have borders.
T   F   6. The AutoSize property has three values.
T   F   7. A label control's borders can be resized at run time by dragging them.
T   F   8. The default value of the Alignment property is 1 - Center.
T   F   9. Clicking a scroll arrow changes the value of the scroll bar by an amount equal to the value of the SmallChange property.
T   F   10. Dragging the scroll box of a scroll bar control causes the scroll bar's Change event to occur.
T   F   11. The WindowState property of a form determines whether the form has a title bar.
T   F   12. All windows must have Minimum and Maximum buttons.
T   F   13. When a form's BorderStyle is set to None, the form does not have a title bar.
T   F   14. A minimized window appears as a button on the taskbar.
T   F   15. A form's Icon property has values of True or False.
T   F   16. IconWorks is a program for creating and editing .ICO files.
T   F   17. A modal dialog box does not have a Control-menu box.
T   F   18. A font cannot be displayed as both bold and italics at the same time.
T   F   19. An image control can be used as a container for graphical images.
T   F   20. The Load Icon dialog box is opened by clicking the Icon button on the toolbar.

STUDENT ASSIGNMENT 2
Multiple Choice

Instructions: Circle the correct response.

1. The _____ property of the line control determines its appearance (solid, dotted, etc).
   a. BorderWidth
   b. LineStyle
   c. BorderStyle
   d. FrameStyle
2. The _____ form is the first form loaded into the computer's memory and displayed on the desktop.
   a. default
   b. Form1
   c. Startup
   d. .FRM
3. Each _____ in an application has its own Code window.
   a. event
   b. control
   c. form
   d. procedure

4. Errors in code are called _____.
   a. glitches
   b. watches
   c. work-arounds
   d. bugs
5. Execution is temporarity halted in_____.
   a. design mode
   b. run mode
   c. break mode
   d. pause mode
6. _____ is a property of scroll bar controls.
   a. Scroll box
   b. Scroll arrow
   c. LargeChange
   d. ScrollChange
7. A shape control can be displayed as a(n) _____.
   a. oval
   b. triangle
   c. both a and b
   d. neither a nor b
8. A scroll bar's Change event occurs when a user _____.
   a. clicks a scroll arrow
   b. drags the scroll box
   c. both a and b
   d. neither a nor b
9. _____ is a Visual Basic financial function.
   a. Ipv
   b. Npr
   c. Pmt
   d. None of these
10. The default value of a label control's BorderStyle property is_____.
    a. 0 - None
    b. True
    c. False
    d. 1 - Fixed Single

STUDENT ASSIGNMENT 3
Understanding the Procedure for Copying Controls

Instructions: Fill in the step numbers below to correctly order the process of making two copies of a control and locating them on a form.

Step _____: Type N for No.

Step _____: Press CTRL+V.

Step _____: Press CTRL+V.

Step _____: Drag the copy of the control to its location.

Step _____: Click the control to be copied.

Step _____: Type N for No.

Step _____: Drag the copy of the control to its location.

Step _____: Press CTRL+C.

STUDENT ASSIGNMENT 4
Understanding Controls and Properties

Instructions: The following table lists several controls and several properties. Place an "X" in the space provided if the control has that property.

PROPERTY	CONTROLS				
	Label	Form	Text Box	Image	Scroll Bar
AutoSize	[ ]	[ ]	[ ]	[ ]	[ ]
BorderStyle	[ ]	[ ]	[ ]	[ ]	[ ]
LargeChange	[ ]	[ ]	[ ]	[ ]	[ ]
Alignment	[ ]	[ ]	[ ]	[ ]	[ ]
MaxButton	[ ]	[ ]	[ ]	[ ]	[ ]
Max	[ ]	[ ]	[ ]	[ ]	[ ]
MinButton	[ ]	[ ]	[ ]	[ ]	[ ]
Min	[ ]	[ ]	[ ]	[ ]	[ ]
SmallChange	[ ]	[ ]	[ ]	[ ]	[ ]
Caption	[ ]	[ ]	[ ]	[ ]	[ ]
Text	[ ]	[ ]	[ ]	[ ]	[ ]
Name	[ ]	[ ]	[ ]	[ ]	[ ]
Value	[ ]	[ ]	[ ]	[ ]	[ ]
Icon	[ ]	[ ]	[ ]	[ ]	[ ]

STUDENT ASSIGNMENT 5
Understanding Code Statements

Instructions: Enter the correct answers.

1. Write a code statement that will center a form named Form1 vertically on the desktop.

Statement: _____

2. Write a code statement that will center a form named Form2 horizontally on the desktop.

Statement: _____

3. Write a code statement that will display a message box titled *My Application*. The message box should display an exclamation point icon and an OK button. The text should read *Important Message*.

Statement: _____

4. Write a code statement that will cause a form named Form3 to appear on the desktop in a modal state.

Statement: _____

5. Write a code statement that will cause a form named Form4 to be removed from the desktop.

Statement: _____

6. Write a code statement that will cause a form named Form5 to be minimized on the desktop.

Statement: _____

STUDENT ASSIGNMENT 6
Understanding Commands in Menus

Instructions: Write the appropriate command name to accomplish each task and the menu in which each command is located.

TASK	COMMAND NAME	MENU NAME
Add a new form to a project	[ ]	[ ]
Begin execution of an application	[ ]	[ ]
Open the dialog box used to specify the Startup Form	[ ]	[ ]
Copy a control or code statements to the Clipboard	[ ]	[ ]
Stop execution of an application	[ ]	[ ]
Save a form to a file	[ ]	[ ]
Copy a control or code statements from the Clipboard	[ ]	[ ]
Add a watch expression	[ ]	[ ]
Close Visual Basic	[ ]	[ ]

C O M P U T E R   L A B O R A T O R Y   E X E R C I S E S

COMPUTER LABORATORY EXERCISE 1
Using Scroll Bar Controls

Instructions: Start Visual Basic. Open the project CLE3-1 from the VB4 folder on the Student Diskette that accompanies this book. Complete the following tasks:

1. Choose the View Form button in the Project window.
2. Add a vertical scroll bar to the form, as shown in Figure CLE3-1 on the next page.
3. Add a horizontal scroll bar to the form, as shown in Figure CLE3-1.

(continued)

COMPUTER LABORATORY EXERCISE 1 (continued)

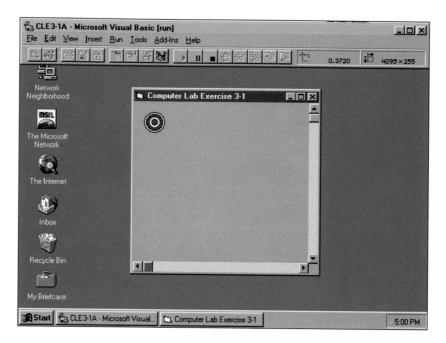

FIGURE CLE3-1

4. Set the following ScrollBars property values:

PROPERTY	CONTROL	
	HSCROLL1	VSCROLL1
Min	480	480
Max	3600	3300
LargeChange	200	200
SmallChange	50	50
Value	480	480

5. Choose the View Code button in the Project window.
6. Choose the HScroll1 control from the Object drop-down list in the Code window.
7. Type `Image1.Width = HScroll1.Value` as the code statement.
8. Choose the VScroll1 control from the Object drop-down list in the Code window.
9. Type `Image1.Height = VScroll1.Value` as the code statement.
10. Save the form using the filename CLE3-1A.FRM, and save the project using the filename CLE3-1A.VBP.
11. Run the application. Stretch the image's size by clicking the scroll arrows, dragging the scroll boxes, and clicking the spaces between the scroll boxes and the scroll arrows. Double-click the form's Control-menu box to stop the application.
12. Check with your instructor for directions on turning in the exercise.

COMPUTER LABORATORY EXERCISE 2
The WindowState of Forms

Instructions: Start Visual Basic. Open the project CLE3-2 from the VB4 folder on the Student Diskette that accompanies this book. Perform the following steps:

1. Add a second form to the project.
2. Size and position the second form so that it fits next the form shown in Figure CLE3-2.
3. Add appropriate code statements to the Click events of the three command buttons to:
   a) show the second form in normal WidowState
   b) show the second form as a modal form
   c) unload the second form
4. Set the BorderStyle of both forms to 1 - Fixed Single.
5. Add a command button to the second form with a Click event that will unload that form.
6. Save the forms as CLE3-2A.FRM and CLE3-2B.FRM.
7. Save the project as CLE3-2A.VBP.
8. Run the application. Click all command buttons in different orders.
9. To end the application, click the End button on the toolbar.
10. Check with your instructor for directions on turning in the exercise.

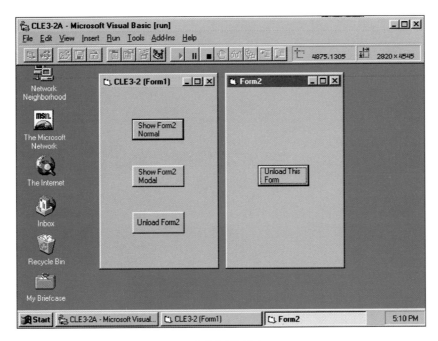

FIGURE CLE3-2

COMPUTER LABORATORY EXERCISE 3
The Alignment Property

Instructions: Start Visual Basic. Open the project CLE3-3 from the VB4 folder on the Student Diskette that accompanies this book. Perform the following steps:

1. Choose the View Form button in the Project window.
2. Draw three option buttons within the frame labeled Alignment, and then set their Caption properties as shown in Figure CLE3-3.

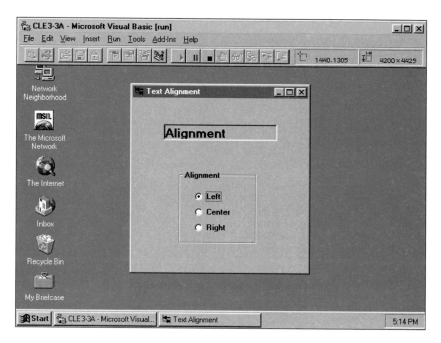

FIGURE CLE3-3

3. Use the Code window to write the following code statements for the Click event for each of the option buttons:

SUBROUTINE	CODE STATEMENT
Option1_Click	Label1.Alignment = 0
Option2_Click	Label1.Alignment = 2
Option3_Click	Label1.Alignment = 1

4. Save the form as CLE3-3A.FRM, and then save the project as CLE3-3A.VBP.
5. Run the application.
6. Click the different option buttons. Minimize the window. Restore the window.
7. End the Alignment application by clicking its Close button.
8. Check with your instructor for directions on turning in the exercise.

COMPUTER LABORATORY ASSIGNMENT 1
Tailor's Calculations

Purpose: To build an application that performs mathematical computations and uses the IsNumeric function and If...Then block.

Problem: A tailor would like to have an application that calculates the average neck size, hat size, and shoe size for male customers, given the customer's weight and waistline. The interface should resemble the one shown in Figure CLA3-1. Text boxes should be used for the inputs, and labels should be used for the outputs. The calculations are as follows:

Neck Size = 3 * (Weight / Waistline)
Hat Size = (3 * Weight) / (2.125 * Waistline)
Shoe Size = 50 * (Waistline / Weight)

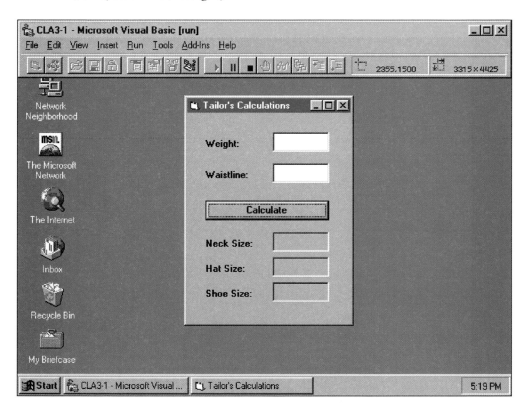

FIGURE CLA3-1

Instructions: Perform the following tasks:

1. Start Visual Basic, or open a new project if Visual Basic is already running.
2. Size and locate the form, as shown in Figure CLA3-1.
3. Add two text boxes, eight labels, and one command button, as shown in Figure CLA3-1.
4. Set the appropriate captions for the form, labels, and command button.
5. Set the text boxes' text values to be blank.
6. Set the BorderStyle of the three labels used for displaying the outputs so that the labels have borders.

(continued)

COMPUTER LABORATORY ASSIGNMENT 1 (continued)

7. Write the code for the command button_Click event. A partial structure for the code is shown below:

```
If IsNumeric(Text1.Text) = False OR IsNumeric(Text2.Text) = False Then
```
(add statements here to clear the text boxes)

```
Else
```
(add statements here to perform the calculations and to display the results in the appropriate labels)

```
End If
```

8. Save the form as CLA3-1.FRM. Save the project as CLA3-1.VBP.
9. Run the application to test it.
10. Check with your instructor for directions on turning in the assignment.

COMPUTER LABORATORY ASSIGNMENT 2
Future Value Calculation

Purpose: To build an application that uses Visual Basic's library of financial functions and the Format$ function.

Problem: Build an application with an interface similar to the one shown in Figure CLA3-2. The application uses the Future Value (FV) function to compute the future value of a series of payments when the interest is compounded on a quarterly basis.

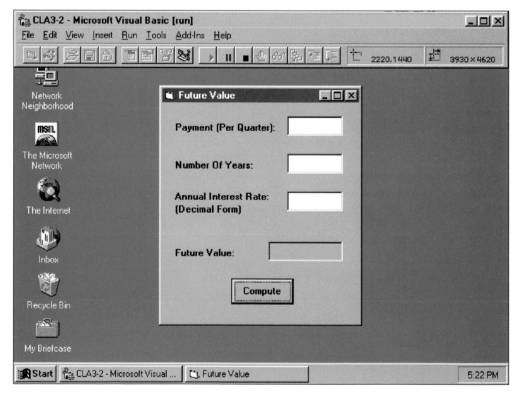

FIGURE CLA3-2

Instructions: Perform the following tasks:

1. Start Visual Basic, or open a new project if Visual Basic is already running.
2. Size and position the form, as shown in Figure CLA3-2.
3. Add the controls shown in Figure CLA3-2.
4. Choose Search For Help On from the Help menu.
5. Type Financial Functions as the entry. Choose the Display button. Click FV Future Value.
6. Scroll through the Help file to see the correct syntax for the FV function. Close the Help window.
7. Write the code for the command button Click event. Use the Format$ function for the output displayed as the future value. ***Note:*** Quarterly compounding means the number of periods is 4 times the number of years, and the rate per period is the annual rate divided by 4.
8. Save the form as CLA3-2.FRM. Save the project as CLA3-2.VBP.
9. Run the application. Click the form's Close button to stop the application.
10. Check with your instructor for directions on turning in the assignment.

COMPUTER LABORATORY ASSIGNMENT 3
An About... Dialog Box

Purpose: To build an application that incorporates a second form.

Problem: Add an About... dialog box similar to the one developed in Project 3 to either Computer Laboratory Assignment 3-1 or Computer Laboratory Assignment 3-2. (Check with your instructor.) You will need to add a command button to the original form and to use the Form.Show and Unload code statements to open and close the About... dialog box.

Instructions: Follow the steps listed below to add an About... dialog box as a second form to a previously completed application.

1. Start Visual Basic if it is not currently running.
2. Open the project that you will modify.
3. Add a command button with the caption About... to the application's form.
4. Choose the New Form command from the File menu.
5. Design the new form to resemble the About... form created in Project 3 (Figure 3-4 on page VB122).
6. Write the appropriate Form.Show code statement for the About... button Click event.
7. Write the appropriate code statement for the About... form's OK button Click event.
8. Resave the main form as CLA3-3A.FRM. Save the About... form as CLA3-3B.FRM. Save the project as CLA3-3.VBP.
9. Check with your instructor for directions on turning in the assignment.

COMPUTER LABORATORY ASSIGNMENT 4
Ideal Age of a Spouse

Purpose: To build an application that incorporates an If...Then statement, IsNumeric function, mathematical calculations, and message box.

Problem: Plato said that the ideal age of a man's wife is one-half the man's age, plus seven years. If this is true, then the ideal age of a woman's husband is two times the woman's age, minus fourteen years. Create an application that will calculate the ideal age of a person's spouse, using Plato's formula.

Instructions: Use your creativity to build an application that calculates the ideal spouse's age as described above. The application must include some method for the user to indicate his or her gender, because the choice of formulas for the spouse's age depends on this fact. Include an IsNumeric function to test the value of age entered by the user. If the input is not numeric, the application should display a message box similar to the one in Project 3 (page VB122) and then clear the input for the user to start over. Include a command button that "clears" the application so that additional calculations can be completed without having to restart the application.

Save the form as CLA3-4.FRM. Save the project as CLA3-4.VBP. Check with your instructor for directions on turning in the assignment.

You Are

male ☐ Female ☐

Your Age is [   ]   [Enter]

Your Ideal Spouse's Age [   ]

USING COLOR, MENUS, THE DATA CONTROL, AND GENERAL PROCEDURES

OBJECTIVES You will have mastered the material in this project when you can:

- ▸ Build applications that contain menus, sub-menus, and pop-up menus
- ▸ Add access keys, separator bars, and check marks to menus
- ▸ Build applications that use the data control
- ▸ Bind data-aware controls to a data control

- ▸ Add color to applications
- ▸ Create control arrays
- ▸ Write code to select records in a database
- ▸ Use the For...Next statement in subroutines
- ▸ Create General procedures
- ▸ Use the Not operator in code statements

▶ INTRODUCTION

O ne of the most powerful features of Visual Basic is the ability to create sophisticated database applications with minimal programming. A **database** is a collection of related facts organized in a systematic manner. A telephone book is an example of a database that contains the names, addresses, and phone numbers of persons and businesses in a community. Many database management products, such as Microsoft Access, are available for personal computers and they allow you to store, maintain, and retrieve data quickly and efficiently.

Visual Basic can be used to build applications that display, edit, and update information from databases created by the following database management products: Microsoft Access, Btrieve, dBase, FoxPro, and Paradox. Project 4 provides an introductory exposure to accessing a database by building an application that displays information from a World Geography database created with Microsoft Access. The World Geography database is included on the Student Diskette that accompanies this text. This project describes only how to display information in a database. You should be aware that Visual Basic can be used to create applications that also query, add, change, or delete information in a database.

Many of the application-building activities in Projects 1 through 3 involved choosing commands from drop-down menus selected from the Visual Basic menu bar. This structure of menus and commands is common in many types of Windows applications. The application built in this project includes a menu bar and drop-down menus.

▶ PROJECT FOUR – GEOGRAPHY DATABASE VIEWER

The application that will be built in this project is shown as it appears on the desktop during run time in Figure 4-1. This application accesses an existing database of information about different countries and displays that information one country at a time. The name of the database is World.

Each characteristic or attribute of a country, such as its name or capital city, is represented in a database by a **field**. In addition to fields that contain text and numbers, the World database has a field that contains a graphical image of each country's flag. Information about a specific country (the values for that country contained in a group of fields) is represented in a database by a single **record**. A group of records within a database that have the same fields is called a **table**. Although databases can contain more than one table, the World database contains only one table, named Countries.

The information contained in the Countries table of the World database is shown in Table 4-1, where each column represents a field, and each row represents a record.

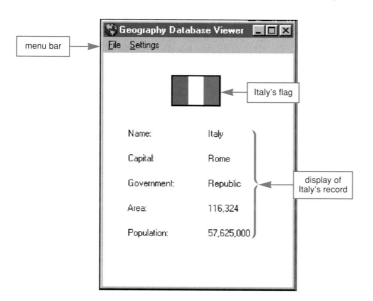

FIGURE 4-1

▶ TABLE 4-1 COUNTRIES TABLE OF THE WORLD DATABASE

NAME	CAPITAL	GOVERNMENT	AREA	POPULATION	FLAG
United States	Washington DC	Federal Republic	3,679,245	250,150,000	Image
Italy	Rome	Republic	116,324	57,625,000	Image
France	Paris	Republic	211,208	52,210,000	Image
Denmark	Copenhagen	Const. Monarchy	2,045	650,000	Image
Turkey	Ankara	Republic	300,948	54,075,000	Image
Mexico	Mexico City	Federal Republic	756,066	85,090,000	Image
Brazil	Brasilia	Federal Republic	3,286,488	148,980,000	Image
Japan	Tokyo	Monarchy	145,870	123,350,000	Image
Ireland	Dublin	Republic	169,235	17,745,000	Image

Unlike the applications built in previous projects, the Geography Database Viewer application does not have any command button, option button, or check box controls for you to initiate events or to choose options during run time (Figure 4-1). The reason for this omission is that all run-time interaction with the application occurs by using menus.

You can view the information in Table 4-1 during run time by moving forward or backward one record (country) at a time or by moving directly to the first record or to the last record. These actions are initiated by choosing the Next, Previous, First, and Last commands in the Select menu (Figure 4-2). The Select menu is a **pop-up menu**, which appears whenever the user right-clicks anywhere on the form during run time. Clicking Color on the Settings menu displays a submenu (Figure 4-3), from which the user can choose one of three background colors for the application. The currently selected color is indicated by a check mark on the menu.

Clicking View on the Settings menu displays a submenu from which the user can choose to display all information about the country or just the flag and name of the country. Because only one choice should be available at a time, the currently displayed choice is disabled or "grayed out" on the menu (Figure 4-4).

The application can be resized, minimized or maximized by the user at run time. The application is closed by clicking the Close button or by clicking Exit on the File menu (Figure 4-5).

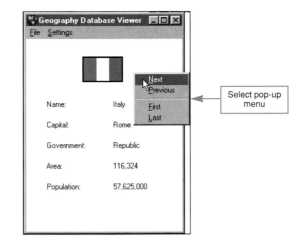

FIGURE 4-2

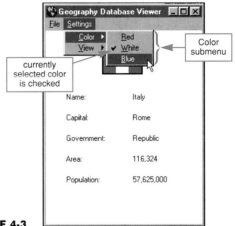

FIGURE 4-3

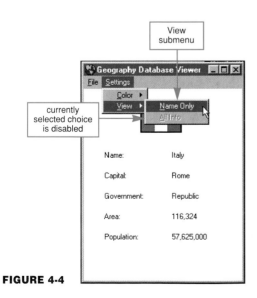

FIGURE 4-4

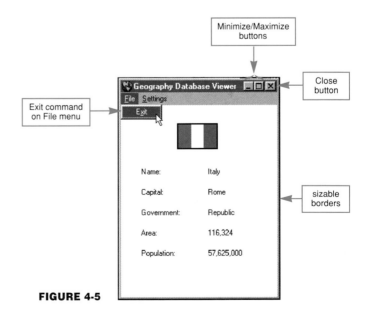

FIGURE 4-5

The Geography Database Viewer application is created in this project by following the same three-step approach used in previous projects:

▸ create the interface
▸ set properties
▸ write code

Getting Started

The database file that is used in this project is contained in the VB4 folder on the Student Diskette that accompanies this book. The file is named WORLD.MDB. Before building the Geography Database Viewer application, this file should be copied to another diskette that will be used later to save the completed application.

If you have any questions about how or where to copy this file, you should see your instructor prior to building the application.

Starting Visual Basic

Begin this project by starting Visual Basic or by beginning a new project if Visual Basic is already running. If necessary, minimize or close other windows and adjust the sizes and locations of the Visual Basic windows to those shown in Figure 4-6. For more information on adjusting the Visual Basic windows, refer to page VB59.

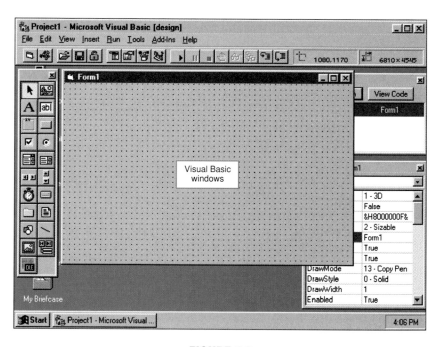

FIGURE 4-6

▶ CREATING THE INTERFACE

In this step, the size and location of the form will be determined, and the controls will be added to the form. The Geography Database Viewer form contains one image control, ten label controls, and one data control. These controls are shown as they appear on the completed form during design time in Figure 4-7. In addition to the new control — the data control — control arrays will be presented for the first time. The menu will be created by using Visual Basic's Menu Editor.

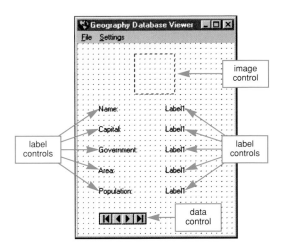

FIGURE 4-7

Setting the Location and Size of the Form

At run time, the form is centered on the desktop. This placement will be accomplished later in the project through code statements, as was done in Project 3. In the steps that follow, the form's size will be set by setting the form's Height and Width properties.

TO SIZE THE FORM

Step 1: Select the form control by clicking it or by selecting its name, Form1, from the Object drop-down list in the Properties window.

Step 2: Double-click the Height property in the Properties list in the Properties window.

Step 3: Type 4900 and press the ENTER key.

Step 4: Double-click the Width property in the Properties list in the Properties window.

Step 5: Type 3800 and press the ENTER key.

Step 6: Drag the form to the center of the desktop to make it easier to use during design time.

The form appears as shown in Figure 4-8.

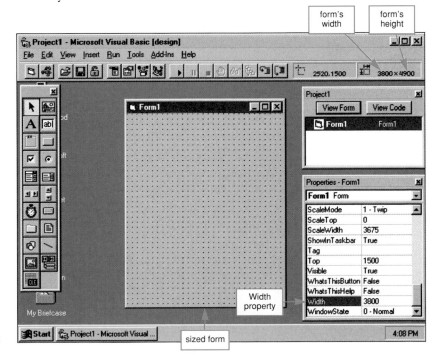

FIGURE 4-8

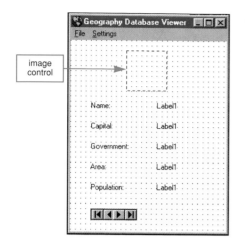

FIGURE 4-9

Adding the Image Control

An image control is used in the Geography Database Viewer application to contain graphical images of the flags of the different countries (Figure 4-9). Perform the following steps to add the image control.

TO ADD THE IMAGE CONTROL

Step 1: Double-click the Image tool in the Toolbox.
Step 2: Drag the control, Image1, to the location shown in Figure 4-10.

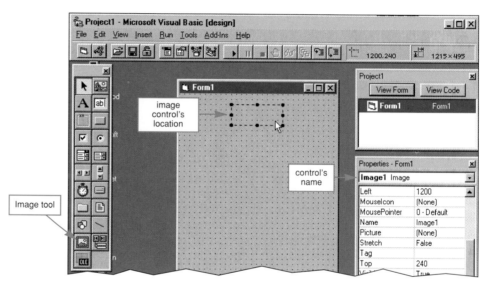

FIGURE 4-10

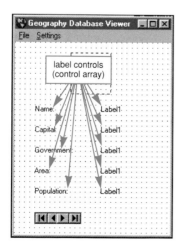

FIGURE 4-11

Adding the Label Control Array

Ten label controls are used in the Geography Database Viewer application (Figure 4-11). The five labels on the left are used to indicate the names of the fields in the database. The five labels on the right are used to display the field values for the current record. The ten labels are added to the form as a control array.

A **control array** is made up of a group of controls of the same type (for example, all labels) that share a common control name and a common set of Event procedures. For example, clicking any label in the array triggers the same Click event subroutine.

Each control in an array has a unique index number assigned by Visual Basic when the array is created. The value of the index begins at zero for the first control and increases by one for each new control. All items in a control array must have the same Name property setting. All other property settings apply only to the individual control. For example, Label1(0) can have a caption and other property settings different from Label1(1).

Arrays make it easier to change a property of a group of controls to a common value during run time. For example, suppose you wanted to change the FontSize of all ten labels to 12 at run time. As separate controls, this change would require ten similar, but separate, code statements. As an array, the FontSize can be changed much more easily through a simple code structure that will be presented later.

The ten labels have their AutoSize property set to True and have the same BackStyle property. Because the controls will be added to the form with the copy method, these two properties will be set for the first control during the interface building step, instead of during the setting properties step. This procedure will eliminate having to set the two properties for each of the ten labels later.

You can use the transparent value of the **BackStyle property** to create transparent controls when you're using a background color on a form. An opaque value of the BackStyle property is used when you want a control to stand out. A control's **BackColor property** is ignored if its BackStyle = 0 (Transparent). The following steps add one label and set its AutoSize and BackStyle properties. The control is then copied nine times to a control array.

TO ADD THE LABEL ARRAY ▼

STEP 1 ▶

Double-click the Label tool in the Toolbox.

A default-sized label, Label1, is added to the form (Figure 4-12).

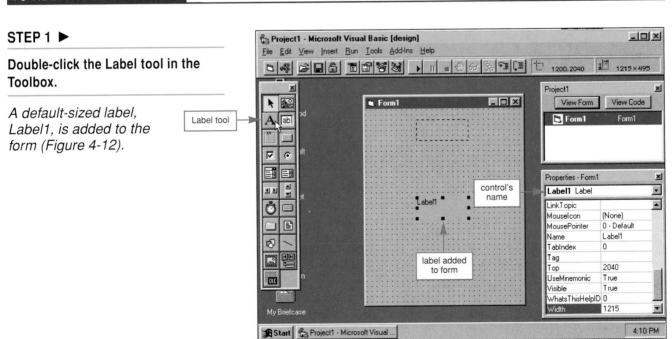

FIGURE 4-12

STEP 2 ▶

Double-click the AutoSize property in the Properties list in the Properties window.

The value of the AutoSize property changes to True (Figure 4-13).

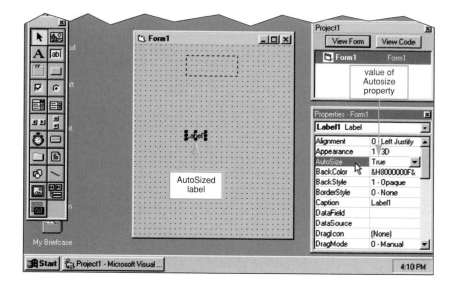

FIGURE 4-13

STEP 3 ▶

Double-click the BackStyle property in the Properties list in the Properties window.

The value of the BackStyle property changes to 0 - Transparent (Figure 4-14).

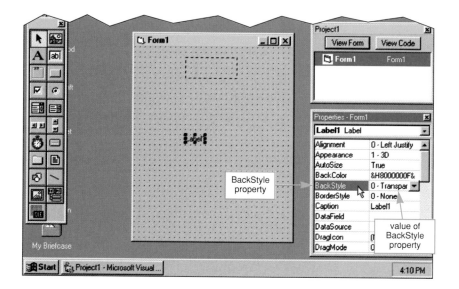

FIGURE 4-14

STEP 4 ▶

Drag the label to the position shown in Figure 4-15 and right-click the label.

A pop-up menu appears next to the control (Figure 4-15).

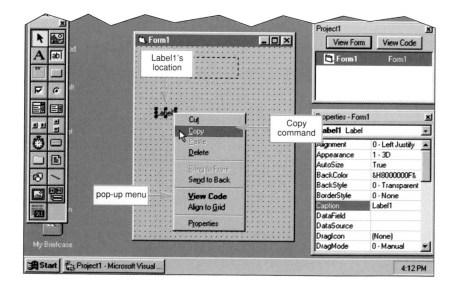

FIGURE 4-15

STEP 5 ▶

Click Copy on the pop-up menu (Figure 4-15).

The control is copied to the Clipboard and the menu closes (Figure 4-16).

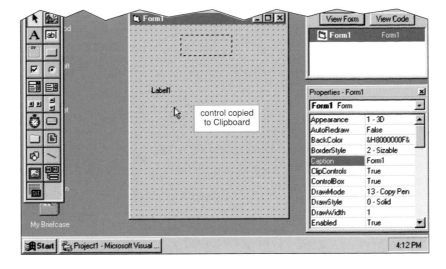

FIGURE 4-16

STEP 6 ▶

Right-click the form.

A pop-up menu appears next to the control (Figure 4-17).

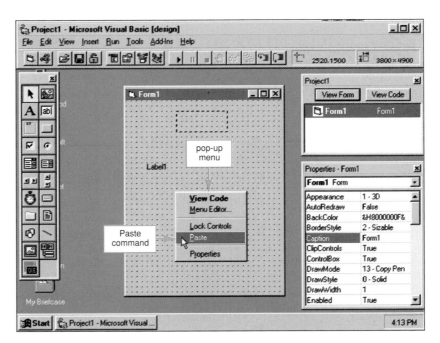

FIGURE 4-17

STEP 7 ▶

Click Paste on the pop-up menu (Figure 4-17).

The Control Array dialog box opens (Figure 4-18).

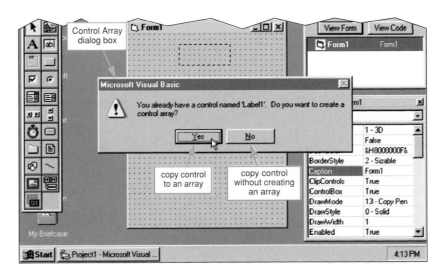

FIGURE 4-18

STEP 8 ▶

Click Yes on the dialog box.

The name of the first label changes to Label1(0). A second label control, Label1(1), is added to the upper left corner of the form (Figure 4-19). The dialog box closes.

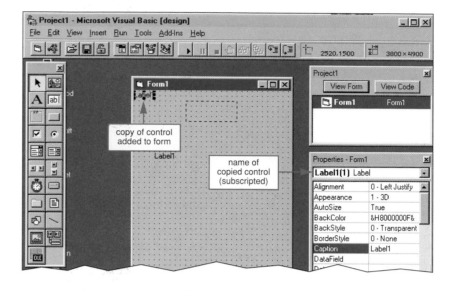

FIGURE 4-19

STEP 9 ▶

Drag the second label control, Label1(1), to the location shown in Figure 4-20.

The property values of the second label control (including the Caption property) are identical to the property values of the control that was copied (Label1(0)).

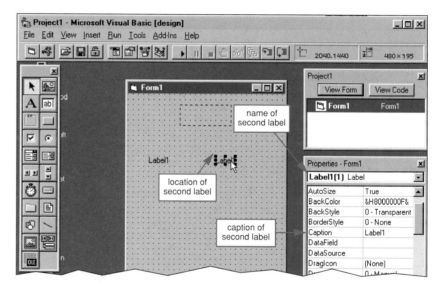

FIGURE 4-20

STEP 10 ▶

Press CTRL+V.

A third label control is added to the form (Figure 4-21).

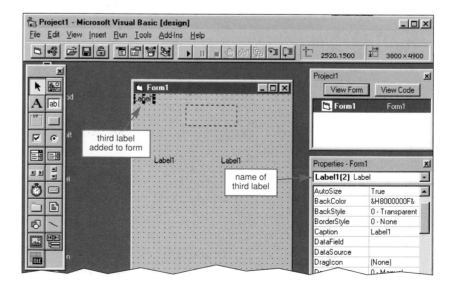

FIGURE 4-21

STEP 11 ►

Repeat Steps 9 and 10 seven times. Drag the labels to the locations shown in Figure 4-22.

Be careful to locate the controls in the order shown in Figure 4-22. They can be confused easily at this point because they have the same caption, Label1.

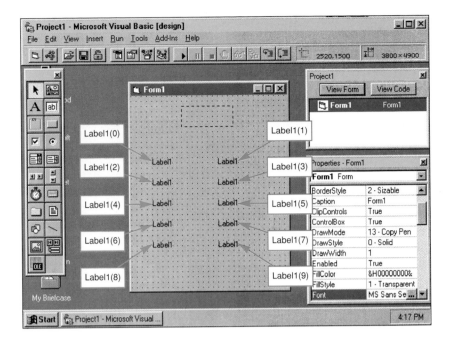

FIGURE 4-22

When controls were copied in previous projects, the Create Array dialog box appeared each time a copy of a control was placed on the form. This is because you responded No to the dialog box each time you were asked if you wanted to start a new control array. Once you responded Yes to the Create Array dialog box in the previous steps, it never appeared again because all subsequent copies were added to the array. If you had wanted to add an additional Label control to the form but not as part of the array, you would have had to use a method other than copying, such as double-clicking the Label tool.

Adding the Data Control

A **data control** is used in Visual Basic applications to provide the necessary links to a database file. The data control is added to a form in the same manner as other controls. A form can contain more than one data control, and generally one data control exists for each database table accessed by the application. The data control has four arrow buttons used during run time to move between records in a database, as shown in Figure 4-23. Perform the steps on the next page to add a data control and to locate it on the form.

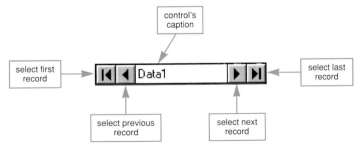

FIGURE 4-23

TO ADD A DATA CONTROL ▼

STEP 1 ▶

Double-click the Data tool in the Toolbox.

A default-sized data control, Data1, is added to the form (Figure 4-24).

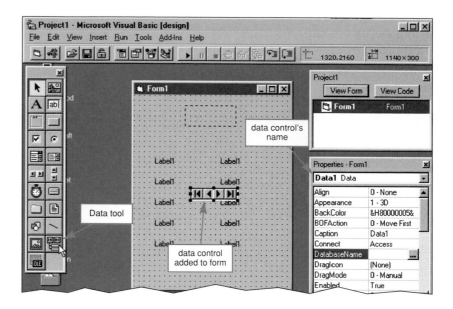

FIGURE 4-24

STEP 2 ▶

Drag the Data1 control to the location shown in Figure 4-25.

The location is not important because the control is not visible at run time in this application.

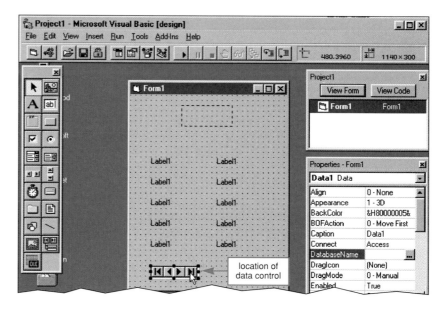

FIGURE 4-25

The Geography Database Viewer application contains a data control to link to the World database. The data control is not visible at run time, however, because record selection is controlled through the Select menu. Later, code will be written that causes the Select menu commands to trigger the data control events that make different records in the database the current record. Even though the Select menu commands initiate the record selection actions in this application, a data control still must be added to make the link between the application and the database.

Creating the Menus

The Geography Database Viewer contains two menus in the menu bar: File, and Settings (Figure 4-26). These menus are selected during run time either by clicking their names in the menu bar or by pressing ALT and an access key. The application also contains one pop-up menu, which is displayed by right-clicking the form.

Access keys allow you to open a menu at run time by pressing the ALT key and a letter. Access key assignments are common in Windows applications and appear as an underlined letter in the menu control's caption. For example, the letter F is the access key for the File menu (Figure 4-26). Access keys also are used in menu choices. However, when a menu is open, you press only the access key of a command (not the ALT key) to choose that command. In the following steps, the three menus in the Geography Database Viewer application are created one at a time.

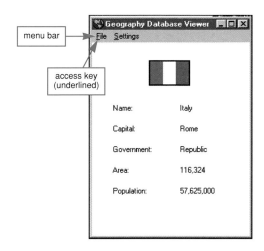

FIGURE 4-26

Creating the File Menu

The File menu in the Visual Basic menu bar follows a standard layout for this type of menu in Windows applications. Although the Visual Basic application can be closed by clicking its Close button, File menus always include an Exit command as an alternate way to close the application. The File menu in the Geography Database Viewer application contains only the Exit command, as shown in Figure 4-27.

Each command you add to a menu is an additional control within the application, and it has a name and a Click event. Menus are created during design time with Visual Basic's **Menu Editor**. The Menu Editor is shown with its major components identified in Figure 4-28. Perform the steps on the next page to create the File menu for the Geography Database Viewer.

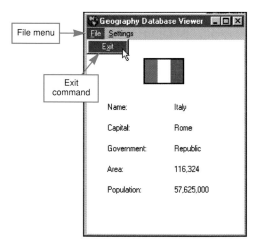

FIGURE 4-27

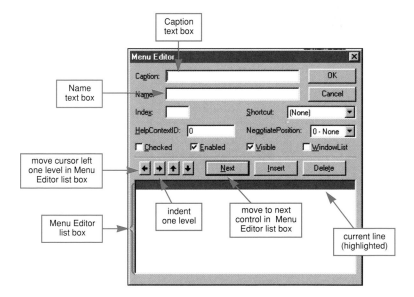

FIGURE 4-28

TO CREATE THE FILE MENU ▼

STEP 1 ▶

Click the Menu Editor button on the toolbar, or choose Menu Editor from the Tools menu.

The Menu Editor opens on the desktop (Figure 4-29).

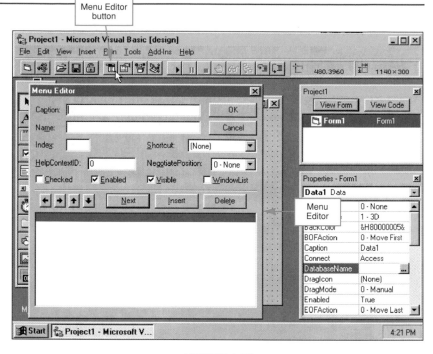

FIGURE 4-29

STEP 2 ▶

Drag the Menu Editor to the center of the desktop. Type &File in the Caption text box.

The caption that will appear on the menu bar appears in the Caption text box and in the Menu Editor list box (Figure 4-30). The ampersand (&) is placed before the letter in the caption to be used as the access key. At run time, the ampersand is not visible, and the access key letter is underlined.

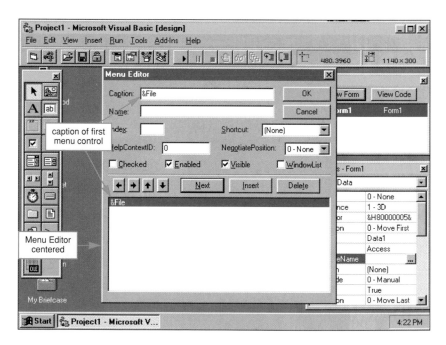

FIGURE 4-30

STEP 3 ▶

Press the TAB key or click the Name text box to move the cursor to that box. Type `mnuFile` and point to the Next button.

The name of the menu control, mnuFile, appears in the Name text box (Figure 4-31).

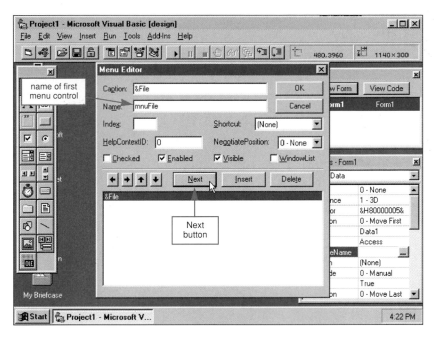

FIGURE 4-31

STEP 4 ▶

Click Next in the Menu Editor.

The highlighted line in the Menu Editor list box advances to the next line, and the Menu Editor properties boxes are blank (Figure 4-32).

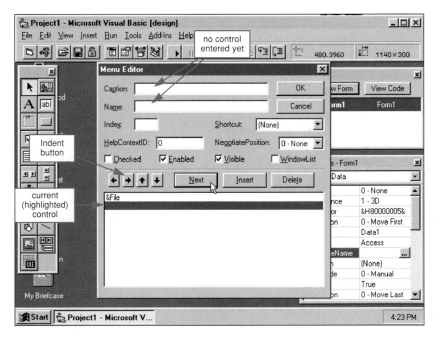

FIGURE 4-32

STEP 5 ▶

Click the right arrow button in the Menu Editor. Select the Caption text box by clicking it. Type `E&xit` **in the Caption text box.**

A new menu control with the run time caption Exit is added. The caption is preceded by a series of four dots in the Menu Editor list box (Figure 4-33). Clicking the right arrow button indents the control's caption and adds dots in the Menu Editor list box. This step is how you indicate Exit is a command within the File menu.

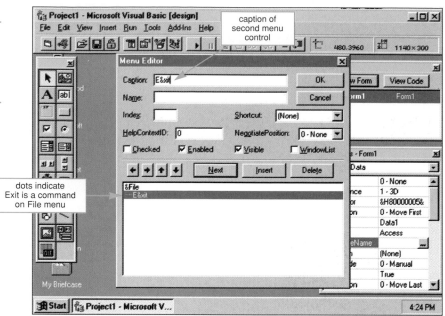

FIGURE 4-33

STEP 6 ▶

Type `mnuExit` **in the Name text box. Choose Next. Click the left arrow button in the Menu Editor.**

Clicking the left arrow button moves the cursor flush left in the Menu Editor list box to indicate the next item will be a new menu (Figure 4-34).

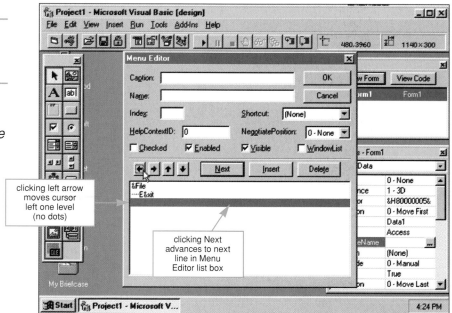

FIGURE 4-34

Creating the Select Menu

The Select pop-up menu is shown in Figure 4-35. The four commands in the menu correspond to the options to move between the records in the database during run time. The Select menu also includes a separator bar. A **separator bar** is a horizontal line used to visually group related commands in a menu. Separator bars are added to the menu at design time by typing a hyphen (–) in the Caption text box in the Menu Editor. The Select menu is not visible on the menu bar. Later in this project, a code statement will be written that causes the Select menu to appear when the user right-clicks the form during run time. Perform the following steps to create the Select menu.

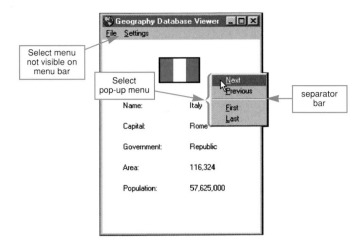

FIGURE 4-35

TO CREATE THE SELECT MENU ▼

STEP 1 ►

Type `Select` in the Caption text box. Type `mnuSelect` in the Name text box. Click the Visible check box to remove the check mark, which makes the Select menu not visible on the menu bar. Click the Next button to advance to a new menu control.

The Menu Editor appears as shown in Figure 4-36.

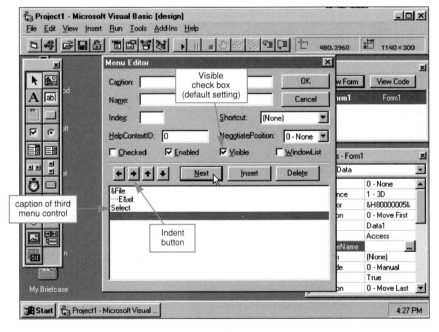

FIGURE 4-36

STEP 2 ▶

Click the right arrow button to indicate a command within the Select menu. Type `&Next` in the Caption text box. Type `mnuNext` in the Name text box. Choose Next. Type `&Previous` in the Caption text box. Type `mnuPrev` in the Name text box. Choose Next.

The Menu Editor appears as shown in Figure 4-37.

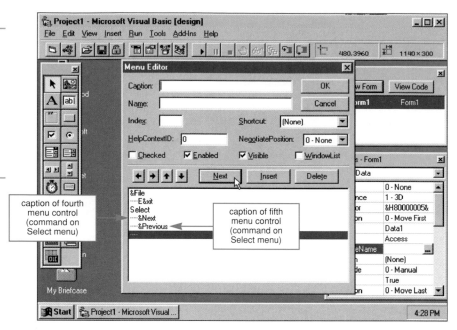

FIGURE 4-37

STEP 3 ▶

Add the separator bar to the Select menu by typing - (a hyphen) in the Caption text box. Type `Separator` in the Name text box. Choose Next. Type `&First` in the Caption text box. Type `mnuFirst` in the Name text box. Choose Next. Type `&Last` in the Caption text box. Type `mnuLast` in the Name text box.

The Menu Editor appears as shown in Figure 4-38. Each separator bar in a menu must be given a unique name even though it doesn't have a function at run time.

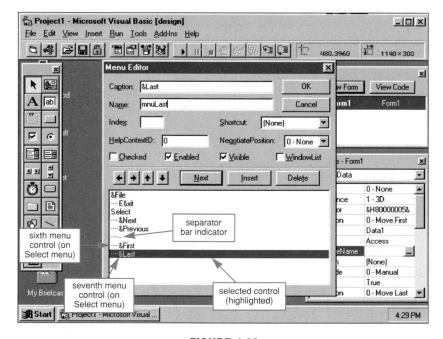

FIGURE 4-38

Creating the Settings Menu

The Settings menu is shown in Figure 4-39. The Settings menu contains two submenus, Color and View. A **submenu** branches off another menu to present an additional set of commands in a separate grouping. Each menu created in Visual Basic can have up to four levels of submenus. Menu choices that display submenus have an arrowhead symbol (▶) at their right edge (Figure 4-39).

The View submenu (Figure 4-40) is used in this application to set whether just the country's name and flag appear during run time. During run time, the status of the choice is indicated by that choice being disabled on the submenu. The following steps create the Settings menu.

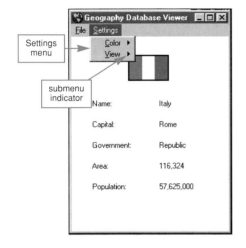

FIGURE 4-39

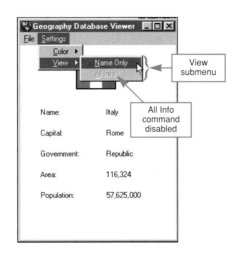

FIGURE 4-40

TO CREATE THE SETTINGS MENU ▼

STEP 1 ▶

Choose Next. Click the left arrow button to move the cursor flush left in the Menu Editor list box. Type &Settings **in the Caption text box. Type** mnuSet **in the Name text box. Choose Next. Click the right arrow.**

The menu control named mnuSet is added. Its caption, &Settings, appears in the menu control list box. The cursor is advanced to the next line and is indented once to indicate the next control added will be a command within the Settings menu (Figure 4-41).

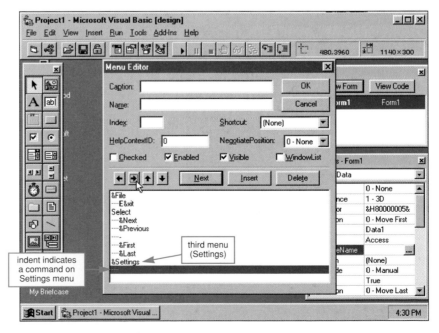

FIGURE 4-41

STEP 2 ▶

Type &Color in the Caption text box. Type mnuColor in the Name text box. Choose Next. Indicate the next control to be added is a submenu by clicking the right arrow button. Type &Red in the Caption text box. Type mnuRed in the Name text box.

The Menu Editor appears as shown in Figure 4-42.

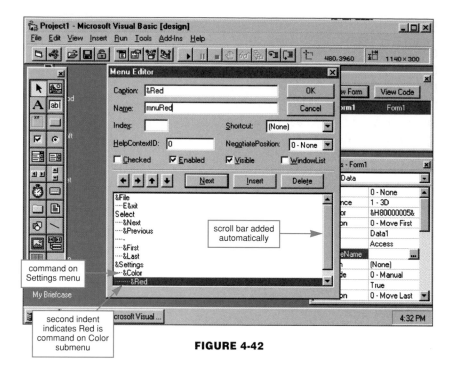

FIGURE 4-42

STEP 3 ▶

Click Next. Type &White in the Caption text box. Type mnuWhite in the Name text box. Click the check box labeled Checked in the Menu Editor.

The menu control appears as shown in Figure 4-43. Checking the Checked box indicates the mnuWhite menu control will have a check mark before it at the start of run time. The form's initial color will be set to white later in the project.

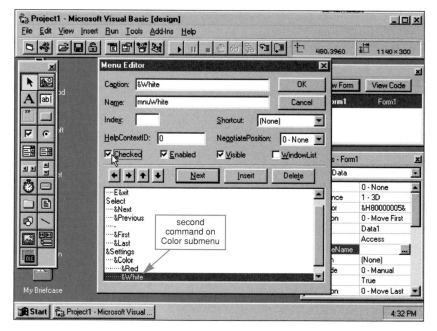

FIGURE 4-43

STEP 4 ▶

Click Next. Type `&Blue` in the Caption text box. Type `mnuBlue` in the Name text box. Click Next. Click the left arrow to move from the Color submenu back to the Settings menu. Type `&View` in the Caption text box. Type `mnuView` in the Name text box.

The Menu Editor appears as shown in Figure 4-44.

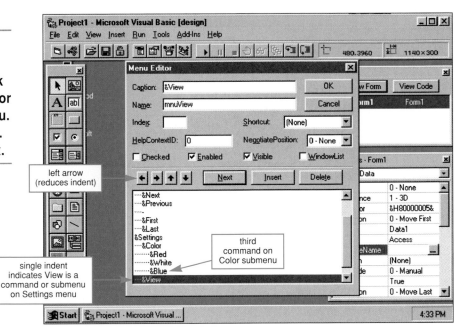

FIGURE 4-44

STEP 5 ▶

Choose Next. Indicate the next control to be added is a submenu item by clicking the right arrow button. Type `&Name Only` in the Caption text box. Type `mnuNameOnly` in the Name text box.

The Menu Editor appears as shown in Figure 4-45.

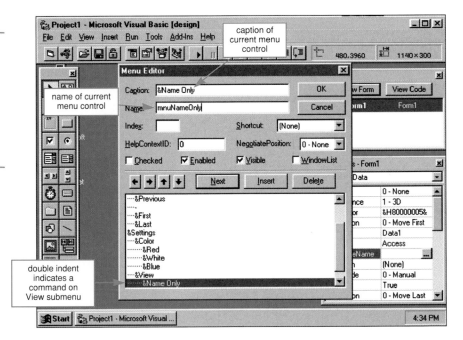

FIGURE 4-45

STEP 6 ▶

Choose Next. Type &All Info **in the Caption text box. Type** mnuAllInfo **in the Name text box. Click the check box labeled Enabled in the Menu Editor.**

The Menu Editor appears as shown in Figure 4-46. Removing the check mark in the Enabled check box indicates that the menu choice All Info will not be available at the start of run time.

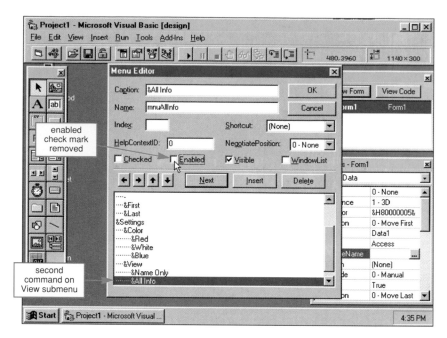

FIGURE 4-46

STEP 7 ▶

Click the OK button in the Menu Editor.

The Menu Editor closes, and the menus appear on the form (Figure 4-47).

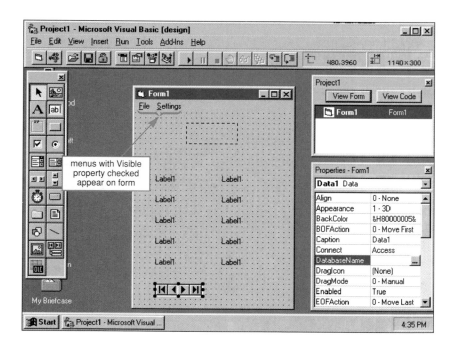

FIGURE 4-47

The menus for the Geography Database Viewer application are complete. During design time, menus can be opened in the Form window by clicking the menu title. Click the menu title for each of the menus you just created.

The interface for the Geography Database Viewer application is now complete. The second step of application development is to set the properties of the form and other controls.

▶ SETTING PROPERTIES

I n this section, control properties are set in the following groups of steps:

- ▶ the properties of the form
- ▶ the properties of the five labels used to display the names of the fields of the database
- ▶ the properties of the data control
- ▶ the properties of the five label controls and one image control used to contain information from the database (the data-aware controls)

Setting Properties of the Form

In the following steps, the name of the form is set. No other control names need to be set because all the labels in the array must have the same name and each of the remaining types of controls appears only once. The form is given a caption to appear in its title bar. Additionally, the form's BackColor property is set to white, and an icon is specified to represent the application. The following steps set these properties for the form control.

TO SET THE FORM'S PROPERTIES ▼

STEP 1 ▶

Select the form by clicking an area that does not contain any other controls. Double-click the Name property in the Properties list. Type `frmGeoView` **and press the** ENTER **key.**

The form's new name appears in both the Project window and the Properties window (Figure 4-48).

FIGURE 4-48

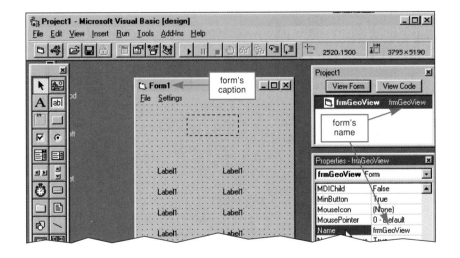

STEP 2 ▶

Double-click the Caption property in the Properties window. Type Geography Database Viewer **and press the** ENTER **key.**

The form's caption appears in the form's title bar (Figure 4-49).

FIGURE 4-49

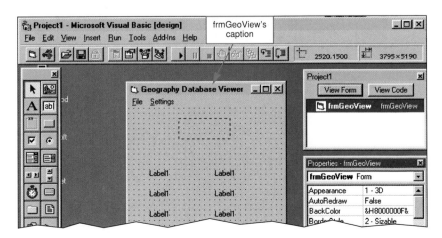

STEP 3 ▶

Double-click the BackColor property in the Properties window. Point to the white color identified in Figure 4-50.

The Color palette opens (Figure 4-50).

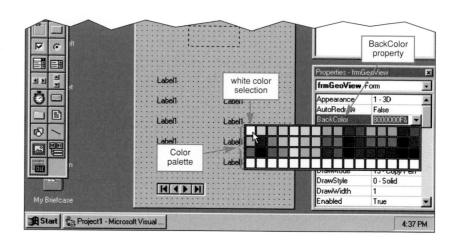

FIGURE 4-50

STEP 4 ▶

Click the left mouse button.

The background color of the form control changes to the selected color, and the Color palette closes (Figure 4-51).

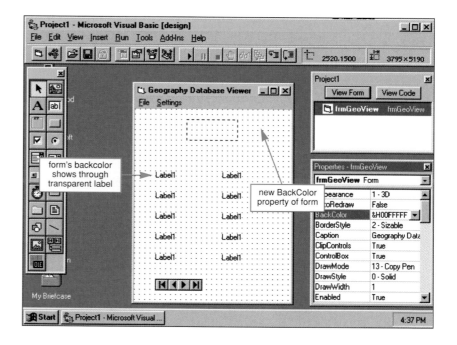

FIGURE 4-51

STEP 5 ▶

Double-click the Icon property in the Properties list.

The Load Icon dialog box opens (Figure 4-52).

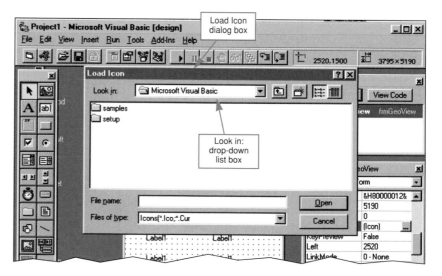

FIGURE 4-52

STEP 6 ▶

Insert the Student Diskette that accompanies this book in the 3½ Floppy [A:] drive. Click 3½ Floppy [A:] in the Look in: drop-down list box. Double-click the VB4 folder. Double-click Earth (Figure 4-53).

Visual Basic loads the icon and closes the Load Icon dialog box.

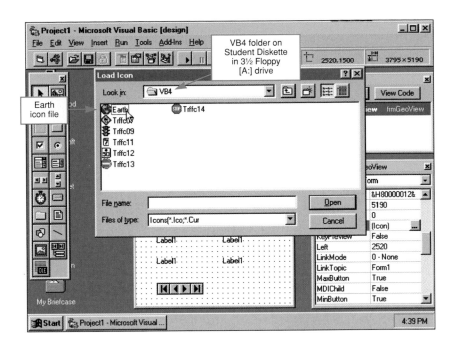

FIGURE 4-53

All of the necessary property settings for the form are complete.

Setting Properties of the Image Control

The image control in this application is used to display the flag of the currently selected country. The flags are part of the World database. By default, an image control will adjust its size to the size of the graphic it contains. However, the size of the flags is smaller than desired, so the image control's height and width will be increased and its **Stretch** property will be set to True. When an image control's Stretch property is set to True, the image it contains is stretched to the size of the control. Perform the following steps to set the image control's properties.

TO SET THE IMAGE CONTROL'S PROPERTIES

Step 1: Click the image control to select it.

Step 2: Double-click the Height property in the Properties window. Type 960 and press ENTER.

Step 3: Scroll down the Properties list and double-click the Width property. Type 960 and press ENTER.

Step 4: Double-click the Stretch property in the Properties list.

Step 5: Drag the image control so that it is centered left to right on the form.

The size of the image control is now enlarged and the flags will be stretched to fit the size of the image control.

Setting Caption Properties

The captions of the five labels in the left column on the form are used to show the names of the fields in the database. The captions of the remaining five labels are used as containers for the values of the corresponding fields in the current record. Perform the following steps to add the field names to the form as captions of the label controls.

TO SET CAPTION PROPERTIES

Step 1: Select Label1(0) by clicking its name in the Object drop-down list in the Properties window. Double-click the Caption property in the Properties list. Type `Name:` and press the ENTER key.

Step 2: Select Label1(2) by clicking its name in the Object drop-down list in the Properties window. Double-click the Caption property in the Properties list. Type `Capital:` and press the ENTER key.

Step 3: Select Label1(4) by clicking its name in the Object drop-down list in the Properties window. Double-click the Caption property in the Properties list. Type `Government:` and press the ENTER key.

Step 4: Select Label1(6) by clicking its name in the Object drop-down list in the Properties window. Double-click the Caption property in the Properties list. Type `Area:` and press the ENTER key.

Step 5: Select Label1(8) by clicking its name in the Object drop-down list in the Properties window. Double-click the Caption property in the Properties list. Type `Population:` and press the ENTER key.

The form appears as shown in Figure 4-54.

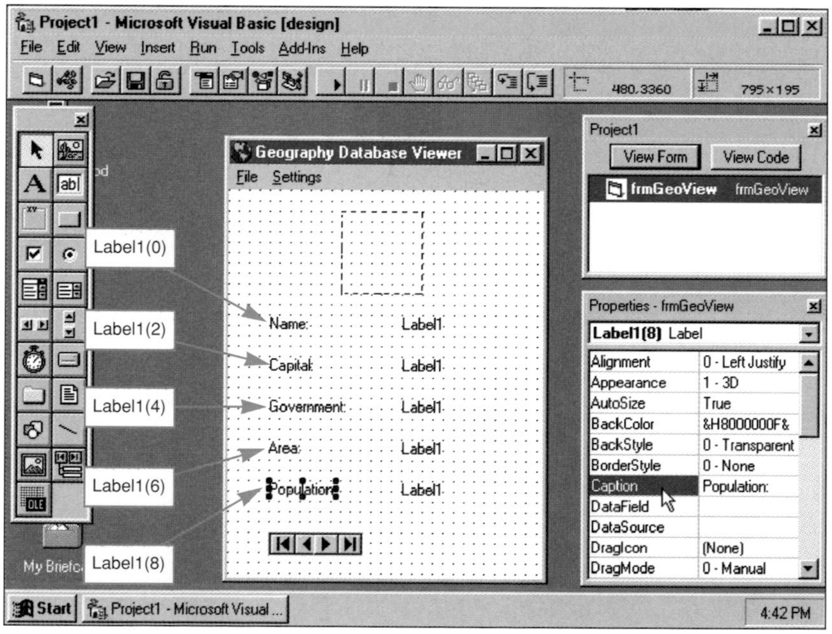

FIGURE 4-54

Setting the Properties of the Data Control

In the following steps, the DatabaseName and RecordSource properties of the data control named Data1 are set. The **DatabaseName property** is used to supply the filename of the database to which the data control is linked. The **Record-Source property** is used to specify the table name in the database to which the data control is linked. The **Connect property** is used to specify the type of database (Microsoft Access, FoxPro, dBASE, etc.). When the database to be accessed is a Microsoft Access database (as in this application), it is not necessary to set the Connect property. The data control's Visible property is set to False so that it will not appear at run time in the Geography Database Viewer application. Perform the following steps to set the properties of the Data1 control.

TO SET THE DATA CONTROL'S PROPERTIES ▼

STEP 1 ▶

Select the data control by clicking it or by clicking its name, Data1, in the Object drop-down list in the Properties window. Double-click the DatabaseName property in the Properties list.

The DatabaseName dialog box appears (Figure 4-55).

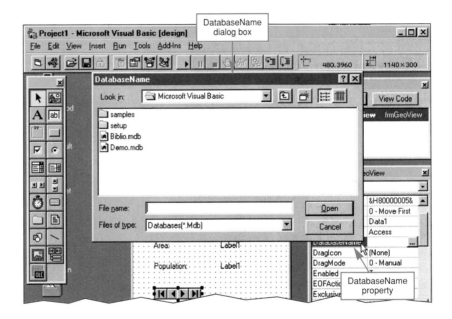

FIGURE 4-55

STEP 2 ▶

Make sure the diskette that you copied the WORLD.MDB file to earlier is in the 3½ Floppy [A:] drive. Click the 3½ Floppy [A:] drive in the Look in: drop-down list box.

The database filename appears in the File name list box (Figure 4-56).

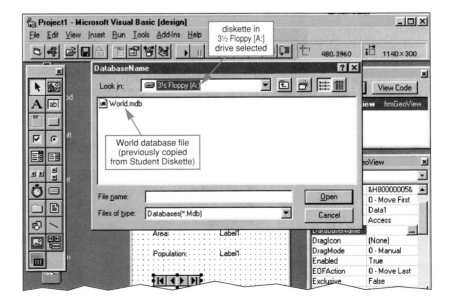

FIGURE 4-56

STEP 3 ▶

Double-click the WORLD.MDB file in the File name list box.

The file's name appears in the Properties list (Figure 4-57).

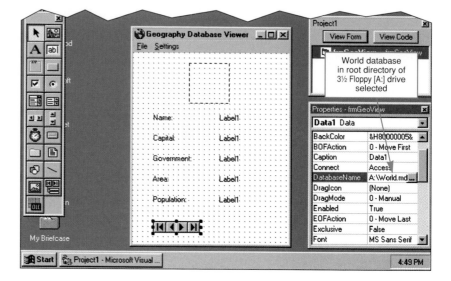

FIGURE 4-57

STEP 4 ▶

Scroll through the Properties list until the RecordSource property is visible. Click the RecordSource property. Click the arrow located to the right of the Settings box.

A Settings drop-down list for the RecordSource property lists all of the tables in the World database (Figure 4-58).

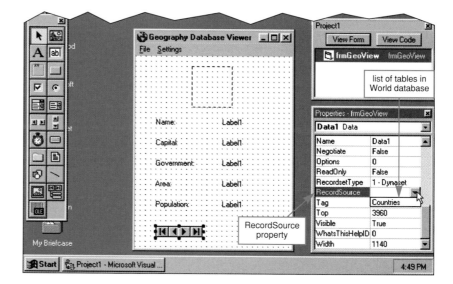

FIGURE 4-58

STEP 5 ▶

Click Countries in the Settings drop-down list.

The drop-down list closes, and the Property setting appears in the Settings box (Figure 4-59).

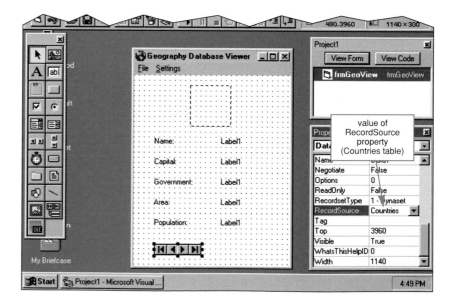

FIGURE 4-59

STEP 6 ▶

Double-click the Visible property in the Properties list.

The value of Data1's Visible property changes to False (Figure 4-60).

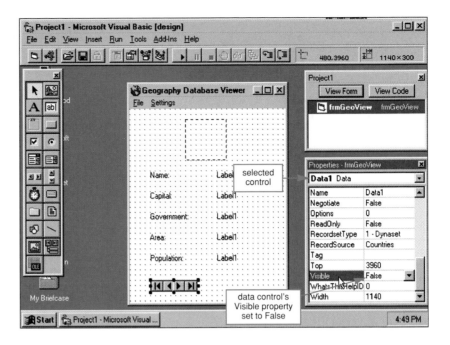

FIGURE 4-60

In Step 4, the Settings drop-down list contained only the name of the Countries table. If the World database contained more than one table, the Settings drop-down list for the RecordSource property would contain all the available tables.

Setting Properties of the Data-Aware Controls

The controls within Visual Basic that can be linked to information in a database are said to be **data-aware**. The data-aware controls are check boxes, images, labels, picture boxes, and text boxes. To use these controls to access a database, the controls must be **bound** to a data control on the form. In a multiform application, the bound control and the data control to which it is bound must be on the same form.

Data-aware controls are bound to a data control by setting their DataSource and DataField properties. The **DataSource property** of a control specifies the name of the data control to which it is bound. The **DataField property** of a bound control specifies the name of a field in the database to which the control is linked. Perform the steps on the next page to bind the five label controls and one image control in the Geography Database Viewer application used to display information from the Countries table of the World database.

TO BIND THE DATA-AWARE CONTROLS ▼

STEP 1 ▶

Select the Label1(1) control by clicking its name in the Object drop-down list in the Properties window. Click the DataSource property in the Properties list. Click the arrow next to the Settings box.

The Settings drop-down list for the DataSource property lists all the data controls on the form (Figure 4-61).

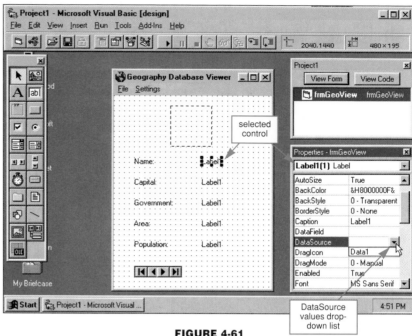

FIGURE 4-61

STEP 2 ▶

Select the Data1 control by clicking its name in the Settings drop-down list. Click the DataField property in the Properties list. Click the arrow next to the Settings box.

The Settings drop-down list for the DataField property lists all the fields in the Countries table of the World database (Figure 4-62).

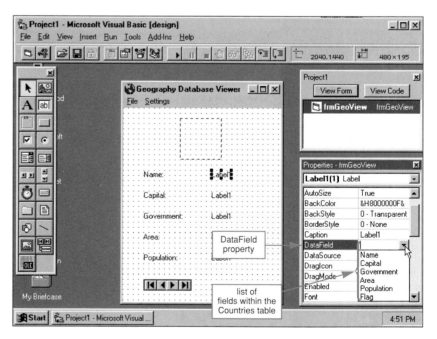

FIGURE 4-62

STEP 3 ▶

Select the Name field by clicking it in the Settings list.

The list closes, and the property value appears in the Settings list (Figure 4-63).

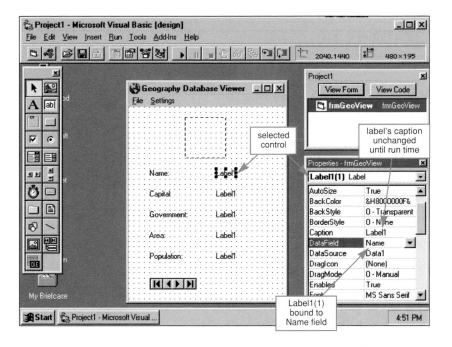

FIGURE 4-63

STEP 4 ▶

Repeat Steps 1 through 3 five times to accomplish the following: bind the Label1(3) control to the Data1 control, and then set the DataField property equal to Capital. Bind the Label1(5) control to the Data1 control, and then set the DataField property equal to Government. Bind the Label1(7) control to the Data1 control, and then set the DataField property equal to Area. Bind the Label1(9) control to the Data1 control, and then set the DataField property equal to Population. Bind the Image1 control to the Data1 control, and then set the DataField property equal to Flag.

The form appears as shown in Figure 4-64.

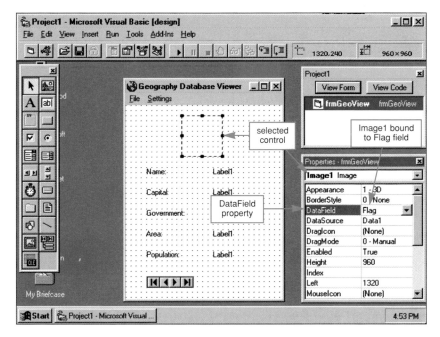

FIGURE 4-64

It is not necessary to change the Caption property of the bound labels to blank because their captions will be given the field values of the first record in the table as soon as the application starts.

The property-setting stage of application development is complete. The third and last stage is to write the code for the application.

▶ WRITING CODE

Code must be written for fourteen Event procedures and one General procedure in the Geography Database Viewer application. The control, procedure, and a description of the action are listed in Table 4-2. The General procedure is presented later.

▸ TABLE 4-2 DATABASE VIEWER EVENT PROCEDURES

CONTROL	PROCEDURE	ACTIONS
frmGeoView	Load	Center form on desktop
mnuExit	Click	Closes the application
mnuNext	Click	Displays the information from the next record in the table
mnuPrev	Click	Displays the information from the previous record in the table
mnuFirst	Click	Displays the information from the first record in the table
mnuLast	Click	Displays the information from the last record in the table
mnuRed	Click	Changes the form's backcolor to red
mnuWhite	Click	Changes the form's backcolor to white
mnuBlue	Click	Changes the form's backcolor to blue
mnuNameOnly	Click	Causes only the country's name and flag to display
mnuAllInfo	Click	Causes all the country's data fields to display
frmGeoView	MouseUp	Displays pop-up menu when right-clicked
Label1()	MouseUp	Displays pop-up menu when right-clicked
Image1	MouseUp	Displays pop-up menu when right-clicked

The code statements (subroutines) for the four menu controls that make up the Select menu are similar. The subroutines for the two menu controls that make up the View submenu also are similar, as are the three color choice subroutines and the three MouseUp subroutines. The code-writing activities for the Geography Database Viewer application are grouped as follows:

- ▸ the frmGeoView_Load subroutine
- ▸ the mnuExit_Click subroutine
- ▸ the Select menu subroutines (mnuNext, mnuPrev, mnuFirst, mnuLast)
- ▸ the mnuColor_Click subroutines (mnuRed, mnuWhite, mnuBlue)
- ▸ the General procedure
- ▸ the View submenu subroutines (mnuNameOnly, mnuAllInfo)
- ▸ the three pop-up menus display subroutines (MouseUp)

The frmGeoView_Load Subroutine

The code in this subroutine causes the GeoView form to be centered on the desktop at the beginning of run time. However, you can drag the form to another location during run time. The same code statements used to center the form in Project 3 are used. Refer to page VB164 for a review of this method. The following steps write the Load procedure for the frmGeoView control.

TO WRITE THE FRMGEOVIEW_LOAD SUBROUTINE

Step 1: Minimize the Form window. Open the Code window by choosing the View Code button in the Project window. Drag the Code window's borders to enlarge it.

Step 2: Select the Form control from the Object drop-down list in the Code window.

Step 3: Enter the following two statements in the Code window:
```
frmGeoView.Top = (Screen.Height - frmGeoView.Height) / 2
frmGeoView.Left = (Screen.Width - frmGeoView.Width) / 2
```

The Code window appears as shown in Figure 4-65.

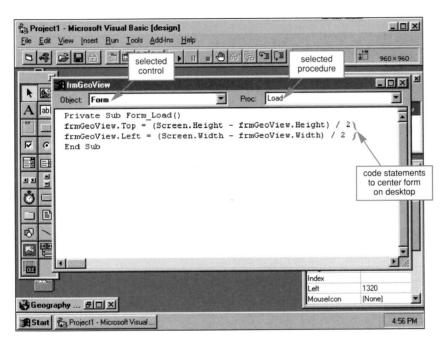

FIGURE 4-65

The mnuExit_Click Subroutine

When you trigger this event during run time by choosing Exit from the File menu, the Geography Database Viewer application closes. This procedure is accomplished in code by using the **End statement**. While the End statement never is required to terminate program execution, it is generally accepted as good programming practice because it closes any files that the application opened, removes forms from the computer's memory, and clears the value of all variables. Perform the steps on the next page to write the mnuExit_Click subroutine.

TO WRITE THE MNUEXIT_CLICK SUBROUTINE

Step 1: Select the mnuExit control from the Object drop-down list in the Code window.
Step 2: Enter the following statement in the Code window:
`End`

The Code window appears as shown in Figure 4-66.

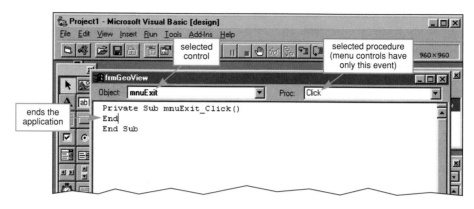

FIGURE 4-66

In the preceding steps, it was not necessary to select the Click event from the Procedure drop-down list in the Code window because menu controls have only the Click procedure.

The Select Menu Subroutines

One event is associated with each of the four commands in the Select menu: mnuNext_Click, mnuPrev_Click, mnuFirst_Click, and mnuLast_Click. When you trigger the mnuNext_Click event during run time by choosing Next from the Select menu, the next record (the one after the current record in the table) becomes the current record, and its information displays in the window. A similar record selection action occurs for each of the other three commands.

As discussed earlier, these actions are the same as if the data control were visible on the form and you clicked on the appropriate arrow button for the next, previous, first, or last record to become the current record. These actions are accomplished in code with the **MoveNext, MovePrevious, MoveFirst,** and **MoveLast** methods. The code statement has the form:

```
DataControlName.Recordset.MoveNext
```

When the current record is the last record in the table and the Next arrow button on a data control is clicked, the last record remains the current record, so nothing happens. However, when the MoveNext method is used, a blank record becomes the current record and the end of file, or **EOF property,** of the recordset changes from False to True. A similar set of events occurs with the MovePrevious method and the beginning of file, or **BOF property**.

The subroutine for the Next command includes an If...Then statement to check if the application has gone past the last record by seeing if the value of EOF is True. If EOF is True, the subroutine makes the first record current. The code to do this procedure is as follows:

```
Data1.Recordset.MoveNext
If Data1.Recordset.EOF = True Then Data1.Recordset.MoveFirst
```

If the MoveNext command causes the current record to move past the last record, then the first record in the table becomes the current record. That is, when the information displayed on the form is from the last country in the table and you choose Next from the Select menu, the information changes to that of the first country in the table. In this way the Geography Database Viewer application "loops" through the records.

A similar code structure is used in the mnuPrev_Click subroutine. The following steps write the subroutines for the four commands in the Select menu of the application.

TO WRITE THE SELECT MENU SUBROUTINES ▼

STEP 1 ►

Select the mnuNext control from the Object drop-down list in the Code window. Enter the following two statements in the Code window:

```
Data1.Recordset.MoveNext
If Data1.Recordset.EOF =
True Then Data1.Recordset.
MoveFirst
```

The Code window appears as shown in Figure 4-67.

FIGURE 4-67

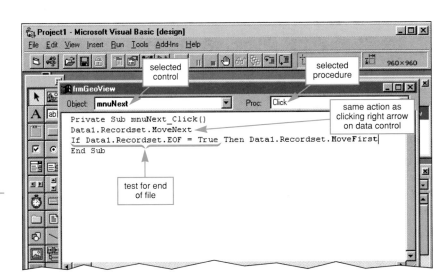

STEP 2 ►

Select the mnuPrev control from the Object drop-down list in the Code window. Enter the following two statements in the Code window:

```
Data1.Recordset.MovePrevious
If Data1.Recordset.BOF = True
Then Data1.Recordset.MoveLast
```

The Code window appears as shown in Figure 4-68.

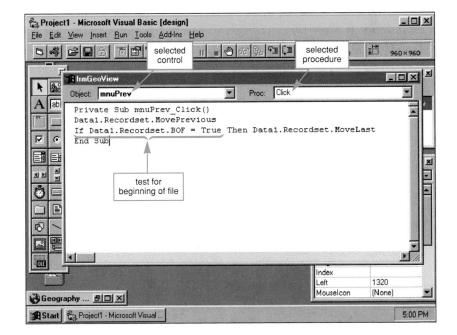

FIGURE 4-68

STEP 3 ▶

Select the mnuFirst control from the Object drop-down list in the Code window. Enter the following statement in the Code window:

`Data1.Recordset.MoveFirst`

The Code window appears as shown in Figure 4-69.

FIGURE 4-69

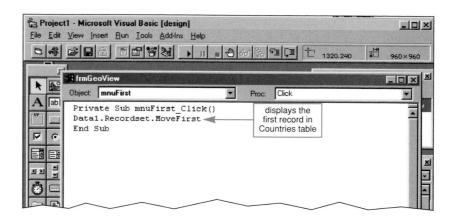

STEP 4 ▶

Select the mnuLast control from the Object drop-down list in the Code window. Enter the following statement in the Code window:

`Data1.Recordset.MoveLast`

The Code window appears as shown in Figure 4-70.

FIGURE 4-70

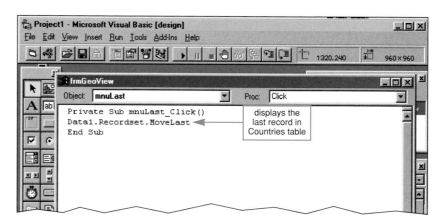

The Color Menu Subroutines

The mnuRed_Click, mnuWhite_Click, and mnuBlue_Click event procedures correspond to the three choices on the Color submenu (Red, White, Blue). They are similar in action in that they cause the form's backcolor to change and cause a check mark to appear on the menu in front of the currently selected color. The check mark also must be removed from the previously selected color choice. The Geography Database Viewer application uses three of Visual Basic's color constants (vbRed, vbWhite, and vbBlue). You can search online Help on Color Constants for a complete list. The backcolor is changed through a simple property assignment statement such as:

```
frmGeoView.BackColor = vbWhite
```

Three additional property assignment statements add the check mark to the menu and remove any previous check mark:

```
mnuRed.Checked = False
mnuWhite.Checked = True
mnuBlue.Checked = False
```

TO WRITE THE MNUWHITE_CLICK SUBROUTINE

Step 1: Select mnuWhite from the Object drop-down list in the Code window.

Step 2: Select the Click event from the Procedure drop-down list in the Code window.

Step 3: Type the following four code statements in the Code window:

```
frmGeoView.BackColor = vbWhite
mnuRed.Checked = False
mnuWhite.Checked = True
mnuBlue.Checked = False
```

The Code window appears as shown in Figure 4-71.

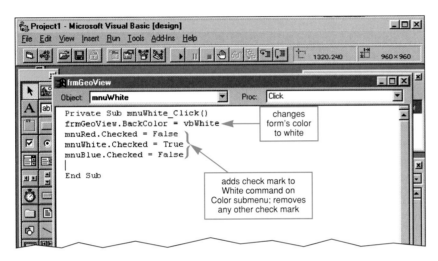

FIGURE 4-71

The subroutines for the other colors are very similar. Complete the following steps to write the other two subroutines.

TO WRITE THE MNURED_CLICK SUBROUTINE

Step 1: Select mnuRed from the Object drop-down list in the Code window.

Step 2: Select the Click event from the Procedure drop-down list in the Code window.

Step 3: Type the following four code statements in the Code window:

```
frmGeoView.BackColor = vbRed
mnuRed.Checked = True
mnuWhite.Checked = False
mnuBlue.Checked = False
```

TO WRITE THE MNUBLUE_CLICK SUBROUTINE

Step 1: Select mnuBlue from the Object drop-down list in the Code window.

Step 2: Select the Click event from the Procedure drop-down list in the Code window.

Step 3: Type the following four code statements in the Code window:

```
frmGeoView.BackColor = vbBlue
mnuRed.Checked = False
mnuWhite.Checked = False
mnuBlue.Checked = True
```

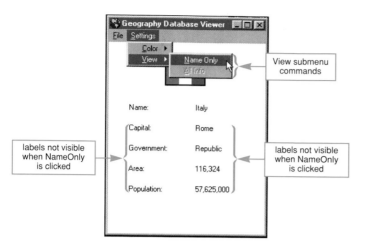

FIGURE 4-72

Writing a General Procedure

Event procedures are triggered when a particular event occurs on a control or form. Those Event procedures can in turn trigger other procedures. A procedure that is not triggered by an Event is called a **General procedure.**

The View submenu contains two choices, Name Only and All Info. Because the flag and country's name are always visible, these two choices turn off and on (toggle) the Visible property of the remaining labels (Figure 4-72). The code statements for these two Event procedures will be identical. Instead of repeating the same code in both Event procedures, a General procedure will be written, which is then triggered by either Event procedure (mnuNameOnly_Click or mnuAllInfo_Click).

The **Not operator** is used to perform logical negation on an expression. For example, if the label with the caption Capital, Label1(2), has its Visible property set to true then the statement:

```
Label1(2).Visible = Not Label1(2).Visible
```

will make its Visible property false. If its Visible property were false, the preceding statement would make its Visible property true.

The eight labels (Figure 4-72) could have their Visible property toggled with eight similar statements. However, a simpler way to accomplish this change is by using a code structure called a For...Next statement. A **For...Next statement**, also called a For...Next loop, repeats a group of code statements a specified number of times. Its syntax is:

```
For counter = start To end
   [statements]
Next
```

The parts of the statement are described in Table 4-3.

▶ **TABLE 4-3 PARTS OF A FOR...NEXT STATEMENT**

PART	DESCRIPTION
For	Begins a For...Next loop control structure; must appear before any other part of the structure
counter	Numeric variable used as the loop counter
start	Initial value of counter
To	Separates start and end values
end	Final value for counter
[statements]	Code statements between For and Next executed the specified number of times
Next	Ends a For...Next loop; causes 1 to be added to counter

A flowchart representation of the For...Next loop is shown to the right.

In the mnuColor_Click subroutine, the *start* and *end* values of the counter are set to the values of the index of the labels whose Visible property will be changed (2 and 9). The counter increases by one each time it performs the statements. However, the statements themselves use the counter's value for the Index value of the label whose Visible property is being changed as follows:

```
For Index = 2 To 9
  Label1(Index).Visible = Not Label1(Index).Visible
Next
```

The last function of the General procedure is to change the enabled property of the View menu choices. Recall that the Enabled property of mnuAllInfo was set to False in the Menu Editor, because all fields are initially displayed when the application starts. The two statements are similar to the one that toggles the Visible property:

```
mnuNameOnly.Enabled = Not mnuNameOnly.Enabled
mnuAllInfo.Enabled = Not mnuAllInfo.Enabled
```

In the following steps, the General procedure will be written. General procedures can be either subroutines or functions. A function is a set of code statements that returns a specific value. The Geography Database Viewer uses a subroutine, which will be named ToggleShow.

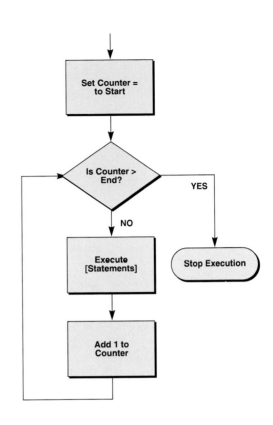

TO WRITE A GENERAL PROCEDURE ▼

STEP 1 ►

Click Insert on the menu bar and point to the Procedure command.

The Insert menu displays (Figure 4-73).

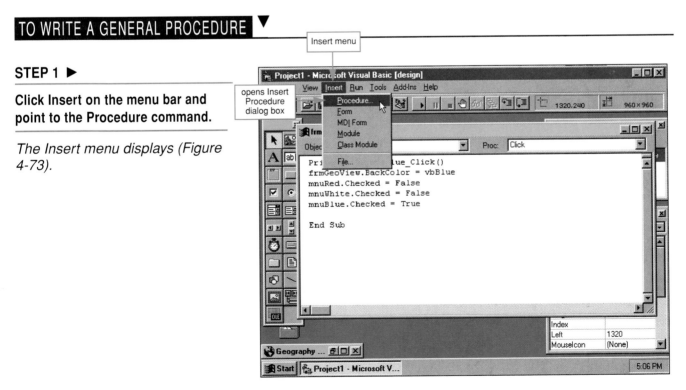

FIGURE 4-73

STEP 2 ▶

Click Procedure on the Insert menu.

The Insert Procedure dialog box appears (Figure 4-74).

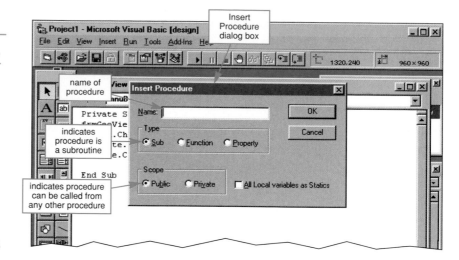

FIGURE 4-74

STEP 3 ▶

Type ToggleShow **in the Name text box and click the OK button.**

The Insert Procedure dialog box closes and the Code window appears as shown in Figure 4-75.

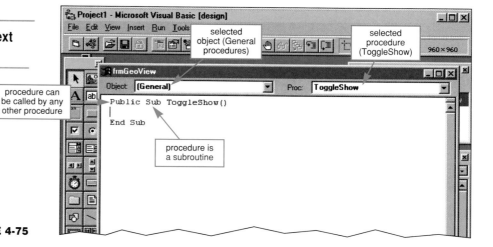

FIGURE 4-75

STEP 4 ▶

Type the following code statements in the Code window as shown in Figure 4-76:

```
For Index = 2 To 9
   Label1(Index).Visible
   = Not Label1(Index).
   Visible
Next
mnuNameOnly.Enabled =
Not mnuNameOnly.Enabled
mnuAllInfo.Enabled = Not
mnuAllInfo.Enabled
```

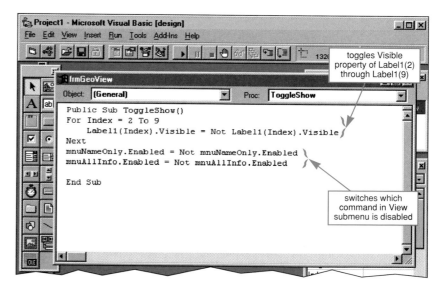

FIGURE 4-76

Calling Subroutines from Other Procedures

Because all of the code to toggle the display of country information is contained in the ToggleShow subroutine, the View menu events (mnuNameOnly_Click and mnuAllInfo_Click) need only to trigger or call the ToggleShow subroutine. You can cause one procedure to initiate another procedure simply by typing the name of the second procedure within the code statements of the first procedure at the point you want the second procedure to begin. After the second procedure is completed, program control returns to the code statement following the one that called the second procedure. Perform the following steps to write the two View menu events.

TO WRITE THE MNUNAMEONLY_CLICK SUBROUTINE

Step 1: Select the mnuNameOnly control from the Object drop-down list in the Code window.
Step 2: Enter the following statement in the Code window:

```
ToggleShow
```

The Code window appears as shown in Figure 4-77.

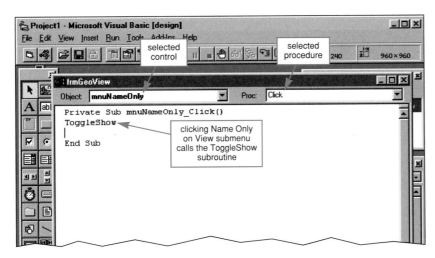

FIGURE 4-77

TO WRITE THE MNUALLINFO_CLICK SUBROUTINE

Step 1: Select the mnuAllInfo control from the Object drop-down list in the Code window.
Step 2: Enter the following statement in the Code window:

```
ToggeShow
```

The MouseUp Event

A **MouseDown** or **MouseUp** event procedure is used to specify actions that will occur when a given mouse button is pressed or released. Unlike the Click and DblClick events, MouseDown and MouseUp events enable you to distinguish between the left, right, and middle mouse buttons. In the Geography Database Viewer application this event is used to cause the Select pop-up menu to appear. Because this action should occur no matter where the mouse pointer is located, a MouseUp event must be written for the form, the image control and the label control array.

Although you can specify where you want the pop-up menu to appear, this application uses the default location, which is wherever the mouse pointer is currently located. This is accomplished through a code statement as follows:

```
PopupMenu menuname
```

where menuname is the name of the menu to be displayed. When a MouseUp event occurs, an integer corresponding to which mouse button was released is passed to the event subroutine as the value of the variable Button. A value of 2 corresponds to the right mouse button. An If...Then statement within the event is used to check for the release of the right mouse button:

```
If Button = 2 Then PopupMenu mnuSelect
```

TO WRITE THE MOUSEUP EVENT PROCEDURES

Step 1: Select the Form control from the Object drop-down list in the Code window.

Step 2: Select the MouseUp event from the Procedure drop-down list in the Code window.

Step 3: Type If Button = 2 Then PopupMenu mnuSelect

The Code window appears as shown in Figure 4-78.

Step 4: Repeat Steps 1 through 3 for the Image1 control.

Step 5: Repeat Steps 1 through 3 for the Label1 control.

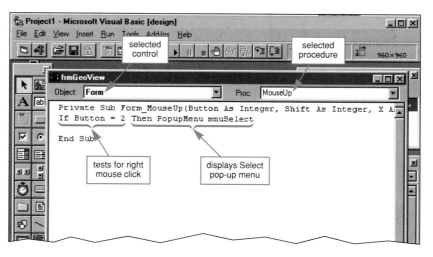

FIGURE 4-78

▶ SAVING THE PROJECT

The Geography Database Viewer project is complete. Before running an application, it always should be saved. Possibly the application contains errors. Depending on the severity of the error, it is possible (although generally not very likely) that the computer will "lock up" when the application runs. If so, all execution stops, and you have no control from the keyboard or mouse. The only recourse in this event is to reboot the computer. If the project has not been saved, all work on the project is lost. If the project has been saved, you can restart Visual Basic, open the project, and begin the process of detecting and correcting errors.

In the following steps, the project is saved to the diskette in the 3½ Floppy [A:] drive that contains the database file, WORLD.MDB. The following steps save the form file and the project file.

TO SAVE THE PROJECT

Step 1: Click the Save Project button on the toolbar.
Step 2: Type `Geoview` in the File name text box in the Save File As dialog box.
Step 3: Select the 3½ Floppy [A:] drive from the Save in drop-down list box in the Save File As dialog box.
Step 4: Click the Save button in the Save File As dialog box.
Step 5: Type `Geoview` in the File name box in the Save Project As dialog box.
Step 6: Click the Save button in the Save Project As dialog box.

The form file is saved on the diskette in the 3½ Floppy [A:] drive as Geoview.frm. The project file is saved on the diskette in the 3½ Floppy [A:] drive as Geoview.vbp.

Even though Save Project was chosen in the preceding Step 1, the Save File As dialog box opened, and then the Save Project As dialog box opened. Visual Basic automatically opened these dialog boxes because neither the form nor the project had been saved previously. With the project saved, it now can be run without risk of losing the work that has been completed.

▶ RUNNING THE APPLICATION

When the Geography Database Viewer application starts, it looks for the World database file (WORLD.MDB) on the diskette in the 3½ Floppy [A:] drive because *A:\WORLD.MDB* is the value assigned to the Database-Name property of the data control in the application. A diskette containing the WORLD.MDB file must be in the 3½ Floppy [A:] drive before running the application. For this reason, the two project files were saved to the diskette, which already contained the WORLD.MDB file.

An alternative to this procedure is to copy the WORLD.MDB file to a directory on the hard disk. However, if this copying is done, the DatabaseName property must be changed to the new drive and directory where the database file is located. Perform the following steps to run the application.

TO RUN THE APPLICATION ▼

STEP 1 ▶

Click the Code window's Close button. Click the Start button on the toolbar, or choose Start on the Run menu.

The application takes a few seconds to load. The first record is read, and the application appears as shown in Figure 4-79.

FIGURE 4-79

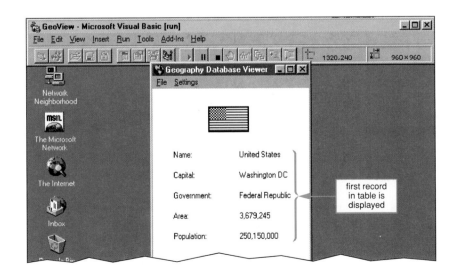

STEP 2 ▶

Right-click anywhere on the form.
Click Last on the Select menu.

*The last country in the table
appears in the window (Figure
4-80).*

FIGURE 4-80

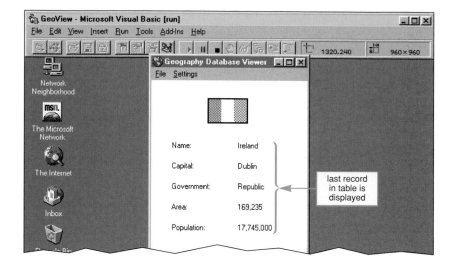

STEP 3 ▶

Click anywhere on the form. Click
Next on the Select menu.

*The record selection "loops" back
to the first record (Figure 4-81).*

STEP 4 ▶

Try all of the different options and
features such as changing the color,
turning off the display
of all info, and minimizing the
application. Choose Exit on the
application's File menu to close the
application.

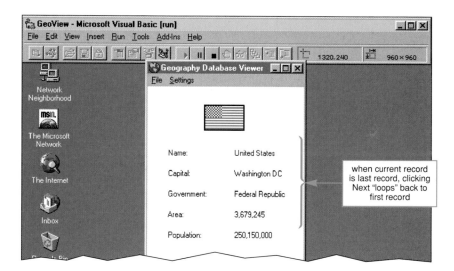

FIGURE 4-81

 PROJECT SUMMARY

Project 4 extended the basics of building applications presented in the first three projects. An application
was built by creating the interface, setting properties and writing code. The data control was introduced
to link the application to a database. The use of color within applications was introduced. Menus were
created for the application using the Menu Editor. The application included the use of a control array and
the For...Next statement. A General procedure was incorporated to keep from repeating the same code
statements in multiple events.

▶ Key Terms and Index

QUICK REFERENCE

In Visual Basic you can accomplish a task in a number of ways. The following table provides a quick reference to each of the major tasks presented for the first time in the project with some of the available options. The commands listed in the Menu column can be executed using either the keyboard or mouse.

Task	Mouse	Menu	Keyboard Shortcuts
Display the Menu Editor	Click Menu Editor button on toolbar	From Tools menu, choose Menu Editor	Press CTRL+E
Open the Code Window for a Selected Object (Form Window Active)	Double-click object on form		Press F7
Open the Color Palette for the Active Control (Design Time)	Double-click ForeColor or BackColor property in Properties window	From View menu, choose Color Palette	

STUDENT ASSIGNMENTS

STUDENT ASSIGNMENT 1
True/False

Instructions: Circle T if the statement is true or F if the statement is false.

T F 1. A database may contain more than one table.
T F 2. In a database, characteristics or attributes of an object are called tables.
T F 3. A control array can contain different types of controls.
T F 4. The Index value of the first control in an array is 1.
T F 5. Controls are copied from the Clipboard by pressing CTRL+Z.

(continued)

STUDENT ASSIGNMENT 1 (continued)

T   F   6. It is not necessary to press the ALT key when using an access key for a command within a menu.
T   F   7. General procedures can be functions or subroutines.
T   F   8. A General procedure is a type of Event procedure.
T   F   9. Separator bars can have Click event subroutines.
T   F   10. The RecordSource property is used to specify the name of the database file to which the data control is linked.
T   F   11. Check box controls are data-aware.
T   F   12. The variable incremented in a For...Next statement is called an index.
T   F   13. Submenus may contain additional submenus.
T   F   14. Data controls never are visible during run time.
T   F   15. All of the controls in an array must have the same name.
T   F   16. Clicking any control that is part of an array will trigger the same Click event subroutine.
T   F   17. Code statements used to center a form on the desktop must be part of the Form_Load subroutine.
T   F   18. Submenus are indicated by a check mark located on the right of the caption.
T   F   19. File menus in Windows applications seldom contain an Exit command.
T   F   20. Control arrays are created by clicking the Array button on the toolbar.

STUDENT ASSIGNMENT 2
Multiple Choice

Instructions: Circle the correct response.

1. The _____ control is not data-aware.
   a. image
   b. text box
   c. common dialog
   d. label
2. Which of the following is/are Visual Basic color constants?
   a. vbRed
   b. vbScrollBars
   c. vbMenuBar
   d. all of the above
3. _____ is a property of data controls.
   a. DatabaseName
   b. DataSource
   c. DataField
   d. All of the above
4. _____ is a property of bound controls.
   a. RecordSource
   b. DataSource
   c. Connect
   d. All of the above
5. Access keys are set by preceding the designated letter in the menu control's caption with _____.
   a. %
   b. $
   c. &
   d. @
6. _____ is not a command button in the Menu Editor.
   a. Next
   b. OK
   c. Previous
   d. Delete

7. The Menu Editor list box contains menu controls' _____.
   a. names
   b. values of the Checked property
   c. captions
   d. all of the above
8. Pop-up menus can be displayed _____ .
   a. on the menu bar
   b. at the mouse pointer's location
   c. at any control
   d. all of the above
9. The _____ property is used to bind a data-aware control to a data control.
   a. DataSource
   b. DatabaseName
   c. RecordSource
   d. Connect
10. The Menu Editor can be opened by _____.
   a. choosing Menu Editor on the Tools menu
   b. clicking the Menu Editor button on the toolbar
   c. both a and b
   d. neither a nor b

STUDENT ASSIGNMENT 3
Understanding the Menu Editor

Instructions: In Figure SA4-3, arrows point to some of the major components in the Menu Editor. Identify these in the spaces provided.

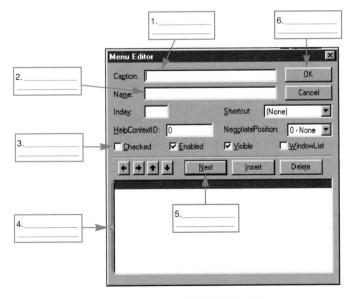

FIGURE SA4-3

STUDENT ASSIGNMENT 4
Understanding Controls and Properties

Instructions: The following table lists several controls and properties. Place an "X" in the spaces provided if the control has that property.

PROPERTIES	DATA CONTROL	IMAGE CONTROL	FORM CONTROL	MENU CONTROL
Stretch	[ ]	[ ]	[ ]	[ ]
Checked	[ ]	[ ]	[ ]	[ ]
BackColor	[ ]	[ ]	[ ]	[ ]
RecordSource	[ ]	[ ]	[ ]	[ ]
Connect	[ ]	[ ]	[ ]	[ ]
DataField	[ ]	[ ]	[ ]	[ ]
Visible	[ ]	[ ]	[ ]	[ ]
MinButton	[ ]	[ ]	[ ]	[ ]
Caption	[ ]	[ ]	[ ]	[ ]
Name	[ ]	[ ]	[ ]	[ ]

STUDENT ASSIGNMENT 5
Understanding Menus

Instructions: The Menu Editor for an application is shown in Figure SA4-5. On a separate sheet of paper draw a picture of the menu bar and the menus for this application. Include submenus, access key markings, separator bars, and check marks.

FIGURE SA4-5

STUDENT ASSIGNMENT 6
Understanding the Visual Basic Toolbar and Toolbox

Instructions: In Figure SA4-6, arrows point to some of the buttons on the toolbar and tools in the Toolbox. Identify these in the spaces provided.

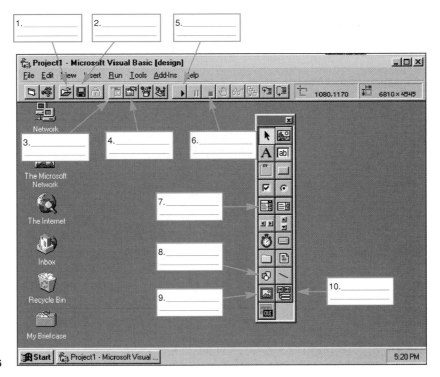

FIGURE SA4-6

COMPUTER LABORATORY EXERCISES

COMPUTER LABORATORY EXERCISE 1
Writing a General Procedure

Instructions: Start Visual Basic. Open the project CLE4-1 from the VB4 folder on the Student Diskette that accompanies this book. Complete the following tasks:

1. Click the Start button on the toolbar. The application appears as shown in Figure CLE4-1.

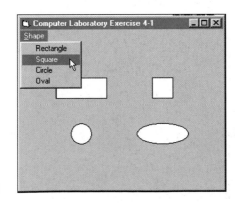

FIGURE CLE4-1

(continued)

COMPUTER LABORATORY ASSIGNMENT 1 (continued)

2. Select one of the shapes from the Shape menu. Select another shape from the Shape menu. Click the Close button to end the application.
3. Click the View Code button in the Project window.
4. Add a General procedure subroutine named ClearAll.
5. Add the following code statements to the ClearAll subroutine:

```
Shape1.BackColor = vbWhite

Shape2.BackColor = vbWhite

Shape3.BackColor = vbWhite

Shape4.BackColor = vbWhite
```

6. Add a code statement to the first line of each of the Click events of the four menu controls that will call the ClearAll subroutine.
7. Run the application again.
8. On a separate piece of paper, describe the action of the ClearAll subroutine.
9. Save the form as CLE4-1A.FRM and save the application as CLE4-1A.VBP.
10. Check with your instructor for directions on turning in the exercise.

COMPUTER LABORATORY EXERCISE 2
Control Arrays and For...Next Loops

Instructions: Start Visual Basic. Open the project CLE4-2 from the VB4 folder on the Student Diskette that accompanies this book. Complete the following tasks:

1. Click the View Form button in the Project window. The form contains an array of 16 labels as shown in Figure CLE4-2.

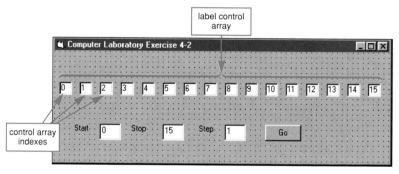

FIGURE CLE4-2

2. Add the following code to the Command1_Click event procedure:

```
For Index = 0 To 15

    Label1(Index).BackColor = vbWhite

Next

For Index = Text1.Text To Text2.Text Step Text3.Text

    Label1(Index).BackColor = vbBlue

Next
```

3. On a separate sheet of paper, describe what each of these two For..Next loops does within the application.
4. Click the Start button to run the application. Click the Go button.
5. Change the values in the Start, Stop, and Step text boxes. Click the Go button.
6. Try several different combinations of Start, Stop, and End values.
7. Click the End button on the toolbar.
8. Save the form as CLE4-2A.FRM and save the project as CLE4-2A.VBP.
9. Check with your instructor for directions on turning in the exercise.

COMPUTER LABORATORY EXERCISE 3
Creating Menus

Instructions: Start Visual Basic. Open the project CLE4-3 from the VB4 folder on the Student Diskette that accompanies this book. In this exercise you will create a menu for the Alignment demo built in Computer Laboratory Exercise 3-3 on page VB188. The completed application will appear as shown in Figure CLE4-3.

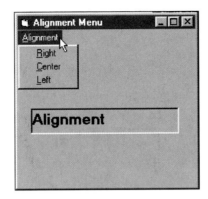

FIGURE CLE4-3

Perform the following steps:

1. Choose the View Form button in the Project window.
2. Open the menu control
3. Add a menu control with the caption &Alignment and the name mnuAlign.
4. Choose Next. Click the right arrow to indent once. Add a menu control with the caption &Right and the name mnuRight.
5. Choose Next. Add a menu control with the caption &Center and the name mnuCenter.
6. Choose Next. Add a menu control with the caption &Left and the name mnuLeft.
7. Choose the OK button in the Menu Editor. Choose the View Code button in the Project window.
8. Select the mnuRight control from the Object drop-down list in the Code window. Write the following mnuRight_Click subroutine statement: `Label1.Alignment = 1`
9. Select the mnuCenter control from the Object drop-down list in the Code window. Write the following mnuCenter_Click subroutine statement: `Label1.Alignment = 2`
10. Select the mnuLeft control from the Object drop-down list in the Code window. Write the following mnuLeft_Click subroutine statement: `Label1.Alignment = 0`
11. Save the form as CLE4-3A.FRM, and save the project as CLE4-3A.VBP.
12. Close the Code window. Run the application. Make menu selections by clicking as well as by using the menu access keys.
13. Close the Alignment application by clicking its Close button or by clicking the End button on the toolbar.
14. Check with your instructor for directions on turning in the exercise.

COMPUTER LABORATORY ASSIGNMENT 1
Tailor's Calculations Revisited

Purpose: To build an application that uses a menu to trigger subroutines that contain mathematical computations.

Problem: A tailor would like to have an application that calculates the average neck size, hat size, and shoe size for male customers, given the customer's weight and waistline. The interface should resemble the one shown in Figure CLA4-1a. Text boxes should be used for the inputs, and a label should be used for the output. The calculations are as shown.

Neck Size = 3 * (Weight / Waistline)
Hat Size = (3 * Weight) / (2.125 * Waistline)
Shoe Size = 50 * (Waistline / Weight)

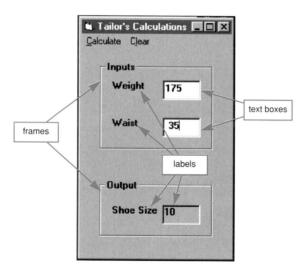

FIGURE CLA4-1a

Instructions: Perform the following tasks:

1. Start Visual Basic, or open a new project if Visual Basic is already running.
2. Size and locate the form, as shown in Figure CLA4-1a.
3. Add two frames, two text boxes, and four labels, as shown in Figure CLA4-1a.
4. Set the appropriate captions for the form and labels.
5. Set the text boxes' Text values to be blank.
6. Set the BorderStyle property of the label used for displaying the outputs so that it is visible.
7. Create a menu, as shown in Figure CLA4-1b.

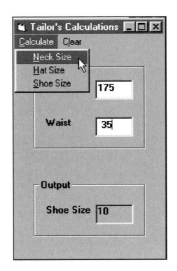

FIGURE CLA4-1b

8. Write the code for the Click event for each of the three commands in the Calculate menu. Each subroutine should perform the appropriate calculation, change the caption of the output label, and display the result.
9. Clicking the Clear choice in the menu bar should clear the data on the form and return the cursor to the first input box. (**Hint:** Use the SetFocus method.)
10. Save the form as CLA4-1.FRM. Save the project as CLA4-1.VBP.
11. Run the application to test it.
12. Check with your instructor for directions on turning in the assignment.

COMPUTER LABORATORY ASSIGNMENT 2
Shape Control Demonstration Revisited

Purpose: To build an application that incorporates menus and submenus.

Problem: You will build the application shown in Figure CLA4-2. The application has one menu used to access the two submenus. One submenu is used to set the Shape property of the shape control on the form, and the other submenu is used to set the BorderStyle property of the shape control.

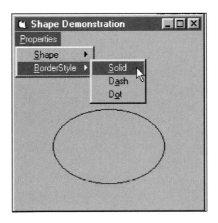

FIGURE CLA4-2

(continued)

Instructions: Perform the following tasks:

1. Start Visual Basic, or open a new project if Visual Basic is already running.
2. Size and position the form, as shown in Figure CLA4-2.
3. Add a shape control, as shown in Figure CLA4-2.
4. Set the form's Caption property.
5. Open the Menu Editor. Create the menu. Include access keys. An outline of the menu is as follows:
   Properties
   > Shape
   >> Rectangle
   >> Square
   >> Oval
   >> Circle
   > BorderStyle
   >> Solid
   >> Dash
   >> Dot
6. Write the Click subroutines for each of the menu commands. The subroutines should change the appropriate property of the shape control to the value listed in the menu control's caption.
7. Save the form as CLA4-2.FRM. Save the project as CLA4-2.VBP.
8. Run the application. Click the form's Close button to stop the application.
9. Check with your instructor for directions on turning in the assignment.

COMPUTER LABORATORY ASSIGNMENT 3
Creating Menus that Include Check Marks

Purpose: To build an application that contains menus with check marks.

Instructions: Build a menu-driven interface for the application described in Computer Laboratory Assignment 4-2. Include three menus in the application's menu bar: File, Shape, and BorderStyle. The File menu should contain one command — Exit. Include access keys. The commands in the Shape and BorderStyle menus should include check marks to indicate the currently selected property value. ***Note:*** You will have to include If...Then blocks in the menu command subroutines that add the check mark to the caption of the command chosen and remove the check mark from the previously chosen command. Save the form as CLA4-3.FRM. Save the project as CLA4-3.VBP. Run the application. Choose Exit on the application's File menu to close the application. Check with your instructor for directions on turning in the assignment.

COMPUTER LABORATORY ASSIGNMENT 4
Accessing a Database

Purpose: To build an application that accesses a database and displays information from that database.

Instructions: The Visual Basic programming system includes a sample database of information about books, authors, and publishers, named BIBLIO.MDB. The database contains several tables. One of the tables, named Publishers, includes the name, address, city, and phone number of several publishing companies. Create an application that will access the Publishers table of the BIBLIO.MDB database and display the information one record at a time. The data control should be used during run time for record selection. The BIBLIO.MDB file is located in the Microsoft Visual Basic folder on your hard disk. Save the form as CLA4-4.FRM. Save the project as CLA4-4.VBP. Check with your instructor for directions on turning in the assignment.

▼

BUILDING APPLICATIONS WITH
DRAG-AND-DROP FUNCTIONALITY

OBJECTIVES You will have mastered the material in this project when you can:

▸ Add drag-and-drop functionality to applications
▸ Write code that calls other subroutines
▸ Copy code using keyboard commands
▸ Understand Visual Basic data types
▸ Include comments in subroutines
▸ Write subroutines with nested code structures

▸ Use the Select Case structure in applications
▸ Use the Do...Loop structure in applications
▸ Use the InputBox and UCase$ functions in applications
▸ Print an application's form and subroutines
▸ Change properties for a group of controls

▶ INTRODUCTION

You interact with many Windows applications by dragging and dropping objects. A good example is Windows' Solitaire game. The application built in this project incorporates the activities necessary to add drag-and-drop functionality to your applications. Additional information about documenting applications is presented.

Project 4 introduced control arrays. In this project, subroutines are written for common events shared by the controls in an array. In addition, a code method is used that allows one event procedure to initiate another event procedure. Several additional code structures are introduced in this project: nested If...Then blocks, Select Case blocks, and Do...Loop statements.

▶ PROJECT FIVE – TRAFFIC SIGN TUTORIAL

T he application built in this project is shown in Figure 5-1 as it appears on the desktop during run time. The application is a tutorial that teaches you the meanings of several traffic signs. At run time, you are presented with several traffic signs and several containers having labels. You are instructed to drag and drop the signs into the correct containers. If you attempt to drop a sign into an incorrect container, the sign snaps back to its original location.

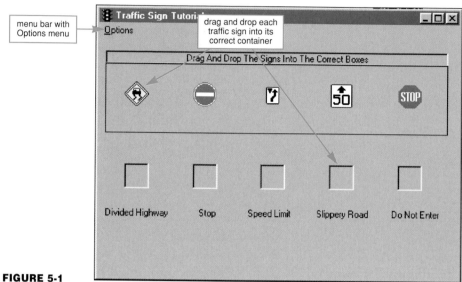

FIGURE 5-1

Three commands are available in the application by choosing the Options menu (Figure 5-2). The menu and commands include access keys, such as the Q in Quiz. Choosing the Clear command returns all the signs to their original locations. Choosing the Show command places all the signs in their correct containers. Choosing the Quiz command presents a series of three questions about the shapes of the signs.

The Traffic Sign Tutorial application is created by following the same three-step approach used in previous projects:

▶ create the interface
▶ set properties
▶ write code

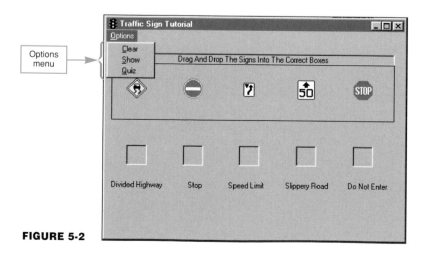

FIGURE 5-2

▶ CREATING THE INTERFACE

I n this step, the size and location of the form is determined, and the controls are added to the form. The Traffic Sign Tutorial form contains one shape control, one individual image control, one individual label control, two arrays of image controls, and one array of label controls, as identified in Figure 5-3. After these controls are added to the form, the menu is created using Visual Basic's Menu Editor.

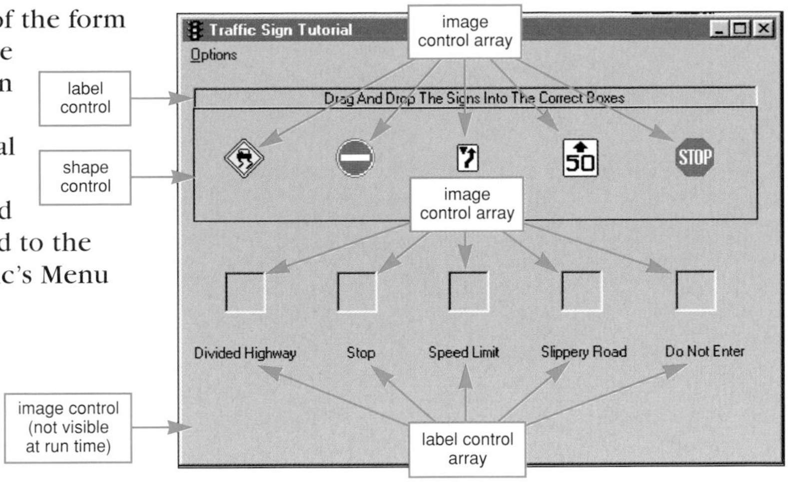

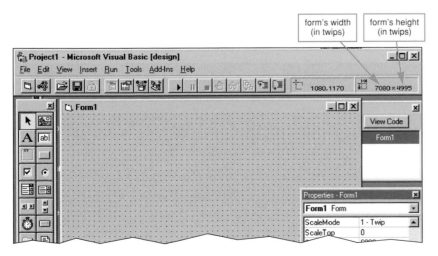

FIGURE 5-3

Setting the Location and Size of the Form

At run time, the form is centered on the desktop. This positioning will be accomplished later in the project through code statements, as was done in Project 4. In the steps that follow, the form is sized by setting the form's Height and Width properties.

TO SIZE THE FORM

Step 1: Select the form control by clicking it.
Step 2: Click the Properties window. Double-click the Height property in the Properties list.
Step 3: Type 4995 and press the ENTER key.
Step 4: Double-click the Width property in the Properties list in the Properties window.
Step 5: Type 7080 and press the ENTER key.

The form's width and height values appear as shown in Figure 5-4.

FIGURE 5-4

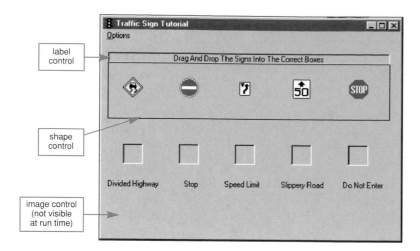

Adding the Individual Label, Shape, and Image Controls

The individual label, shape, and image controls are identified in Figure 5-5. The label control is used to contain the run-time instructions for the application. The shape control is used to visually group the traffic signs that are to be dragged and dropped. The individual image control is left blank and is not visible at run time. Its purpose is explained later in this project.

FIGURE 5-5

TO ADD THE INDIVIDUAL CONTROLS

Step 1: Add a label control to the form by double-clicking the Label tool on the Toolbox. Adjust the label's size to that shown in Figure 5-6, and then drag it to the location shown.

Step 2: Add a shape control to the form by double-clicking the Shape tool on the Toolbox. Adjust the shape control's size to that shown in Figure 5-6, and then drag it to the location shown.

Step 3: Add an image control to the form by double-clicking the Image tool on the Toolbox. Drag it to the location shown in Figure 5-6.

The form appears as shown in Figure 5-6.

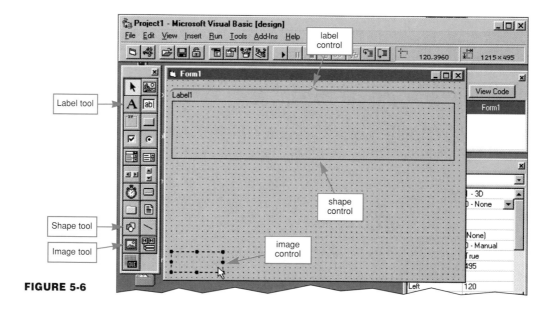

FIGURE 5-6

Adding the imgSign Array

Run-time dragging and dropping of a control does not automatically change its location. When the left mouse button is released to drop the control, the control retains its original position. Any relocation must be specifically programmed with code statements to occur when the left mouse button is released. Many times the control does not actually relocate. The control only appears to relocate by changing the properties of it and other controls, such as the Visible property.

In Visual Basic, the control being dragged is called the **source control**. The control over which the source control is located during the dragging operation is called the **target control**.

In the Traffic Sign Tutorial application, a sign appears to move into a container by changing the Picture property of the container from being blank to being equal to the Picture property of the image being dropped. Much of the apparent movement in the Traffic Sign Tutorial application is the result of changing the values of the Picture and Visible properties of image controls on the form.

The first set of image controls in this application contains the graphical images of the five signs (Figure 5-7). These controls are grouped in an array to simplify the code writing later. The control array is given the name imgSign.

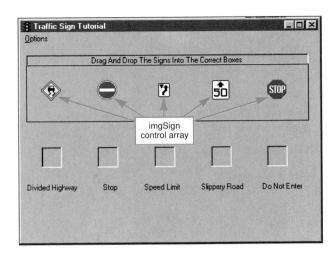

FIGURE 5-7

The ability to drag a control during run time is determined by the value of the control's **DragMode property.** When the DragMode property is set to Automatic, the dragging operation is initiated during run time by positioning the mouse pointer on the control and pressing the left mouse button. The DragMode property can be set through code statements or in the Properties window. In this application, the DragMode property is set to Automatic for the first image control in the array so that the property will be copied to all image controls in the array. The following steps add the imgSign control array.

TO ADD THE IMGSIGN ARRAY ▼

STEP 1 ▶

Double-click the Image tool on the Toolbox.

A default-sized image control, Image2, is added to the form (Figure 5-8).

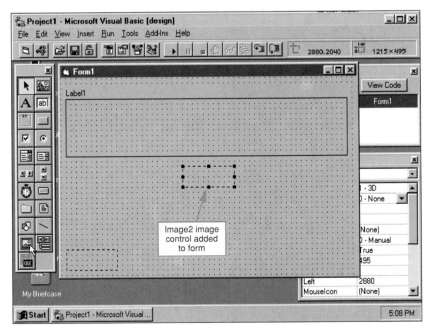

FIGURE 5-8

STEP 2 ▶

Drag the image control to the location shown in Figure 5-9.

Its size will be adjusted later.

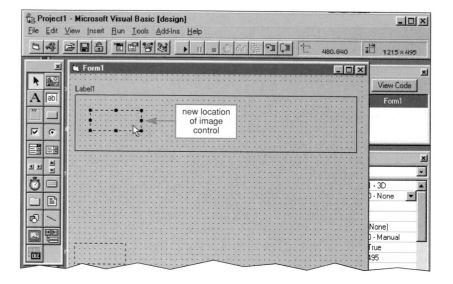

FIGURE 5-9

STEP 3 ▶

Click the Properties window. Double-click the Name property in the Properties list. Type `imgSign` and press the ENTER key. Double-click the DragMode property in the Properties list.

The control's new name (imgSign) appears in the Object box, and the value of the DragMode property changes to 1 - Automatic (Figure 5-10).

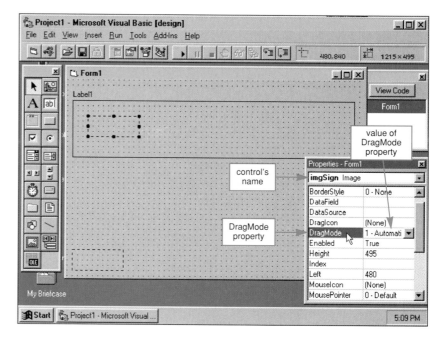

FIGURE 5-10

STEP 4 ▶

Click the imgSign control on the form. Press CTRL+C to copy the control to the Clipboard. Press CTRL+V to paste the contents of the Clipboard to the form. Choose Yes from the dialog box to begin a control array.

The name of the first image changes to imgSign(0). A second image control, imgSign(1), is added to the upper left corner of the form (Figure 5-11).

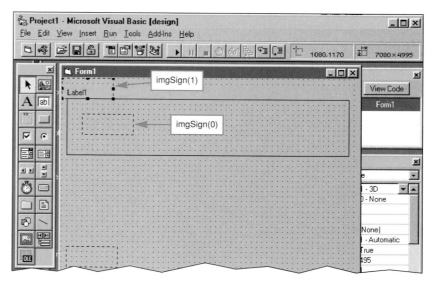

FIGURE 5-11

STEP 5 ▶

Drag the second image control, imgSign(1), from the upper left corner of the form to the location shown in Figure 5-12. Press CTRL+V to paste the Clipboard contents to the form.

A third label control, imgSign(2), is added to the form (Figure 5-12).

FIGURE 5-12

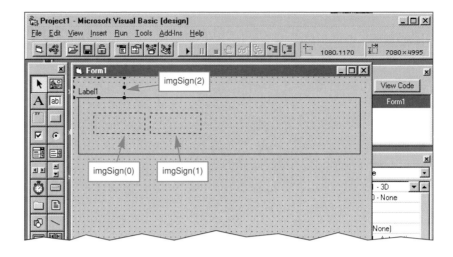

STEP 6 ▶

Drag the third image control in the array to the location shown in Figure 5-13. Press CTRL+V. Drag the fourth image control, imgSign(3), to the position shown in Figure 5-13. Press CTRL+V to paste the Clipboard contents to the form. Drag the fifth image control, imgSign(4), to the position shown in Figure 5-13.

Locating the controls in the order shown in Figure 5-13 is important. They easily can be confused because they all have the same appearance on the form.

FIGURE 5-13

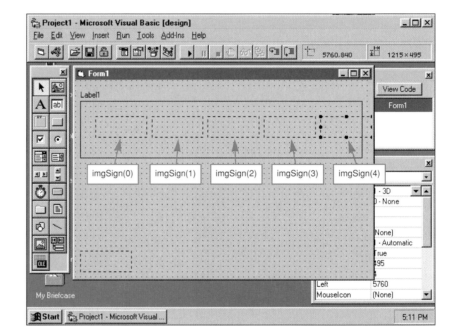

Adding the imgContainer Control Array

The second set of image controls is indicated in Figure 5-14. These controls also are grouped as an array and act as the containers into which the signs will be dropped. These controls have their Border-Style set to Fixed Single to display as empty boxes. Perform the steps on the next page to create this array, imgContainer, and to locate the controls on the form.

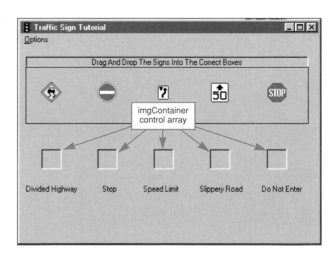

FIGURE 5-14

TO ADD THE IMGCONTAINER ARRAY

Step 1: Double-click the Image tool on the Toolbox.

Step 2: Double-click the Name property in the Properties list in the Properties window. Type `imgContainer` and press the ENTER key. Drag the image control to the location shown in Figure 5-15.

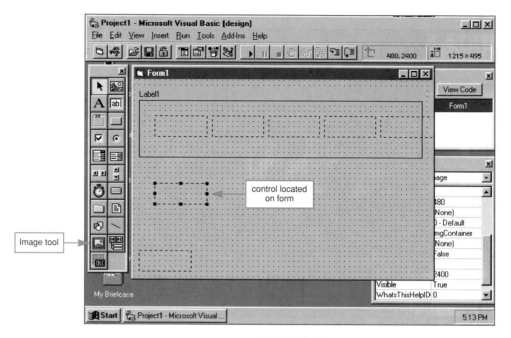

FIGURE 5-15

Step 3: Click the imgContainer control on the form. Press CTRL+C to copy the control to the Clipboard. Press CTRL+V to paste the Clipboard's contents to the form. Choose Yes from the dialog box to start a control array.

Step 4: Drag the second image control, imgContainer(1), to the location shown in Figure 5-16.

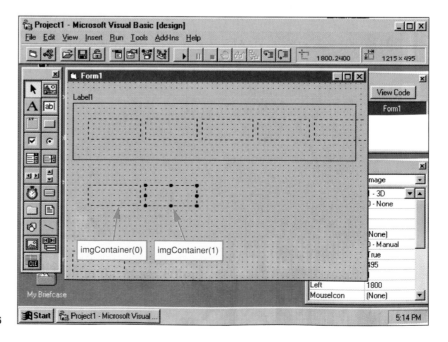

FIGURE 5-16

Step 5: Press CTRL+V to paste the Clipboard's contents to the form. Drag the third image control to the location shown in Figure 5-17.

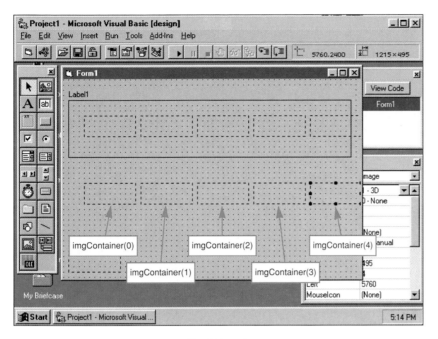

FIGURE 5-17

Step 6: Repeat Step 5 two times, dragging the controls to the locations shown in Figure 5-17.

Locating the controls in the order shown in Figure 5-17 is important. They easily can be confused because they all have the same appearance on the form.

Adding the Label Control Array

The label control array is indicated in Figure 5-18. These controls are used for the names of the containers. The labels in the array have their AutoSize property set to True. The steps on the next page create this array using the default name Label2 and locate the controls on the form.

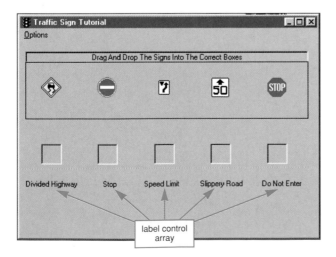

FIGURE 5-18

TO ADD THE LABEL2 ARRAY

Step 1: Double-click the Label tool on the Toolbox.

Step 2: Double-click the AutoSize property in the Properties list to change the value to True. Drag the label control to the location shown in Figure 5-19.

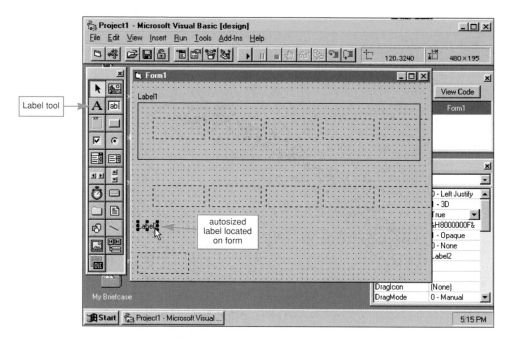

FIGURE 5-19

Step 3: Click the Label2 control on the form. Press CTRL+C to copy the control to the Clipboard. Press CTRL+V to paste the Clipboard's contents to the form. Choose Yes from the dialog box.

Step 4: Drag the second label control, Label2(1), to the location shown in Figure 5-20.

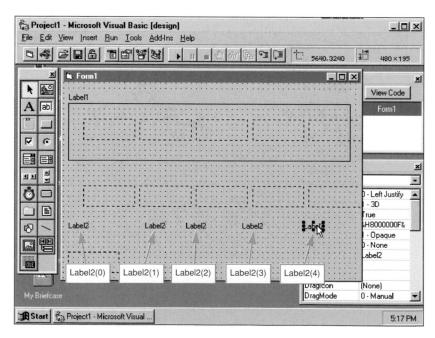

Step 5: Press CTRL+V to paste the Clipboard's contents to the form. Drag the third label control to the location shown in Figure 5-20.

Step 6: Repeat Step 5 two times, dragging the label controls to the locations shown in Figure 5-20.

Locating the controls in the order shown in Figure 5-20 is important. They easily can be confused because they all have the same caption, Label2.

FIGURE 5-20

Creating the Menu

The Options menu in the Traffic Sign Tutorial application contains three commands, as shown in Figure 5-21. Access keys are designated for the menu selection and command choices. The following steps create the menu using the Menu Editor.

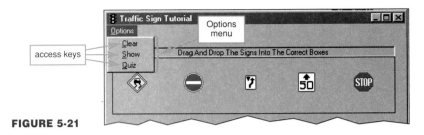

FIGURE 5-21

TO CREATE THE MENU ▼

STEP 1 ▶

Click the Menu Editor button on the toolbar, or choose Menu Editor from the Tools menu.

The Menu Editor opens on the desktop (Figure 5-22).

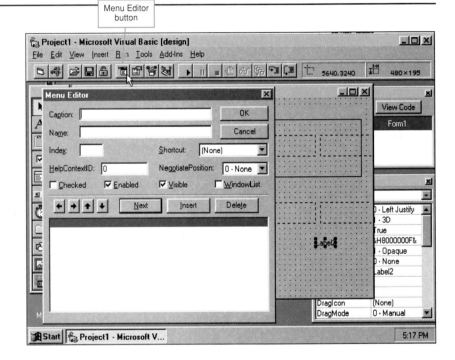

FIGURE 5-22

STEP 2 ▶

Type &Options in the Caption box. Press the TAB key. Type mnuOptions in the Name box. Click Next.

The mnuOptions control is added to the menu. Its caption appears in the Menu Editor list box. The cursor advances to the next line in the Menu Editor list box (Figure 5-23).

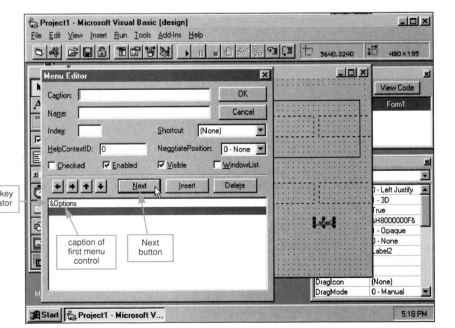

FIGURE 5-23

STEP 3 ▶

Click the right arrow button in the **Menu Editor** list box. Type &Clear in the Caption box. Press the TAB key. Type mnuClear in the Name box. Click Next.

The Menu Editor appears as shown in Figure 5-24.

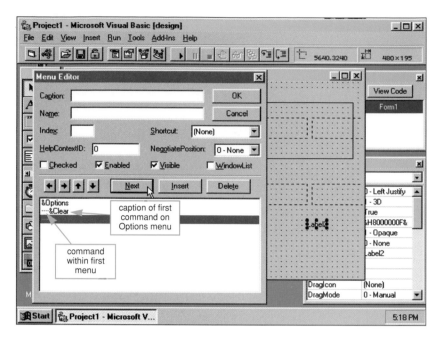

FIGURE 5-24

STEP 4 ▶

Type &Show in the Caption box. Press the TAB key. Type mnuShow in the Name box. Click Next.

The Menu Editor appears as shown in Figure 5-25.

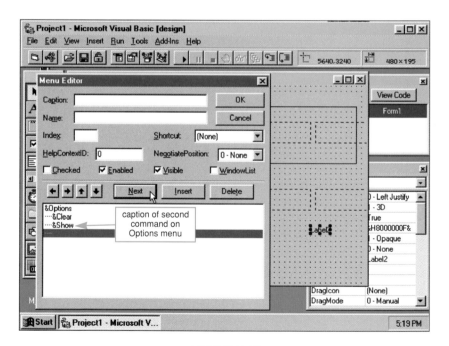

FIGURE 5-25

STEP 5 ▶

Type &Quiz **in the Caption box. Press the TAB key. Type** mnuQuiz **in the Name box. Click the OK button.**

The Menu Editor closes, and the menu is added to the form (Figure 5-26).

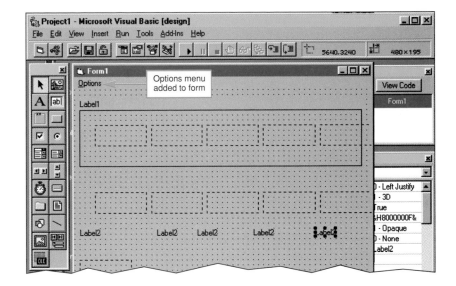

FIGURE 5-26

STEP 6 ▶

Click the menu title, Options, to view the menu structure.

Menus can be viewed during design time, as shown in Figure 5-27. Click anywhere on the form, or press the ESC key to close the menu.

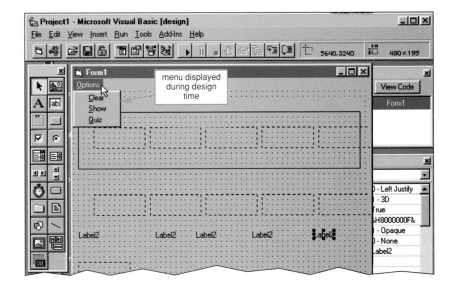

FIGURE 5-27

The interface for the Traffic Sign Tutorial application is now complete. The next step of application development is to set the properties of the form and other controls.

▶ SETTING PROPERTIES

n this section, control properties are set in the following groups of steps:

- ▶ the properties of the form
- ▶ the properties of the five label controls used to display the names of the containers
- ▶ the properties of the controls in the imgSign array
- ▶ the properties of the controls in the imgContainer array
- ▶ the properties of the individual image and label controls

Setting Name, Caption, and Icon Properties of the Form

In the following steps, the name of the form is set, it is given a caption to appear in its title bar and an icon is specified to represent it when it is minimized. The following steps set these properties for the form control.

TO SET THE FORM'S PROPERTIES ▼

STEP 1 ▶

Make the Properties window visible by clicking it. Select the Form1 control from the Object drop-down list. Double-click the Name property in the Properties list. Type `frmTraffic` and press the ENTER key. Click the Project window to make it visible.

The form's new name appears in both the Project window and the Properties window. The form is given a default filename even though it has not yet been saved (Figure 5-28).

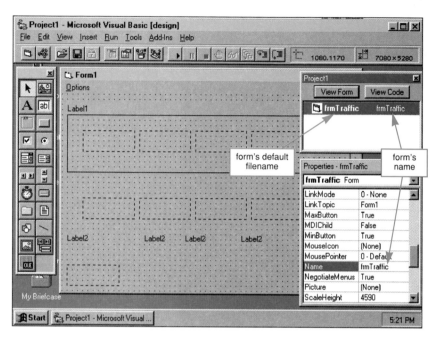

FIGURE 5-28

STEP 2 ▶

Double-click the Caption property in the Properties window. Type `Traffic Sign Tutorial` and press the ENTER key. Double-click the Icon property in the Properties list.

The Load Icon dialog box opens (Figure 5-29).

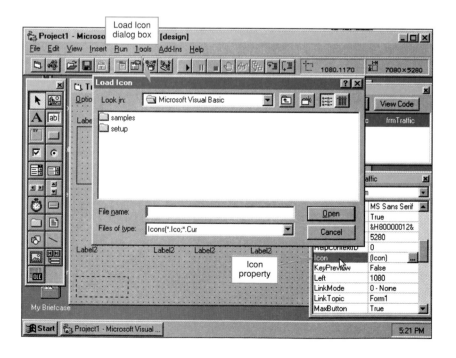

FIGURE 5-29

STEP 3 ▶

With the Student Diskette that accompanies this book in the 3½ Floppy [A:] drive, click 3½ Floppy [A:] in the Look in: drop-down list box. Double-click the VB4 folder. Point to the Trffc09 icon file in the File list box (Figure 5-30).

The traffic sign icons used in this project will be loaded from the VB4 folder on the Student Diskette.

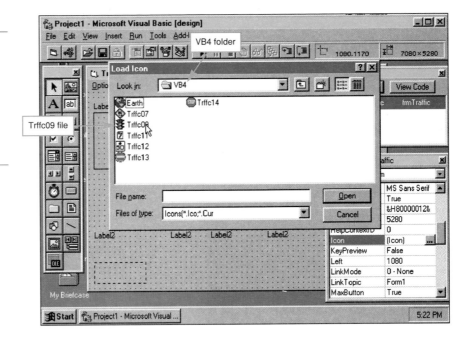

FIGURE 5-30

STEP 4 ▶

Double-click Trffc09.

The Load Icon dialog box closes and the icon is added to the form (Figure 5-31).

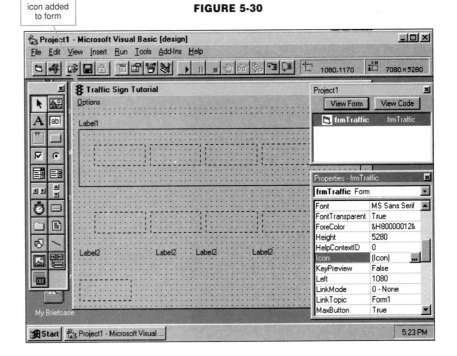

FIGURE 5-31

Setting the Captions of the Label Array Controls

The following steps set the captions of the label controls to reflect the names of the sign containers.

TO SET THE LABELS' CAPTIONS

Step 1: Select the Label2(0) control by clicking its name in the Object drop-down list in the Properties window. Double-click the Caption property. Type `Divided Highway` and press the ENTER key.

Step 2: Select the Label2(1) control by clicking its name in the Object drop-down list in the Properties window. Double-click the Caption property. Type `Stop` and press the ENTER key.

Step 3: Select the Label2(2) control by clicking its name in the Object drop-down list in the Properties window. Double-click the Caption property. Type `Speed Limit` and press the ENTER key.

Step 4: Select the Label2(3) control by clicking its name in the Object drop-down list in the Properties window. Double-click the Caption property. Type `Slippery Road` and press the ENTER key.

Step 5: Select the Label2(4) control by clicking its name in the Object drop-down list in the Properties window. Double-click the Caption property. Type `Do Not Enter` and press the ENTER key.

Step 6: Click the form to place it on top of the Properties window.

The labels' captions appear on the form. If necessary, adjust the location of the labels for even spacing, as shown in Figure 5-32.

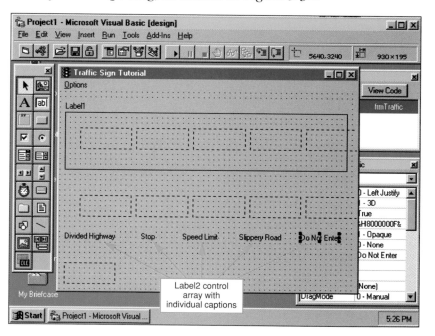

FIGURE 5-32

Setting the Properties of the imgSign Array Controls

Controls in an array must have a common value for their Name property. There is no similar restriction on any other properties of controls in an array. The following steps load some of Visual Basic's traffic sign icons into the image controls in the imgSign array by setting the Picture property of each of these image controls.

When dragging is initiated during run time, only an outline of the control is moved across the desktop. An image other than the control's outline can appear as the control is being dragged by setting the control's **DragIcon property**. Double-clicking the DragIcon property in the Properties list opens the Load Icon dialog box that was used to set the form's Icon property. In this application, the DragIcon property is set with code statements that will be added later. Perform the following steps to load the traffic icons into the image controls in the imgSign array.

TO SET THE PICTURE PROPERTY OF THE IMGSIGN ARRAY CONTROLS

Step 1: Select the imgSign(0) control from the Object drop-down list in the Properties window. Double-click the Picture property in the Properties list.

Step 2: Double-click the *trffc11.ico* (Divided Highway) icon in the File list box.

Step 3: Select the imgSign(1) control. Double-click the Picture property. Double-click the *trffc14.ico* (Stop) icon in the File list box.

Step 4: Select the imgSign(2) control. Double-click the Picture property. Double-click the *trffc12.ico* (Speed Limit) icon in the File list box.

Step 5: Select the imgSign(3) control. Double-click the Picture property. Double-click the *trffc07.ico* (Slippery Road) icon in the File list box.

Step 6: Select the imgSign(4) control. Double-click the Picture property. Double-click the *trffc13.ico* (Do Not Enter) icon in the File list box. Click the form to move it on top of the Properties window.

The traffic icons are loaded into the controls in the imgSign array, as shown in Figure 5-33.

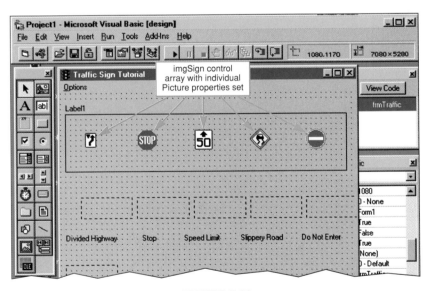

FIGURE 5-33

To load the icons in the previous steps, Visual Basic had to access the .ICO files. Once icons are loaded, they are saved as part of the form file, and the .ICO files are not used again.

Setting Properties for a Group of Controls (imgContainer Array)

The values of the BorderStyle, Height and Width properties of the image controls in the imgContainer array need to be adjusted. In order for these controls to appear as containers, the BorderStyle will be set to 1 - Fixed Single, and the Height and Width properties both will be set to 480 (Figure 5-34).

These properties could be set individually for each control, as has been done many times previously. However, there is an easier way to set a property for a group of controls when the property value will be the same for all the controls in the group. Complete the following steps to select a group of controls and change their property values.

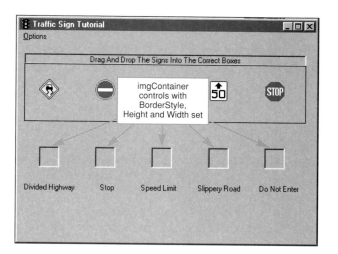

FIGURE 5-34

TO SET PROPERTIES FOR A GROUP OF CONTROLS ▼

STEP 1 ▶

Click the imgContainer(0) control.

The control is selected (Figure 5-35).

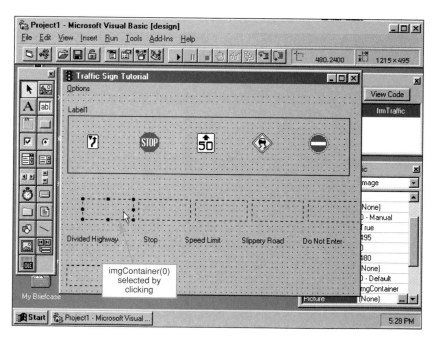

FIGURE 5-35

STEP 2 ▶

With the control selected, press and hold down the CTRL key, and then click each additional control in the imgContainer array.

As additional controls are selected, gray sizing handles appear around the selected control (Figure 5-36).

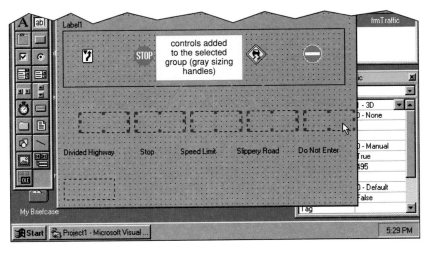

FIGURE 5-36

STEP 3 ▶

Double-click the BorderStyle property in the Properties window.

The BorderStyle of all selected controls changes (Figure 5-37).

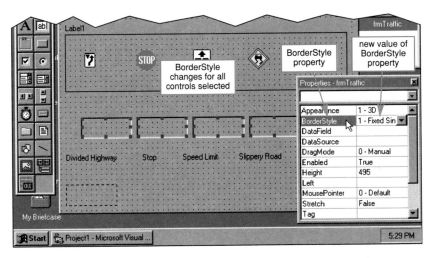

FIGURE 5-37

STEP 4 ▶

Double-click the Height property. Type 480 and press ENTER.

The height of all selected controls changes (Figure 5-38).

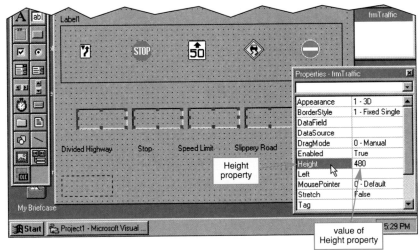

FIGURE 5-38

STEP 5 ▶

Double-click the Width property. Type 480 and press ENTER. Click an empty area of the form.

The width of all selected controls changes and the group of controls is de-selected (Figure 5-39).

FIGURE 5-39

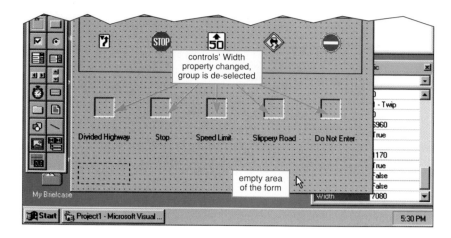

In the preceding steps, properties for all of the image controls in the imgContainer array were changed at the same time by first selecting those controls as a group. This same procedure can be applied to a group of dissimilar controls (for example a text box and a label). However, only the properties those controls have in common can be changed as a group. You can cancel the selection of a specific control in a group by holding down the CTRL key and clicking the control. A group of controls also can be selected by holding down the left mouse button and dragging a box around the controls you want to select as a group.

Setting Properties for the Individual Label and Image Controls

The one label control that is not part of the label array is used to contain the run-time instructions for the Traffic Sign Tutorial application. The instructions are centered in the control by setting the Alignment property.

The individual image control (lower left corner of the form in Figure 5-39) is not visible at run time. It contains a blank picture that is assigned to other image controls through code statements to make them appear to move. The control is named imgBlank to aid in understanding the functions of the code statements in which its name is used. The following steps set the properties for these two controls.

TO SET THE LABEL AND IMAGE CONTROLS' PROPERTIES

Step 1: Select the label control by clicking it or by clicking its name, Label1, in the Object drop-down list in the Properties window.

Step 2: Double-click the Caption property. Type `Drag And Drop The Signs Into The Correct Boxes` and press the ENTER key.

Step 3: Double-click the Alignment property in the Properties window. Double-click the Alignment property in the Properties window a second time to center the text.

Step 4: Double-click the BorderStyle property in the Properties list to change the value to 1 - Fixed Single.

Step 5: Select the Image1 image control by clicking it (located in the bottom left of the Form window) or by clicking its current name, Image1, in the Object drop-down list in the Properties window.

Step 6: Double-click the Name property in the Properties list. Type `imgBlank` and press the ENTER key.

Step 7: Double-click the Visible property in the Properties list to change the value to False.

The new property settings are visible in the Properties window (Figure 5-40).

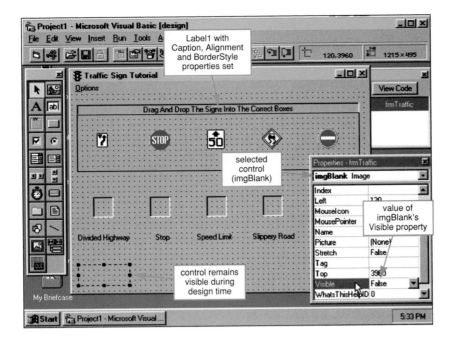

FIGURE 5-40

The design-time property setting is complete. The third phase in application development is to write the code. Before proceeding, save the form using the following steps.

TO SAVE THE FORM

Step 1: Insert a formatted diskette in the 3½ Floppy [A:] drive.
Step 2: Choose Save File As from the File menu.
Step 3: Type Traffic in the File name box in the Save File As dialog box.
Step 4: Click 3½ Floppy [A:] in the Look in: drop-down list.
Step 5: Click the Save button in the Save File As dialog box.

The form is saved as TRAFFIC.FRM. Click the Project window to see the form's filename (Figure 5-41).

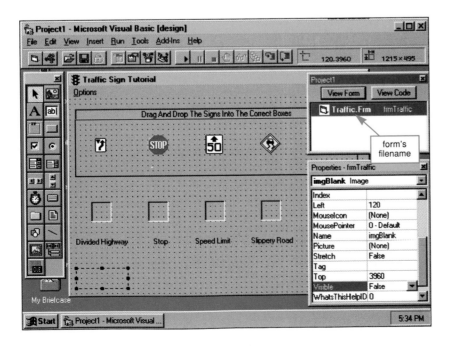

FIGURE 5-41

▶ Writing Code

The code-writing activities for the Traffic Sign Tutorial application include two new events: the DragOver event and the DragDrop event. The **DragOver event** occurs when a drag-and-drop operation is in progress. The mouse pointer position determines which target object receives this event. For example, when an image control (such as, Image1) is dragged over a form (such as, Form1), the Form_DragOver event is initiated. The source is Image1. The target is Form1.

You can write a code statement that applies to any control being dragged over the target by using the word `source` in the code statement. For example, the statement `Source.Visible = False` in a DragOver event subroutine sets the Visible property to False for any control being dragged over the target control. Note that changing the source control's Visible property to False does not affect the source control's DragIcon property. That is, the drag icon is still visible. Changing the source control's Visible property to False gives the effect that the source control is being picked up and moved.

Visual Basic automatically adds the following first line to a DragOver subroutine:

```
Private Sub ctrlName_DragOver (Source As Control, X As Single, Y As Single, State As Integer)
```

The different parts of the DragOver procedure, called **arguments**, are listed in Table 5-1.

▶ TABLE 5-1 DRAGOVER PROCEDURE ARGUMENTS

ARGUMENT	DESCRIPTION
ctrlName	The control being dragged over (the target).
Source	The control being dragged.
X, Y	The current horizontal (X) and vertical (Y) position of the mouse pointer within the target form or control.
State	The transition state of the control being dragged in relation to a target form or control: 0 — Enter (source control is being dragged within the range of a target) 1 — Leave (source control is being dragged out of the range of a target) 2 — Over (source control has moved from one position in the target to another)

The **DragDrop event** occurs when a drag-and-drop operation is completed as a result of dragging a control over a form or control and then releasing the left mouse button. Visual Basic automatically adds the following first line to a DragDrop subroutine:

```
Private Sub ctrlName_DragDrop (Source As Control, X As Single, Y As Single)
```

The arguments of the DragDrop procedure are listed in Table 5-2.

▶ **TABLE 5-2 DRAGDROP PROCEDURE ARGUMENTS**

ARGUMENT	DESCRIPTION
ctrlName	The control over which the mouse pointer is located when the left mouse button is released (the target).
Source	The control being dragged. You can refer to properties and methods with this argument (for example, Source.Visible = False).
X, Y	The current horizontal (X) and vertical (Y) position of the mouse pointer within the target form or control.

The DragDrop event procedure is used to control what happens after a drag-and-drop operation has been completed. For example, you can use the DragDrop event to move the source control to a new location or change the Visible property of the source control.

Code must be written for eleven events in the Traffic Sign Tutorial application. The control name, procedure, and the action's description are listed in Table 5-3.

▶ **TABLE 5-3 TRAFFIC SIGN TUTORIAL EVENTS**

CONTROL NAME	PROCEDURE	ACTION
general	Declarations	Declares variables used within the subroutines.
frmTraffic	Load	Center the form on the desktop. Sets the DragIcon property for image controls in the imgSign array.
frmTraffic	DragOver	Occurs when dragging one of the signs is initiated. Changes the source control's Visible property to False.
frmTraffic	DragDrop	Dropping a sign on the form (not in a container) is an incorrect placement of a sign. The source control's Visible property is set to True so the control appears to "snap back" to its original position.
imgSign	DragDrop	Dropping a sign on another sign is also an incorrect placement. Same action as the form's DragDrop event.
Label1	DragDrop	Dropping a sign on a label is also an incorrect placement. Same action as form's DragDrop event.
Label2	DragDrop	Same as Label1_DragDrop event.
imgContainer	DragDrop	Evaluates whether placement is correct or not. If correct, sets container's picture; if not, sets source Visible property to True.
mnuClear	Click	Clears all pictures from containers; sets all imgSign( ) Visible properties to True.
mnuShow	Click	Sets all imgSign( ) properties to False; sets imgContainer( ) Picture properties equal to correct signs.
mnuQuiz	Click	Hides Traffic form; displays three questions (one at a time); keeps displaying question until a correct answer is given; shows Traffic form.

The subroutines for the frmTraffic_DragDrop, imgSign_DragDrop, Label1_DragDrop, and Label2_DragDrop are identical and are written using the same set of steps. The code-writing activities for the Traffic Sign Tutorial application are grouped as follows:

- ▶ General_Declarations subroutine
- ▶ frmTraffic_Load subroutine
- ▶ frmTraffic_DragOver subroutine
- ▶ Label1, Label2, form, and imgSign DragDrop subroutines
- ▶ imgContainer_DragDrop subroutine
- ▶ mnuClear_Click subroutine
- ▶ mnuShow_Click subroutine
- ▶ mnuQuiz_Click subroutine

The subroutines written in the sections that follow include remark statements. **Remarks**, also called **comments**, are explanatory statements within a subroutine. A remark can be any text you want to include in your program. Spaces and punctuation are permitted. Comments are used to **document** (provide a written record of) how your code works or to provide any other information with your code. A remark statement must begin with either the word **REM** or an apostrophe (') to indicate to Visual Basic that the statement is not executable. When the application runs, all REM statements are ignored as if they weren't in the subroutine.

Writing the General_Declarations Subroutine

The Traffic Sign Tutorial application keeps a count of the number of correct sign placements by adding the number 1 to a variable named NumCorrect each time a correct placement is made. Because the value of NumCorrect must be available to more than one subroutine, it must be declared. The concept of declaring variables was introduced in Project 2 (page VB94). Recall that variable declarations must include a data type.

Visual Basic allows variables to have a **Variant data type**, so a given variable can store numbers, text, dates, or times. The Variant data type handles all types of data and converts them automatically. Declaring a data type other than Variant restricts the use of the variable but conserves some memory and makes the code run slightly faster. Visual Basic data types are listed in Table 5-4.

▶ **TABLE 5-4 VISUAL BASIC DATA TYPES**

TYPE	STORAGE	RANGE OF VALUES
Integer	2 bytes	-32,768 to 32,767
Long	4 bytes	-2,147,483,648 to 2,147,483,647
Single	4 bytes	-3.402823E38 to -1.401298E-45 for negative values; 1.401298E-45 to 3.402823E38 for positive values
Double	8 bytes	-1.79769313486232E308 to -4.94065645841247E-324 for negative values
Currency	8 bytes	-922,337,203,685,477.5808 to 922,337,203,685,477.5807
String	1 byte/chr	0 to approximately 65,500 bytes (some storage overhead is required)
Variant	As needed	Any numeric value up to the range of a Double or any character text

For more information about data types, click Search For Help On.. on the Visual Basic Help menu. Type `Data Type` and click the Display button.

TO WRITE THE GENERAL_DECLARATIONS SUBROUTINE

Step 1: Minimize the Form window.
Step 2: Click the View Code button in the Project window.
Step 3: Enter the following statement in the General_Declarations subroutine:
```
Dim NumCorrect As Integer
```
Step 4: Press ENTER.

The minimized Form window and the Code window appear as shown in Figure 5-42.

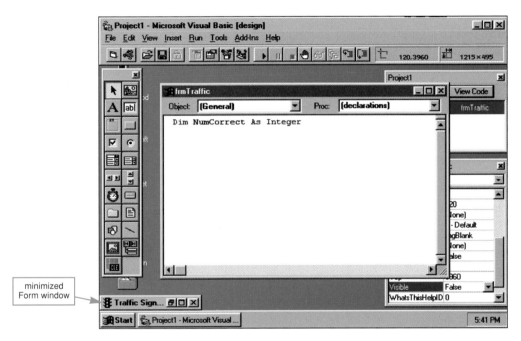

FIGURE 5-42

Writing the frmTraffic_Load Subroutine

The code in this subroutine causes the Traffic form to be centered on the desktop at the beginning of run time. The same code statements used to center the forms in previous projects are used in this project.

This subroutine also assigns a picture to the DragIcon property of each of the controls in the imgSign array. Recall that the default property setting for a drag icon is simply an outline of the control. In the following steps, the DragIcon property for each image is set equal to that image's Picture property. For example, the Picture property for imgSign(0) is the Divided Highway sign. The statement

```
imgSign(0).DragIcon = imgSign(0).Picture
```

sets the drag icon for that control to the Divided Highway icon. Because this assignment must be done for all five signs, the For...Next code structure presented in Project 4 is used. Perform the steps on the next page to write the Load procedure for the frmTraffic control.

TO WRITE THE FRMTRAFFIC_LOAD SUBROUTINE

Step 1: Select the form control from the Object drop-down list in the Code window. Drag the Code window's right border to extend the width of the Code window.

Step 2: Enter the following statements in the Code window:

```
Rem Center form on desktop
frmTraffic.Top = (Screen.Height - frmTraffic.Height) / 2
frmTraffic.Left = (Screen.Width - frmTraffic.Width) / 2
Rem Set dragicons for signs
For Index = 0 To 4
    imgSign(Index).DragIcon = imgSign(Index).Picture
Next
```

The Code window appears as shown in Figure 5-43.

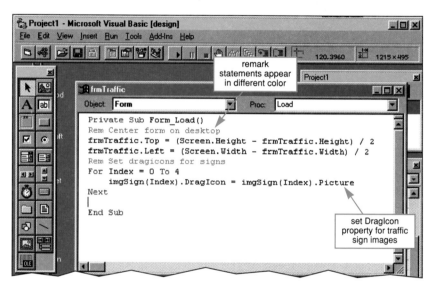

FIGURE 5-43

In the preceding steps, two remarks were added to help clarify the code statements that follow them. Note that when the ENTER key is pressed after a REM statement, Visual Basic changes the color of the statement to further set it apart from executable statements.

Writing the Form_DragOver Subroutine

This subroutine is executed whenever a control is dragged over the form. Because a shape control does not have a DragOver event, this event occurs in the Traffic Sign Tutorial application when one of the traffic signs is dragged from its original position. To give the appearance that the sign is being moved, this event is used to change the Visible property of the source control to False. In this way, the source control's drag icon is visible when dragging occurs, but the source control is not visible in its original location.

The following steps write the code statement to set the Visible property to False when the drag-and-drop operation begins.

TO WRITE THE FORM_DRAGOVER EVENT

Step 1: Select the DragOver procedure from the Procedure drop-down list in the Code window.

Step 2: Enter the following statements in the Code window:
```
Rem Set sign to invisible when dragging begins
Source.Visible = False
```

The Code window appears as shown in Figure 5-44.

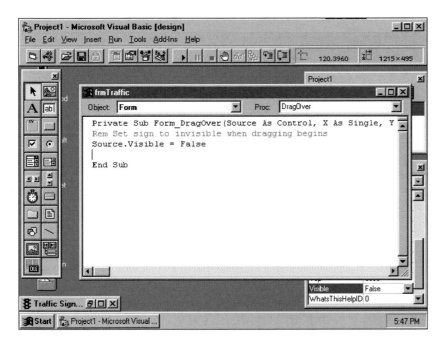

FIGURE 5-44

It is important to note that the Form_DragOver event is the first event to occur during the drag-and-drop operation in this application because the form is the first control that a source is dragged across when dragging is initiated.

Writing the Form, Label1, Label2, and imgSign DragDrop Subroutines

During the drag-and-drop operation in the Traffic Sign Tutorial application, a control can be dropped on any of the controls listed above or on one of the controls in the imgContainer array. Recall that the Visible property of the source control (image being dragged) was set to False at the beginning of the drag-and-drop operation in the Form_DragOver event.

The DragDrop event occurs at the end of a drag-and-drop operation when the left mouse button is released. If the control (traffic sign) being dragged is dropped on any control other than an imgContainer, the placement is incorrect. When this error occurs, setting the source control's Visible property back to True makes the control appear to snap back to its original location. The code statements to do this are written in the steps on the next page. The following steps also show how one event applies to all controls in an array.

TO WRITE THE DRAGDROP SUBROUTINES ▼

STEP 1 ▶

Select DragDrop from the Procedure drop-down list in the Code window.

The Form_DragDrop subroutine appears in the Code window (Figure 5-45).

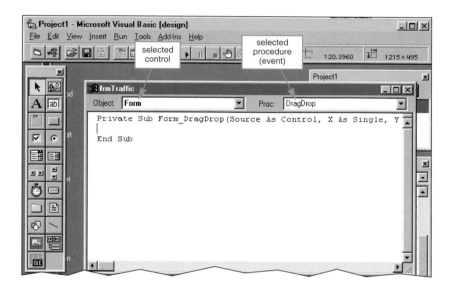

FIGURE 5-45

STEP 2 ▶

Enter the following two statements in the Code window:

```
Rem Unallowable drop; return
sign to original location
Source.Visible = True
```

The Code window appears as shown in Figure 5-46.

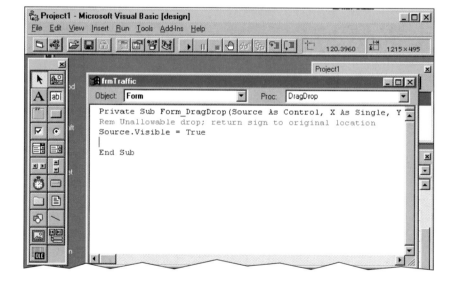

FIGURE 5-46

STEP 3 ▶

Move the cursor to the left of the R in Rem. Press and hold the SHIFT key. Press the cursor down arrow key twice. Release the SHIFT key.

The two code statements written in Step 2 are highlighted (Figure 5-47).

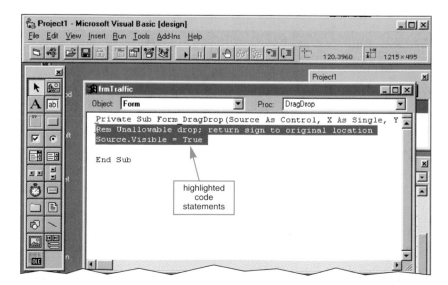

FIGURE 5-47

STEP 4 ▶

Press CTRL+C to copy the highlighted text to the Clipboard. Select the Label1_DragDrop subroutine by clicking Label1 in the Object drop-down list and clicking DragDrop in the Procedure drop-down list. Press CTRL+V to paste the Clipboard's contents inside the active Code window.

The highlighted code statements are copied to the Clipboard and then pasted to the Label1_Drag-Drop subroutine (Figure 5-48).

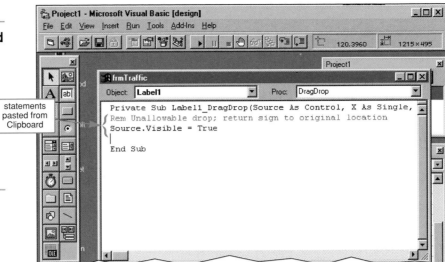

FIGURE 5-48

STEP 5 ▶

Select the Label2_DragDrop subroutine by clicking Label2() in the Object drop-down list and clicking DragDrop in the Procedure drop-down list. Press CTRL+V to paste the Clipboard's contents inside the active Code window.

The highlighted code statements are pasted to the Label2_Drag-Drop subroutine (Figure 5-49).

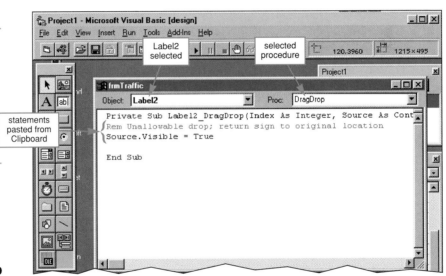

FIGURE 5-49

STEP 6 ▶

Select the imgSign_DragDrop subroutine by clicking imgSign() in the Object drop-down list and clicking DragDrop in the Procedure drop-down list. Press CTRL+V to paste the Clipboard's contents inside the active Code window.

The highlighted code statements are pasted to the imgSign_Drag-Drop subroutine (Figure 5-50).

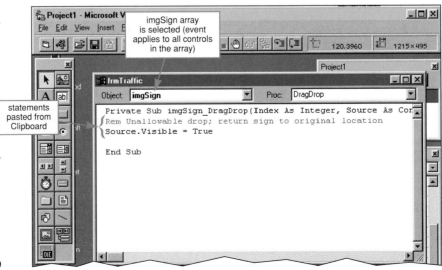

FIGURE 5-50

Project 2 presented a method for copying code between subroutines using the mouse and commands in the Edit menu. The preceding steps presented an alternate method for copying code using keyboard commands only. These same keyboard commands were used to copy and paste controls earlier in this project.

Writing the imgContainer_DragDrop Subroutine

Dropping a sign on one of the containers may or may not be a correct placement of the sign. Care was taken to add the controls in the arrays to the form in a certain order and to assign the pictures of the imgSign array and captions of the Label2 array in the same order.

For example, the Picture property of imgSign(0) is the Divided Highway sign. Label2(0) appears on the form below the imgContainer(0) control, and its caption is Divided Highway (Figure 5-51). By maintaining this consistency in array indexes, the "correctness" of dropping one of the imgSign controls on one of the imgContainer controls is determined by whether their indexes match. Recall that Index is a property of the source control when the source control is part of an array, and that Index also is an argument of the DragDrop event that identifies the specific target control when the target control is part of an array. Later, the imgSign controls will be rearranged on the form to make the tutorial more challenging, but this change will not affect their indexes.

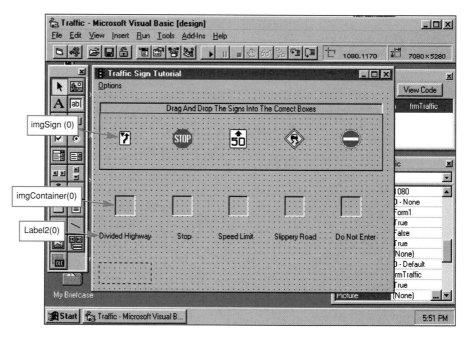

FIGURE 5-51

In the Traffic Sign Tutorial application, certain actions occur if the placement is correct, and other actions occur if it is not. This type of logical selection is represented in code with the If...Then...Else structure used in previous projects. One of the actions if the placement is correct is to **increment** (add 1 to) the NumCorrect variable, which is used as a **counter**. Because the number of signs is five, additional actions are initiated if the counter's value = 5. This logic also is structured as an If...Then statement, but the condition NumCorrect = 5 is evaluated only if the current placement is correct. This If...Then structure within an If...Then...Else structure is called **nested**.

The logical flow of the nested If...Then structure for the Traffic Sign Tutorial application is diagrammed in Figure 5-52. The dialog box that indicates all signs have been placed correctly (Figure 5-53) is created using the MsgBox statement.

When the OK button is clicked in the dialog box, the signs are returned to their original positions. This same action occurs when the Clear command is chosen from Options menu in the application. Instead of repeating the code statements in both subroutines, you can execute a second subroutine by **calling** the event procedure for the second subroutine from the first. For example, when Visual Basic encounters the statement `mnuClear_Click` within the imgContainer_DragDrop subroutine, it immediately executes all the code within the mnuClear_Click subroutine and then returns to execute the next code statement in the imgContainer_DragDrop subroutine.

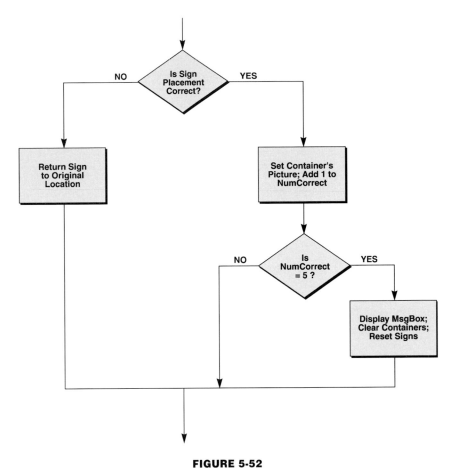

FIGURE 5-52

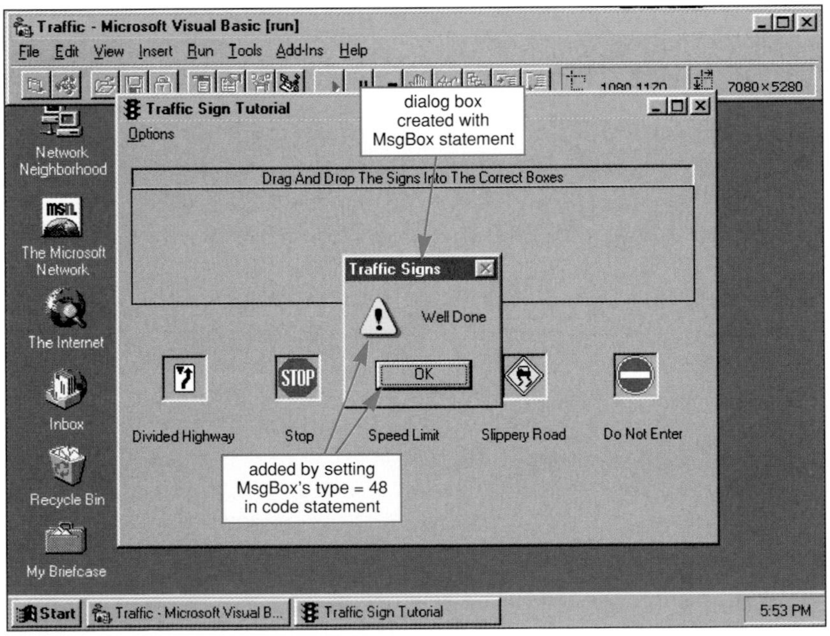

FIGURE 5-53

The following steps write the imgContainer_DragDrop subroutine using the nested If...Then structure.

TO WRITE THE IMGCONTAINER_DRAGDROP SUBROUTINE

Step 1: Select the imgContainer control array from the Object drop-down list in the Code window. Select the DragDrop procedure from the Procedure drop-down list.

Step 2: Enter the following statements in the Code window:

```
Rem Check for correct drop (indexes match)
If Source.Index = Index Then
    Rem Place sign in container; increment NumCorrect
    imgContainer(Index).Picture = Source.Picture
    NumCorrect = NumCorrect + 1
    Rem Check for last sign
    If NumCorrect = 5 Then
        Rem Display message; clear form
        MsgBox "Well Done", 48, "Traffic Signs"
        mnuClear_Click
    End If
Else
    Rem Incorrect drop; return sign to original location
    Source.Visible = True
End If
```

The maximized Code window appears as shown in Figure 5-54.

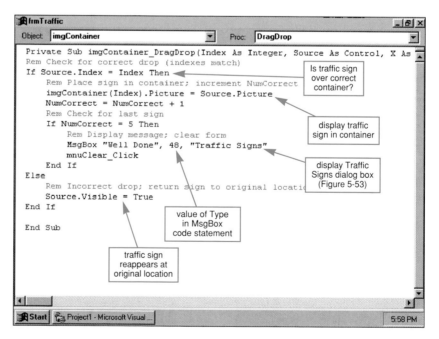

FIGURE 5-54

Writing the mnuClear_Click Subroutine

When the user of the Traffic Sign Tutorial application chooses this command, all signs currently in containers are returned to their original locations. This command actually involves two actions: clearing any pictures from the container images and setting the Visible property of the imgSign controls. This subroutine also resets the value of NumCorrect to 0.

Each container is cleared by setting its Picture property equal to the Picture property of the imgBlank control. Each sign appears to return to its original locations by setting the Visible property of the controls in the imgSign array to True.

Because the property setting must be done for each control in the two arrays, the following steps write the subroutine using the For...Next loop presented on page VB229.

TO WRITE THE MNUCLEAR_CLICK SUBROUTINE

Step 1: Select the mnuClear control from the Object drop-down list in the Code window.

Step 2: Enter the following statements in the Code window:

```
Rem Clear containers and reset signs to original locations
For Index = 0 To 4
    imgContainer(Index).Picture = imgBlank.Picture
    imgSign(Index).Visible = True
Next
Rem Reset counter
NumCorrect = 0
```

The Code window appears as shown in Figure 5-55.

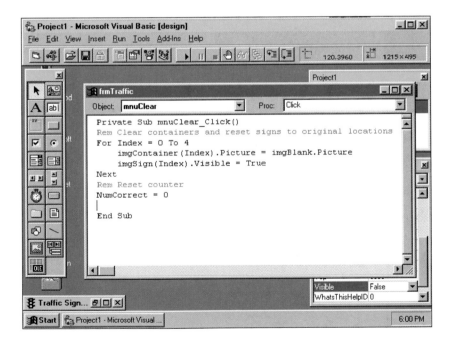

FIGURE 5-55

The mnuShow_Click Subroutine

When the Show command is chosen from the Options menu, all the signs appear to move from their original locations to the correct containers. This move is accomplished by setting the imgSign controls' Visible property to False and by setting each imgContainer's Picture property equal to the Picture property of the imgSign control's corresponding index.

You can choose the Show command any time during run time. Therefore, movements for all controls must be programmed because you don't know which signs have been placed correctly and which ones have not. The following steps use a For...Next loop to perform these tasks.

TO WRITE THE MNUSHOW_CLICK SUBROUTINE

Step 1: Select the mnuShow control from the Object drop-down list in the Code window.

Step 2: Enter the following statements in the Code window:

```
Rem Move all signs to correct containers
For Index = 0 To 4
    imgContainer(Index).Picture = imgSign(Index).Picture
    imgSign(Index).Visible = False
Next
```

The Code window appears as shown in Figure 5-56.

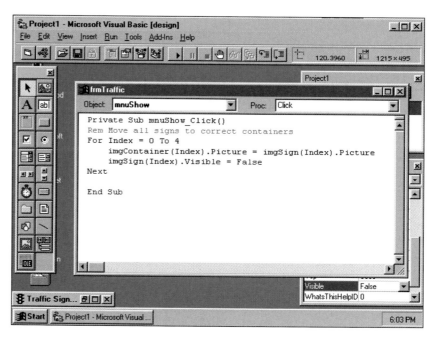

FIGURE 5-56

Writing the mnuQuiz_Click Subroutine

When you choose the Quiz command from the Options menu, you initiate a subroutine that contains several code structures, some of which are nested. The Quiz subroutine presents a series of three questions about the shapes of some signs. A For...Next loop is used to repeat the process of presenting a question and processing an answer.

When the Quiz is displayed, the main form is removed from the desktop. This is accomplished using the Hide method. The **Hide method** removes a form from the screen and its Visible property is set to False. However, unlike the Unload method used in Project 3 (VB173), the form is not removed from the computer's memory and the hidden form's controls are available to the running Visual Basic application. After the Quiz is completed, the form is added back to the desktop using the Show method presented in Project 3 (VB172).

The questions are displayed using a dialog box (Figure 5-57). An **InputBox function** displays a prompt in a dialog box, waits for the user to input text or to choose a button, and then returns the contents of the text box to the subroutine.

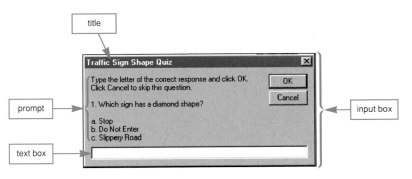

FIGURE 5-57

The syntax of the simplest form of the InputBox function is:

InputBox*(prompt, title)*

The arguments of the InputBox function are described in Table 5-5.

▸ **TABLE 5-5 ARGUMENTS OF THE INPUTBOX FUNCTION**

ARGUMENT	DESCRIPTION
prompt	String expression displayed as the message in the dialog box. The maximum length is approximately 255 characters depending on the width of the characters used.
title	String expression displayed in the title bar of the dialog box. If the title is omitted, nothing is placed in the title bar.

The prompt in Figure 5-57 consists of the question and all possible answers. A new line is started for each answer by using the carriage return and linefeed control characters presented on page VB104. This time their use is simplified, however, by creating and using a variable named NL (for new line) that is given the value of the control characters as follows:

```
NL = Chr$(13) & Chr$(10)
```

The variable's name, NL, now can be used in code statements in place of the control code characters themselves.

If the user chooses the OK button or presses the ENTER key, the InputBox function returns whatever is in the text box. If the user chooses the Cancel button, the function returns a zero-length string (""). More complex InputBox functions are available in Visual Basic. For more information, refer to Visual Basic's online Help.

Each time the subroutine loops through the For...Next structure it must select the appropriate question. Project 3 presented the If...Then...Else statement as a method of selection within code. This project uses an additional selection structure, the Select Case statement. The **Select Case statement** executes one of several statement blocks depending on the value of an expression. In its simplest form, its syntax is:

Select Case *testexpression*
Case *expression1*
    statementblock-1
Case *expression2*
    statementblock-2
Case *Else*
    statementblock-n
End *Select*

The parts of the Select Case statement are described in Table 5-6 on the next page.

▸ **TABLE 5-6 PARTS OF THE SELECT CASE STATEMENT**

PART	DESCRIPTION
Select Case	Begins the Select Case structure. Must appear on a separate line before any other part of the Select Case structure.
testexpression	The name of a variable or any numeric or *string expression* whose value is compared to the *expressions* that follow the word Case in each block (e.g. *expression1, expression2, etc.*). If *testexpression* matches the *expression* associated with a Case clause, the *statementblock* following that Case clause is executed.
Case	Begins a Case clause setting a group of Visual Basic statements to be executed if the *expression* following the word Case matches *testexpression*.
expression	The value of *testexpression* that leads to a different *statementblock* being executed. Similar to the *condition* in an If...Then statement.
statementblock	Any number of Visual Basic code statements.
Case *Else*	Optional keyword indicating the *statementblock* to be executed if no match is found between the *testexpression* and an *expression* in any of the other Case selections.
End *Select*	Ends the Select Case structure. Must appear on a separate line after all other statements in the Select Case structure.

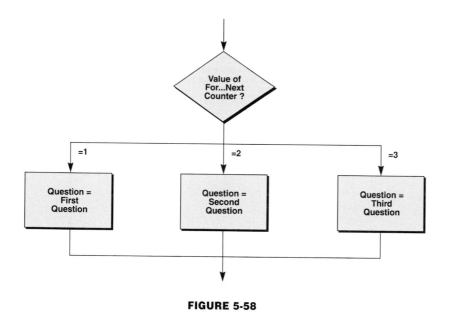

FIGURE 5-58

In the Traffic Sign Tutorial application, the counter in the For...Next loop is used as the *testexpression*, and the values from 1 to 3 are used in the *expressions* to select the appropriate question. The logical flow is diagrammed in Figure 5-58.

Although the question displayed in the Traffic Tutorial Quiz InputBox changes, the instructions and the set of possible answers remain the same each time. Code writing is simplified by creating three variables, named *inst1, inst2* and *answers*. The *inst1* and *inst2* variables hold the text of the instructions and the codes for new lines. The *answers* variable holds the text of the set of answers. The variables' names then are used in place of all the text. The code statements to create these variables are:

```
inst1 = "Type the letter of the correct response and click OK. "
inst2 = "Click Cancel to skip this question." & NL & NL
answers = "a. Stop" & NL & "b. Do Not Enter" & NL & "c. Slippery Road"
```

The code statements and explanatory remarks for the first part of the mnuQuiz subroutine are as follows:

```
Rem Create newline variable
NL = Chr$(13) & Chr$(10)
Rem Create instructions variables
inst1 = "Type the letter of the correct response and click OK. "
inst2 = "Click Cancel to skip this question." & NL & NL
Rem Create answers variable
answers = "a. Stop" & NL & "b. Do Not Enter" & NL & "c. Slippery Road"
Rem Hide traffic form
frmTraffic.Hide
Rem Loop for three questions
For QuesNum = 1 To 3
    Rem Assign value to variable Question and variable CorrectAnswer
    Select Case QuesNum
      Case Is = 1
          question = "1. Which sign has a diamond shape?" & NL & NL & answers
          CorrectAnswer = "C"
      Case Is = 2
          question = "2. Which sign has an octagonal shape?" & NL & NL & answers
          CorrectAnswer = "A"
      Case Is = 3
          question = "3. Which sign has a round shape?" & NL & NL & answers
          CorrectAnswer = "B"
    End Select
```

At this point in the code's execution during run time, the For...Next loop has begun. The first question has been assigned to the variable Question, and the correct answer to the first question has been assigned to the variable CorrectAnswer.

Next, the question must be displayed and the user's answer processed. An InputBox function is used to display the question and to get the user's answer. Whatever the user has typed in the text box of the dialog box is assigned as the value of a variable when the OK button is clicked. The variable can be given any valid variable name. This variable is named *Response* in the Traffic Sign Tutorial.

If the user has entered an incorrect answer and has clicked the OK button, the value of the variable Response does not match the value of the variable CorrectAnswer. The Traffic Sign Tutorial application then displays the message box shown in Figure 5-59.

The application continues to redisplay the message box and the same question until the correct answer is given or until the user clicks the Cancel button. A For...Next loop is not an appropriate structure of repetition for this activity because the number of repetitions is not known in advance. A **Do...Loop** repeats a block of statements while a condition is True or until a condition is met. In this application, the incorrect answer message box and question are displayed until the answer is correct or until the Cancel button has been clicked. One form of the Do...Loop, called a **Do Until loop,** is used. The syntax is as follows:

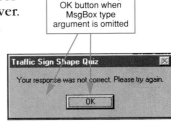

no icon and only OK button when MsgBox type argument is omitted

FIGURE 5-59

```
Do Until condition
    statementblock
Loop
```

The parts of the Do Until loop are described in Table 5-7.

▶ **TABLE 5-7 PARTS OF THE DO UNTIL LOOP**

PART	DESCRIPTION
Do	Must be the first statement in a Do...Loop control structure.
statementblock	Program lines between the Do and Loop statements that are repeated while or until condition is True.
Until	Indicates the loop is executed until condition is True.
condition	Numeric or string expression that evaluates to True.

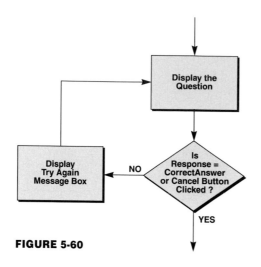

FIGURE 5-60

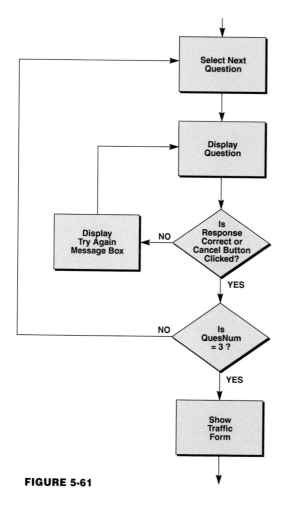

FIGURE 5-61

The logical flow of this Do Until loop is diagrammed in Figure 5-60. Notice that if the user responds correctly the first time or clicks the Cancel button, the condition is True immediately and the statements inside the loop (statementblock) are not executed. The online Help contains information on other variations of Do...Loop statements.

The condition evaluated in the Traffic Shape Quiz is whether the value of the variable Response equals the value of the variable CorrectAnswer or the value (""). Recall that the zero length string value ("") means the Cancel button was clicked. Notice in the code on page VB283 that the value assigned to the variable CorrectAnswer in Case = 1 is the character uppercase C. If the user enters a lowercase c, the condition will evaluate to False and the loop will continue. A way to account for a user responding in either lower or uppercase is to use the UCase$ function.

The **UCase$ function** returns a string with all letters of the argument uppercase. Its syntax is:

UCase$(*stringexpr*)

The argument *stringexpr* can be any string expression. Only lowercase letters are converted to uppercase; all uppercase letters and nonletter characters remain unchanged.

An InputBox statement is placed before the Do Until loop to provide the first opportunity for the user to respond. The loop executes until a correct answer is given *for each question*. That is, the Do...Loop is nested within the For...Next loop, as diagrammed in Figure 5-61. The additional code for the mnuQuiz_Click subroutine is as follows:

```
Rem Display question; assign returned value to
    variable Response
Response = InputBox(inst1 & inst2 & question,
    "Traffic Sign Shape Quiz")
Rem Begin loop for correct answer or Cancel button
Do Until UCase$(Response) = CorrectAnswer Or
    Response = ""
    Rem Create variable named TryAgain to hold text
        of message box for wrong answer
    TryAgain = "Your response was not correct.
        Please try again."
    Rem Display message box for wrong answer
    MsgBox TryAgain, , "Traffic Sign Shape Quiz"
    Rem Display question; assign returned value to
        variable Response
    Response = InputBox(inst1 & inst2 & question,
        "Traffic Sign Shape Quiz")
Loop
Rem Add 1 to counter in for next loop
Next
Rem Redisplay main form after 3rd question
frmTraffic.Show
```

With the second section of code on page VB284, the mnuQuiz_Click subroutine is complete. In the following steps the mnuQuiz_Click subroutine is entered in the Code window.

TO WRITE THE MNUQUIZ_CLICK SUBROUTINE

Step 1: Select the mnuQuiz control from the Object drop-down list in the Code window.

Step 2: Enter the code for the subroutine, as shown in Figure 5-62.

```
frmTraffic                                                      _ |8| X|
Object: mnuQuiz                      ▼   Proc: Click                  ▼

Private Sub mnuQuiz_Click()
Rem Create newline variable
NL = Chr$(13) & Chr$(10)
Rem Create instructions variables
inst1 = "Type the letter of the correct response and click OK. "
inst2 = "Click Cancel to skip this question." & NL & NL
Rem Create answers variable
answers = "a. Stop" & NL & "b. Do Not Enter" & NL & "c. Slippery Road"
Rem Hide traffic form
frmTraffic.Hide
Rem Loop for three questions
For QuesNum = 1 To 3
    Rem Assign value to variable Question and variable CorrectAnswer
    Select Case QuesNum
      Case Is = 1
          question = "1. Which sign has a diamond shape?" & NL & NL & answers
          CorrectAnswer = "C"
      Case Is = 2
          question = "2. Which sign has an octagonal shape?" & NL & NL & answe
          CorrectAnswer = "A"
      Case Is = 3
          question = "3. Which sign has a round shape?" & NL & NL & answers
          CorrectAnswer = "B"
    End Select
    Rem Display question; assign returned value to variable Response
    Response = InputBox(inst1 & inst2 & question, "Traffic Sign Shape Quiz")
    Rem Begin loop for correct answer or CANCEL button
    Do Until UCase$(Response) = CorrectAnswer Or Response = ""
        Rem Create variable named TryAgain to hold text of message box for wron
        TryAgain = "Your response was not correct. Please try again."
        Rem Display message box for wrong answer
        MsgBox TryAgain, , "Traffic Sign Shape Quiz"
        Rem Display question; assign returned value to variable Response
        Response = InputBox(inst1 & inst2 & question, "Traffic Sign Shape Quiz"
    Loop
Rem Add 1 to counter in for next loop
Next
Rem Redisplay main form after 3rd question
frmTraffic.Show

End Sub
```
```
Start  | Project1 - Microsoft Visual ...                        6:31 PM
```

FIGURE 5-62

One last activity must be done before the Traffic Sign Tutorial is complete. In its current state (Figure 5-63), the correct container for each sign is directly below the sign. The steps on the next page rearrange the imgSign controls to make the tutorial more challenging.

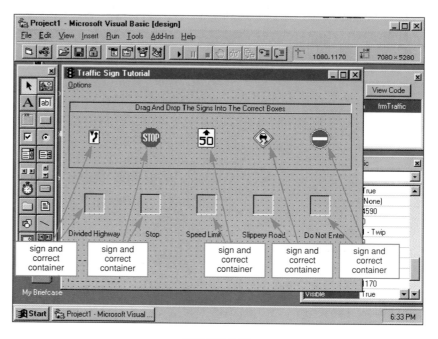

FIGURE 5-63

TO REARRANGE THE IMGSIGN CONTROLS

Step 1: Close the Code window by clicking its Close button.
Step 2: Restore the Form window by clicking the form's button on the taskbar.
Step 3: Rearrange the imgSign controls by dragging them to the positions shown in Figure 5-64.

This rearrangement does not affect the controls' indexes and therefore will have no effect on the function of the Tutorial.

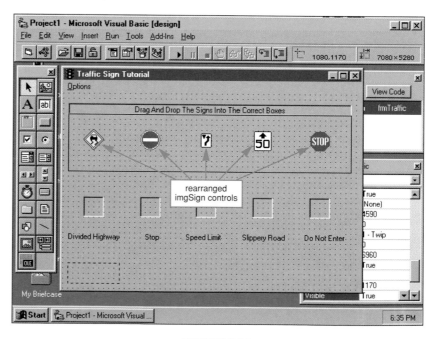

FIGURE 5-64

▶ SAVING, RUNNING, AND DOCUMENTING THE APPLICATION

T he Traffic Sign Tutorial project is complete. Before running the application, the form should be resaved and the project should be saved. The application is documented by generating a written record of the application's form and code.

Saving the Project

The following steps resave the form file with the added code and save the project file to the diskette in the 3½ Floppy [A:] drive.

TO SAVE THE PROJECT

Step 1: Choose Save Project from the File menu, or click the Save Project button on the toolbar.

Step 2: Type Traffic in the File name box in the Save Project As dialog box.

Step 3: Click the Save button in the Save Project As dialog box.

The form file is resaved on the diskette in the 3½ Floppy [A:] drive as TRAF-FIC.FRM. The project file is saved on the diskette in the 3½ Floppy [A:] drive as TRAFFIC.VBP.

Running the Application

With the application saved to a diskette, it can be run and tested. If Visual Basic encounters an error while reading or executing the code, it will halt execution and display and highlight the error in the Code window. The error can be corrected, and the application can be restarted. If you detect and correct any errors in this manner, be certain to resave the project.

The steps on the next page run the Traffic Sign Tutorial application and test its functionality.

TO RUN THE APPLICATION ▼

STEP 1 ▶

Click the Start button on the toolbar, or choose Start from the Run menu.

The application appears (Figure 5-65).

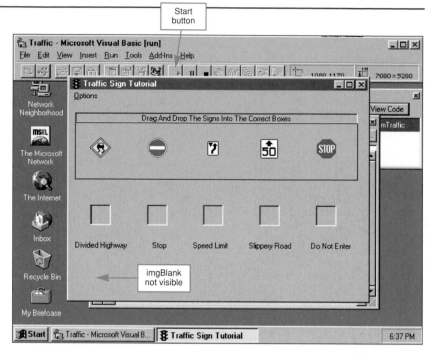

FIGURE 5-65

STEP 2 ▶

Click Show on the Options menu.

The signs move to the correct containers (Figure 5-66).

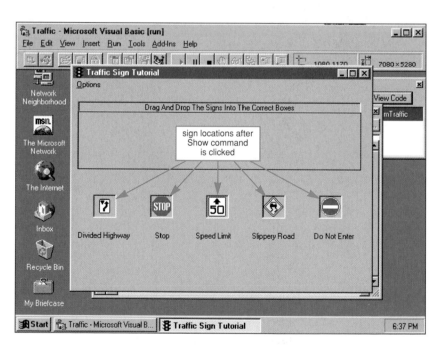

FIGURE 5-66

STEP 3 ▶

Choose Clear from the Options menu to return the signs to their original locations. Drag and drop one of the signs anywhere on the form other than its correct container.

During the drag operation the sign appears to move from its original location (Figure 5-67). When dropped incorrectly, it returns to its original position.

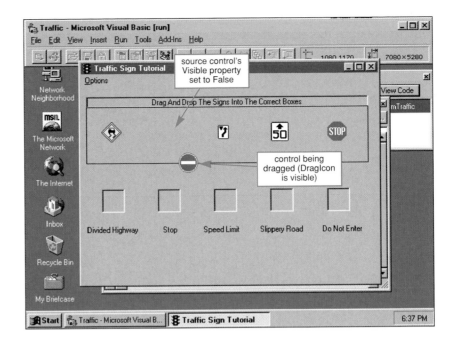

FIGURE 5-67

STEP 4 ▶

Choose Quiz from the Options menu. Enter a (an incorrect answer) and then click the OK button. When the dialog box indicating an incorrect response appears, click the OK button.

The question is redisplayed until a correct answer is given (Figure 5-68).

STEP 5 ▶

Complete the quiz, and then test the other features of the application. To end the application, click the Traffic Sign Tutorial's Close button or click the End button on the toolbar.

Because the dialog box is a modal form, you cannot perform any other function (including stopping the application) until the form is closed by entering the correct answer or clicking Cancel.

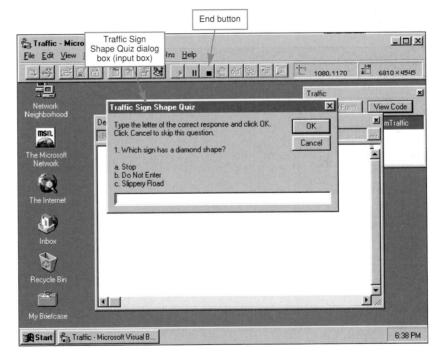

FIGURE 5-68

Documenting the Application

In this project, remarks were added within subroutines to make the code statements more understandable. Also, variable names were chosen that reflected the purpose of the variable, such as QuesNum instead of x or y. Using these methods to aid understanding is called making the code **self-documenting**.

Documenting the application refers to generating a written record of the application. The following steps can be used to print a record of the application when the computer is connected to a printer.

TO PRINT A RECORD OF THE APPLICATION ▼

STEP 1 ▶

Select the File menu from the menu bar.

The File menu opens (Figure 5-69).

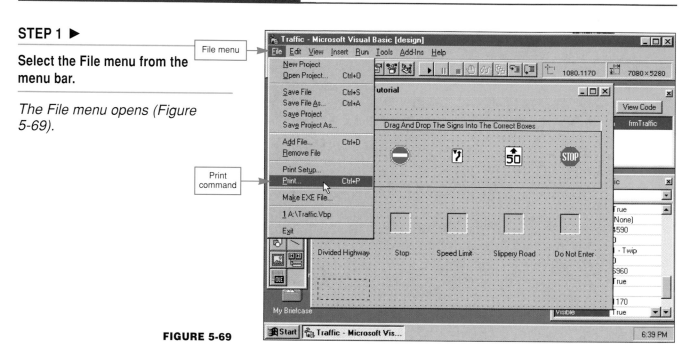

FIGURE 5-69

STEP 2 ▶

Choose the Print command.

The Print dialog box opens (Figure 5-70).

STEP 3 ▶

Click the Project option button. Click the Form Image check box. Click the Code check box. Click the OK button.

The Traffic form and code subroutines are printed.

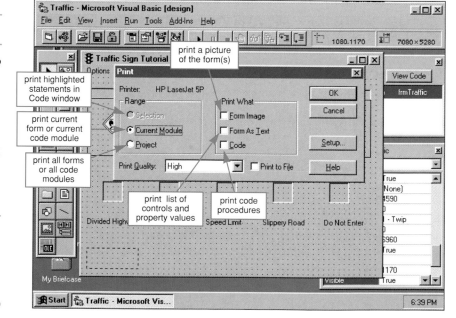

FIGURE 5-70

▶ **PROJECT SUMMARY**

In Project 5, the three-step approach was used to build another Windows application. The InputBox and UCase$ functions were used in the code statements. More complex code was written using nested structures, the Select Case structure, and the Do...Loop structure. Remarks were added to aid in understanding the code, and a printed record of the application was generated.

▶ **KEY TERMS AND INDEX**

arguments *(VB268)*
calling subroutines *(VB277)*
comments *(VB270)*
counter *(VB276)*
Do...Loop *(VB283)*
Do Until loop *(VB283)*
document *(VB270)*
DragDrop event *(VB268)*

DragIcon property *(VB263)*
DragMode property *(VB251)*
DragOver event *(VB268)*
Hide method *(VB280)*
increment *(VB276)*
InputBox function *(VB281)*
nested *(VB276)*
REM *(VB270)*

remarks *(VB270)*
Select Case statement *(VB281)*
self-documenting *(VB290)*
source control *(VB251)*
target control *(VB251)*
UCase$ function *(VB284)*
Variant data type *(VB270)*

Q U I C K   R E F E R E N C E

In Visual Basic you can accomplish a task in a number of ways. The following table provides a quick reference to each of the major tasks presented for the first time in the project with some of the available options. The commands listed in the Menu column can be executed using either the keyboard or mouse.

Task	Mouse	Menu	Keyboard Shortcuts
Copy Code From the Clipboard to a Selected Code Window		From Edit menu, choose Paste	Press CTRL+V
Copy Highlighted Code to the Clipboard		From Edit menu, choose Copy	Press CTRL+C
Highlight (Select) Code Statements in the Code Window	Drag mouse across code block to be selected		Press SHIFT+ARROW keys
Open the Print Dialog Box		From File menu, choose Print	Press CTRL+P

STUDENT ASSIGNMENT 1
True/False

Instructions: Circle T if the statement is true or F if the statement is false.

T   F   1. A Do...Until loop always executes the same number of times.
T   F   2. The Unload and Hide methods perform the same function.
T   F   3. A control being dragged is called the source control.
T   F   4. The control over which another control is being dragged is called the object control.
T   F   5. Run-time dragging of a control automatically changes its location.
T   F   6. Design-time dragging of a control automatically changes its location.
T   F   7. CTRL+V can be used to copy a control to the Clipboard.
T   F   8. After a control is copied to the Clipboard, it can be pasted only once.
T   F   9. A shape control does not have a DragOver event.
T   F   10. Menus can be selected only during run time.
T   F   11. The default value of an image control's DragIcon property is the value of its Picture property.
T   F   12. Only image controls can have DragIcons.
T   F   13. The different parts of a function or procedure are called arguables.
T   F   14. A control's DragDrop event is executed when the control is the target during a dragging operation and the left mouse button is released.
T   F   15. REM statements must begin with the letters REM or with a comma.
T   F   16. Variables with a Variant data type must be declared.
T   F   17. Variables used by more than one subroutine must be declared.
T   F   18. Generally, variables with a data type other than Variant require less memory space.
T   F   19. Nesting refers to writing one code structure within another.
T   F   20. One control event cannot be used to initiate other controls' events.

STUDENT ASSIGNMENT 2
Multiple Choice

Instructions: Circle the correct response.

1. The _____ argument of the MsgBox function determines which icon is displayed in the message box.
    a. style   c. type
    b. prompt   d. icon
2. _____ is a function that converts a string to all uppercase letters.
    a. UPPER$ c. CASE ELSE
    b. CASE$ d. UCASE$
3. _____ is the keyboard command to paste a control from the Clipboard to a form.
    a. CTRL+C   c. CTRL+V
    b. CTRL+X   d. CTRL+P
4. The ability to drag an object during run time is controlled by its _____ property.
    a. DragOver   c. DragIcon
    b. DragDrop   d. DragMode
5. During a drag-and-drop operation, the DragOver event and DragDrop event belong to the _____ control.
    a. source   c. dragged
    b. target   d. form

6. Comment statements within code must be preceded by _____.
   a. REM
   b. '
   c. neither a nor b
   d. either a or b
7. _____ is not a valid data type.
   a. Integer
   b. Long
   c. Short
   d. Double
8. A variable used in code to keep track of the number of times something has occurred is called a(n) _____.
   a. flag
   b. increment
   c. nest
   d. counter
9. The Select Case statement is a code structure used for _____.
   a. repetition
   b. selection
   c. sequence
   d. none of the above
10. An InputBox function always contains a(n) _____.
    a. text box
    b. OK button
    c. Cancel button
    d. all of the above

STUDENT ASSIGNMENT 3
Understanding Code Structures

Instructions: Figure SA5-3 shows an interface for an application that calculates the total cost of the purchase of ball point pens. The unit price depends on the quantity ordered, as follows:

QUANTITY	PRICE PER UNIT
< 150	.55
151-250	.48
251-500	.42
> 500	.40

FIGURE SA5-3

Draw a flowchart and write a subroutine to calculate the total price. Use a Select Case statement within the subroutine to select the appropriate unit price before calculating the total price.

STUDENT ASSIGNMENT 4
Understanding Code Structures

Instructions: Figure SA5-4 shows an interface for an application that computes weekly pay, given the number of hours worked and the hourly pay rate. If the number of hours worked exceeds 40, the person is paid an overtime rate of 1.5 times the normal rate. If a person works more than 40 hours and his pay rate is less than $4.50, he receives a $10 bonus for that week in addition to the regular and overtime pay.

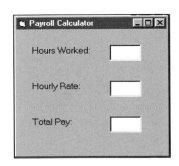

Draw a flowchart and write a subroutine to compute the week's pay. Use a nested If...Then structure to determine whether the $10 bonus is added to the pay.

FIGURE SA5-4

STUDENT ASSIGNMENT 5
Understanding Code Structures

Instructions: Draw a flowchart and write a subroutine to perform the following actions:

Display an input box that prompts the user to supply an examination score. After a score is entered, the input box should prompt for another score. After the fifth score is entered, the average of the five scores should be displayed using a MsgBox statement.

STUDENT ASSIGNMENT 6
Understanding Code Structures

Instructions: A bank computes its monthly service charge based on the number of checks written. The service charge is computed as $.25 plus $.09 on the first ten checks plus $.08 on the next ten checks plus $.07 on the next ten checks plus $.06 on any additional checks.

Write two subroutines that calculate the service charge, given the number of checks. The first subroutine should use a Select Case statement. The second subroutine should perform the same calculation using an If...Then...Else block.

C O M P U T E R   L A B O R A T O R Y   E X E R C I S E S

COMPUTER LABORATORY EXERCISE 1
DragMode and DragIcon Properties

Instructions: Start Visual Basic. Open the project CLE5-1 from the VB4 folder on the Student Diskette that accompanies this book. Complete the following tasks.

1. Choose the View Form button. The form contains two image controls, two frames, and five Option buttons, as shown in Figure CLE5-1.
2. Set the Visible property of the Image2 control to False.
3. Set the following captions as shown in the table below.

CONTROL	CAPTION
Frame1	DragMode
Frame2	DragIcon
Option1	Manual
Option2	Automatic
Option3	None
Option4	Image1
Option5	Image2

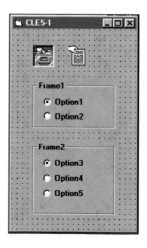

FIGURE CLE5-1

4. Enter the subroutines listed in the table to the right for the Option button Click events.

EVENT	SUBROUTINE
Option1_Click	Image1.DragMode = 0
Option2_Click	Image1.DragMode = 1
Option3_Click	Rem Image2.DragIcon is blank Image1.DragIcon = Image2.DragIcon
Option4_Click	Image1.DragIcon = Image1.Picture
Option5_Click	Image1.DragIcon = Image2.Picture

5. Save the form as CLE5-1A.FRM, and save the project as CLE5-1A.VBP. Close the Code window.
6. Run the application. Select the Manual DragMode Option button. Drag the image around the desktop. What happens?
7. Select the Automatic DragMode option button. Drag the image around the desktop. What happens?
8. Select each of the three DragIcon option buttons, and drag the image around the desktop. What happens?
9. To end the application, click the End button on the toolbar, or click the form's Close button.
10. Check with your instructor for directions on turning in the exercise.

COMPUTER LABORATORY EXERCISE 2
The DragOver Event

Instructions: Start Visual Basic. Open the project CLE5-2 from the VB4 folder on the Student Diskette that accompanies this book.

Perform the following steps.

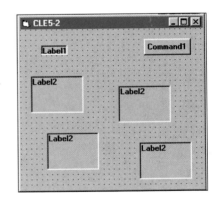

FIGURE CLE5-2

1. Choose the View Form button in the Project window. The form contains one label, one command button, and one label control array, as shown in Figure CLE5-2.
2. Set the control properties as shown in the table below and to the bottom right.
3. Enter the following Command1_Click subroutine:

```
For Index = 0 To 3
  Label2(Index).Caption = ""
Next
```

4. Write the following Label2_DragOver subroutine:

```
If State = 2 Then
   Label2(Index).Caption = "Target"
Else
   Label2(Index).Caption = ""
End If
```

5. Save the form as CLE5-2A.FRM, and then save the project as CLE5-2A.VBP. Close the Code window.
6. Start the application. Click the Clear button.
7. Drag the Label1 control (with the caption Source) around the form. What happens?
8. Drop the label on the form. Click the Clear button. Drag the label again.
9. To end the application, click the End button on the toolbar, or click the form's Close button.
10. Check with your instructor for directions on turning in the exercise.

CONTROL	PROPERTY	VALUE
Label1	Caption	Source
Label1	DragMode	Automatic
Command1	Caption	Clear

COMPUTER LABORATORY EXERCISE 3
The DragDrop Event

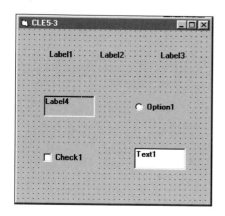

FIGURE CLE5-3

Instructions: Start Visual Basic. Open the project CLE5-3 from the VB4 folder on the Student Diskette that accompanies this book.

Perform the following steps.

1. Choose the View Form button in the Project window. The form contains four label controls, one text box, one check box, and one option button, as shown in Figure CLE5-3.
2. Double-click Label1's BackColor property in the Properties window. Use the Color palette to set Label1's BackColor to red.
3. Repeat Step 2 twice to set Label2's BackColor to yellow and Label3's BackColor to green.
4. Set the DragMode to Automatic for Label1, Label2, and Label3.
5. Write the following subroutine for the Label4_DragDrop event:
   ```
   Label4.BackColor = Source.BackColor
   ```
6. Write the following subroutine for the Text1_DragDrop event:
```
Text1.BackColor = Source.BackColor
```
7. Write the following subroutine for the Option1_DragDrop event:
```
Option1.BackColor = Source.BackColor
```
8. Write the following subroutine for the Check1_DragDrop event:
```
Check1.BackColor = Source.BackColor
```
9. Write the following subroutine for the Form_DragDrop event:
```
Form1.BackColor = Source.BackColor
```
10. Save the form as CLE5-3A.FRM, and then save the project as CLE5-3A.VBP. Close the Code window.
11. Run the application. Drag and drop the three labels on the different controls on the form. What happens?
12. Close the application by clicking its Close button or by clicking the End button on the toolbar.
13. Check with your instructor for directions on turning in the exercise.

COMPUTER LABORATORY ASSIGNMENTS

COMPUTER LABORATORY ASSIGNMENT 1
Team Assignment Application

Purpose: To build an application that uses drag-and-drop functionality to add text to list boxes.

Problem: You have been put in charge of organizing the tug-of-war event at the annual company picnic. As people call to let you know they want to participate, you assign them to one of two teams. You would like to have a computer application to keep track of these assignments. You want to be able to type in the name and then drag and drop the person's name on one of two scrollable lists.

Instructions: Perform the following tasks.

1. Start Visual Basic, or open a new project if Visual Basic already is running.
2. Create an interface with three labels, one text box, two simple list boxes, and caption, as shown in Figure CLA5-1.
3. Set the TabStop property of the list boxes to False.
4. Set the appropriate captions for the form and labels.
5. Set the DragMode of the text box to Automatic.

6. Write the DragDrop event for each of the list boxes. Dropping the text box on the list should add the name to that list and clear the name from the text box. ***Hint:*** Use the AddItem method to add Text1.Text, and then set Text1.Text equal to "".
7. Save the form as CLA5-1.FRM. Save the project as CLA5-1.VBP.
8. Run the application to test it.
9. Check with your instructor for directions on turning in the assignment.

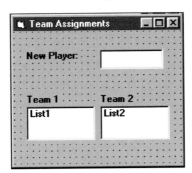

FIGURE CLA5-1

COMPUTER LABORATORY ASSIGNMENT 2
Security Subroutine

Purpose: To build an application that uses InputBox statements, MsgBox statements, and a Do...Loop.

Problem: You want to design a password checking subroutine that will be part of the Form_Load procedure for an application.

Instructions: Perform the following tasks:

1. Start Visual Basic, or open a new project if Visual Basic already is running.
2. Set the form's Caption property to Security Check. All actions for the password check will be part of the Form_Load subroutine, so you needn't do anything else to the form.
3. The subroutine should prompt the user with a dialog box similar to the one shown in Figure CLA5-2a.
4. If the password is correctly entered (it is "pass"), the message box in Figure CLA5-2b should display. ***Hint:*** This MsgBox *Type* is 16. If the password is not correct, the message box shown in Figure CLA5-2c should appear. If the user clicks the Cancel button, the application should end.
5. If the user enters an incorrect password a third time, the application should end. ***Hint:*** Each time the input box is displayed, a counter variable should be incremented.
6. Use a Do...Loop in the subroutine. ***Hint***: The input box keeps displaying until the password is correct OR the number of incorrect tries is three OR the user clicks the Cancel button.
7. Save the form as CLA5-2.FRM. Save the project as CLA5-2.VBP.
8. Run the application by clicking the Start button on the toolbar.
9. Check with your instructor for directions on turning in the assignment.

FIGURE CLA5-2a   **FIGURE CLA5-2b**   **FIGURE CLA5-2c**

COMPUTER LABORATORY ASSIGNMENT 3
Custom Traffic Quiz Input Box

Purpose: To build and use a custom input box.

Problem: In the Traffic Sign Tutorial application built in Project 5, the questions in the Traffic Sign Shape Quiz were presented to the user by using an InputBox function. You would like to have a customized input box where the input area (text box) is not so wide.

Instructions: Start a new application with a form that has a single command button labeled Quiz. Clicking the Quiz button should initiate the series of three questions and message boxes described in Project 5. However, you should create a second form to display the question and to receive the user's answer instead of using the InputBox function.

Save the main form as CLA5-3A.FRM. Save the input form as CLA5-3B.FRM. Save the project as CLA5-3.VBP If you completed the application in Project 5, it can be revised by adding CLA5-3B.FRM to the TRAFFIC.VBP project and replacing the mnuQuiz_Click subroutine with the Command1_Click subroutine written in this assignment. Check with your instructor about revising the TRAFFIC.VBP application and for directions on turning in the assignment.

COMPUTER LABORATORY ASSIGNMENT 4
Currency Exchange

Purpose: To build an application that uses the ListIndex value of a drop-down list box and uses a Select Case structure within code.

Problem: You would like to add some additional sophistication to the Currency Exchange application that was built and revised in previous assignments. Specifically, you would like the conversion to take place at the same time the type of currency is selected from a drop-down list.

Create an interface similar to the one shown in Figure CLA5-4. The drop-down list should contain the names of the different currencies. Clicking the Clear button should clear all boxes on the form.
Hint: The combo box's Click event is triggered when an item is selected from the drop-down list. The value of the combo box's ListIndex property corresponds to the item selected; the appropriate conversion could be made by selecting different actions based on the value of Combo1.ListIndex. A combo box's text is cleared by setting its ListIndex equal to -1.

Use the following exchange rates. One dollar equals:

   1.4920 pounds
   1.6250 guilders
   1.4506 marks
   1.3757 Canadian dollars

Save the form as CLA5-4.FRM. Save the project as CLA5-4.VBP. Check with your instructor for directions on turning in the assignment.

FIGURE CLA5-4

MICROSOFT VISUAL BASIC 4 FOR WINDOWS

APPENDIX A

Visual Basic 4.0 Working Model

System Requirements:

▸ Personal computer with a 386DX/25 or higher processor (486 or higher recommended)

▸ Microsoft Windows 95 or Windows NT Workstation 3.51 or later operating system

▸ 6MB of memory (8MB or more recommended) if using Windows 95; 16 MB if using Windows NT

▸ Available hard disk space: minimum installation 20 MB

▸ A CD-ROM drive

▸ VGA or higher resolution monitor

▸ Microsoft mouse or compatible pointing device

Differences from Standard Edition:

▸ Fewer controls

▸ No Make EXE command

▸ No Data Manager

▸ Projects limited to two modules (Forms, MDI Forms, Modules, Classes)

Installation:

▸ Run the Setup program on the Visual Basic 4.0 Working Model CD

INDEX